D1825738

*The Lutterworth Guide*
*to*

# Activity and Study Holidays 1993

**The Lutterworth Press**
**Cambridge**

The Lutterworth Press
P.O. Box 60
Cambridge
CB1 2NT

*British Library Cataloguing-in-Publication Data*
A catalogue record for this book is available from the British Library

ISBN 0-7188-2867-3

Printed in Great Britain by
Hillman Printers (Frome) Ltd, Somerset

Cover design by Sarah Brierley
Photographs reproduced with kind permission from:
*Acorn Activities*
*Bearsports Outdoor Centres*
*Field Studies Council (Tony Thomas)*
*Millfield School Village of Education (T & J Lea Design & Print)*
*Rock Lea Activity Centre*
*West Dean College*

# Contents

# Index of Photographs

# Introduction

For most of us, our leisure time is seen as a break from working; a time to continue and develop an existing interest or to take up a new one; or simply to get away and enjoy ourselves. Consequently more and more people are moving away from the 'sun and sand' type holiday simply lazing around and are looking closer to home for a more challenging and fulfilling way of spending their free time.

This book is a new directory of activity and special interest holidays offering hundreds of ideas organised by over 500 centres in England, Scotland and Wales. Anyone, of whatever age or level of experience will find something to interest them, whether looking for ideas for a residential weekend or holiday-with-a-difference, or having a specific course in mind but just not sure where in Britain to find it.

You may be looking for an exciting adventure holiday, abseiling in Wales or white-water canoeing in Scotland for instance. Or you may prefer a more relaxing weekend basket making in the West Country or landscape painting in Suffolk; or perhaps you want to satisfy your curiosity about aromatherapy or industrial architecture. Whatever your inclination, there is a vast range of courses in this book from which to choose including sections on arts, crafts, photography, sports, outdoor pursuits, natural history, music and dance, food and drink, fitness, games, personal development - or a combination of any of these in a multiactivity holiday. There is even a section on organisations catering just for children. Some of the courses (particularly in the sports section) lead to recognised certificates, some are study subjects, some are just for fun, but all are taken primarily for enjoyment rather than academic or professional reasons.

## Accommodation

The courses listed vary in length from two days to a week or longer but, in all cases include a stay away from home, doing something different in an interesting location, with the benefit of expert tuition or instruction but still within a holiday atmosphere. They are almost all residential, either staying on site in an outdoor centre, university campus, country mansion, private home or even on board a boat; or the organisation hosting the course will either arrange accommodation for you in the locality or provide lists of local hotels, guest houses and camping sites.

## How to use the book

This book is divided into two sections. The first section is a listing of courses. Beneath the subject heading is the name of the organisation, the location of the course, the duration and which months of the year they are held. Where applicable, there is information on how many people are in the group, at what level the course is aimed, and the minimum suitable age recommended. Additionally, each organisation has a Centre number - this is the number referring you to the **Centres Index** where you can find the contact details and information about accommodation. Please note that the location of the course may not be where the organisation is based, therefore in all cases the reader is advised to phone the organisation for further details and to request a brochure, which is almost always free of charge.

The second section is the **Centres Index**. It includes the contact address and telephone number, the kind of accommodation offered or organised by them, and in some cases the possible leisure facilities available. The ⚇ symbol shows that the centre can accommodate children and the ♿ symbol indicates that there are facilities for the disabled, although these vary from centre to centre and should always be checked in advance. The 🐕 symbol indicates that the organisation can accommodate pets.

The details for inclusion have been compiled from returned entry forms and by information supplied by phone and letter, but are not intended to be a fully comprehensive review of what is being offered. It is always advisable to check with the Centre first as this guide cannot be held responsible for the accuracy of the details of each holiday. The entries are free of charge although a small amount has been charged for including additional information (in italics) in the **Centres Index.**

Finally, if you organise courses and would like to be included in future editions of this book, please write with details to the editor at The Lutterworth Press, PO Box 60, Cambridge, CB1 2NT.

Sarah Brierley
Editor

## Acknowledgements

The editor would like to thank the following people for their assistance: Christine Hutchinson, Amy Sutter, Cathy Curwood and Penny O'Dell.

# Arts, Crafts, Photography and Video

Many people do not have the time or opportunity to realise their artistic potential. What better then than to devote a few days, a week or even longer to your chosen art or craft, when you would have the time in relaxed surroundings and an inspiring location to concentrate on acquiring new techniques or developing an existing skill, under the careful supervision of an experienced artist.

There is a vast range of courses to choose from. Many are located in areas of outstanding natural beauty to provide that inspiration which may not come easily elsewhere. They may be undertaken in residential centres, or even in the artists' own home. Coaching is often in small groups to ensure personal attention and encouragement, which will benefit equally the complete beginner and the more experienced.

Amongst the most popular courses are painting and drawing, but you can also do pottery, sculpture, photography or woodturning; or there are the more practical crafts of upholstery, furniture restoration or rugmaking. There is also a wide variety of needlecrafts on offer - tapestry, embroidery, crochet, as well as the more traditional skills of weaving, spinning and dyeing. You could even have a go at a more unusual craft - glass blowing, metalwork, pyrography or clogmaking! There is something for everyone, and complete novices or the less confident should not be put off as many of these courses are aimed at the complete beginner. Whatever you are looking for, the following section will provide you with ideas to discover the creative ability that lies in all of us.

# Arts

## Calligraphy

**Acorn Activities**      **Centre 3**
Location: Herefordshire/Pembrokeshire
Duration: 2 days, April/June/September
Levels: all
*A basic grounding in a variety of styles.*

**Alston Hall Residential
College**      **Centre 16**
Location: Lancashire
Duration: 5 days, June
Levels: all
Min. age: 16

**Braziers Adult College**      **Centre 53**
Location: Oxon
Duration: 2 days, March/June/September
Max. in group: 10
Levels: all

**British Universities Accommodation
Consortium Ltd**      **Centre 61**
Location: various universities in Britain
Duration: varies, June-September
Levels: all
*Ring for locations.*

**Burton Manor College**      **Centre 70**
Location: Cheshire
Duration: 5 days, July
Max. in group: 16
Levels: all
Min. age: 14

**Diana Hoare Letter Carver**      **Centre 130**
Location: Herefordshire
Duration: 1-3 days, all year
Max. in group: 6
Levels: all
Min. age: 10
*Course for basic understanding of forms
leading to completion of a finished piece.*

**Flatford Mill Field Centre**      **Centre 169**
Location: Essex
Duration: 3-7 days, February-November
Levels: all
Min. age: 16
*Instruction given on popular styles : making
reed and quill pens with individual tuition
for particular interests.*

**Hawkwood College**      **Centre 200**
Location: Gloucestershire
Duration: 4 days, June
Max. in group: 20
Levels: all
Min. age: 18

**Higham Hall Residential
Study Centre**      **Centre 214**
Location: Cumbria
Duration: 2 days, January
Levels: all
Min. age: mostly 16

## Calligraphy continued

**Lands End**                          **Centre 256**
Location: Cumbria
Duration: 2 days, all year
Max. in group: 15
Levels: all
Min. age: 16
*Courses on the Foundational Hand and Roman Capitals with exploration of the variations of letter forms.*

**Preston Montford**
**Field Centre**                       **Centre 357**
Location: Shropshire
Duration: 3 days, February-October
Levels: beginners/intermediate
Min. age: 16
*Courses covering elements of design and layout for complete beginners or improvers.*

**University of Birmingham**           **Centre 455**
Location: Worcestershire
Duration: 2 days, September
Max. in group: 25
Levels: beginners
Min. age: 18
*Practical course designed to help beginners explore the materials and techniques.*

**University of Stirling**             **Centre 459**
Location: Stirling
Duration: 2 days, June
Max. in group: 20
Levels: beginners/intermediate
Min. age: 16
*Studio work consisting of the study of Foundational Hand and will lead to the production of a finished piece of work.*

**Wethersfield Arts Centre**           **Centre 483**
Location: Essex
Duration: 2 days, June-July

*Acorn Activities*

Max. in group: 14
Levels: beginners/intermediate
Min. age: 14
*Course on calligraphy applications and lettering techniques. Individual and group demonstrations.*

# Cartoon Art

**Cartoon School (The)**               **Centre 89**
Location: Yorkshire
Duration: 3 days, March
Max. in group: 20
Levels: all
Min. age: 18
*Course to encourage newcomers to develop all types of cartoon drawing and caricature.*

**HF Holidays Ltd**                    **Centre 207**
Location: Nationwide
Duration: 4-7 days, April-October
Max. in group: 20
Levels: all

# Chinese Brush Painting

**Alston Hall Residential
College**                    Centre 16
Location: Lancashire
Duration: 2 days, August
Levels: all
Min. age: 16

**Broadlands Arts Centre**    Centre 62
Location: Norfolk
Duration: 2 days, May
Max. in group: 15
Levels: all
Min. age: 16
*Practical course to learn the techniques of
brush strokes with demonstrations and videos.*

**Burton Manor College**      Centre 70
Location: Cheshire
Duration: 2 days, April/August
Max. in group: 16
Levels: all
Min. age: 14

**Cinderhill House**          Centre 95
Location: Gloucestershire
Duration: 3 days, October-April
Max. in group: 10
Levels: all
Min. age: 18

**Hawkwood College**          Centre 200
Location: Gloucestershire
Duration: 2 days, November
Max. in group: 15
Levels: all
Min. age: 18

**Malham Tarn Field Centre**  Centre 278
Location: Yorkshire
Duration: 3 days, October
Levels: all
Min. age: 16

> **Please refer to the Centres Index
> for details about accommodation**

**University of Birmingham**   Centre 455
Location: Shropshire
Duration: 2 days, March
Max. in group: 24
Levels: beginners
Min. age: 18
*An introduction to basic brush strokes using
bamboo.*

# Drawing

**Broadlands Arts Centre**    Centre 62
Location: Norfolk
Duration: 2 days, June
Max. in group: 18
Levels: intermediate/advanced
Min. age: 16
*Intensive nude life drawing course using
numerous drawing methods to explore tone,
form, structure and movement.*

**Slapton Ley Field Centre**  Centre 406
Location: Devon
Duration: 7 days, August
Levels: all
Min. age: 16
*Scenery, geology, flora and fauna are ex-
plored in a combination of walking and draw-
ing.*

**Wethersfield Arts Centre**  Centre 483
Location: Essex
Duration: 2 days, April-October
Max. in group: 14
Levels: beginners/intermediate
Min. age: 14
*Tuition on all techniques of drawing
applied to a wide range of subjects.
Individual help and group demonstrations.*

# Fine Art & Art History

**British Universities**
**Accommodation Consortium     Centre 61**
Location: various universities in Britain
Duration: varies, June-September
Ring for programme.

**Inscape Fine Art Tours     Centre 227**
Location: Nationwide
Duration: 4/6/8 days, all year
Max. in group: 20
Levels: all
Min. age: 18
*Small groups taken to view art collections and architecture encouraging discussion, participation and art appreciation.*

**University of Birmingham     Centre 455**
Location: Oxford
Duration: 2 days, August
Max. in group: 25
Levels: all
Min. age: 18
*Based in an Oxford College this course will combine visits to the Ashmolean Museum and Christ Church Picture Gallery.*

**University of Manchester     Centre 457**
Location: Manchester
Duration: 2 days, July/August
Levels: all
*Various courses. Ring for details.*

**University of Oxford     Centre 458**
Location: Oxford
Duration: 7 days, July-August
Max. in group: 12
Levels: all
Min. age: 18
*Seminars on art history and appreciation. Full details available in brochure. No practical courses offered.*

**University of Cambridge     Centre 456**
Location: Cambridgeshire
Duration: 2 days, all year
Max. in group: 15
Levels: all
Min. age: 18
*A variety of art history courses covering many different periods and styles.*

**Wessex Fine Arts Summer**
**Study Course     Centre 478**
Location: Nationwide
Duration: 5 days, June
Max. in group: 42
Levels: all
Min. age: 21
*A study of English architecture, interior design and furnishing.*

# Illustration

**Dale Fort Field Centre     Centre 121**
Location: Pembrokeshire
Duration: 7 days, May
Levels: all
Min. age: 16
*Botanical illustration using watercolour and drawing. Enthusiasm and interest in flowers the primary qualification.*

**Flatford Mill Field Centre     Centre 169**
Location: Essex
Duration: 3-7 days, February-November
Levels: all
Min. age: 16
*A variety of courses covering botanical illustration, landscape and wildlife.*

**Nettlecombe Court**
**Field Centre     Centre 314**
Location: Somerset
Duration: 7 days, April-October
Levels: intermediate/advanced
Min. age: 16

*Practical instruction on portraying plants, plus illustrated talks on their history.*

# Mixed Media

### Edinburgh College of Art Festival
### Summer School                    Centre 151
Location: Edinburgh
Duration: 20 days, August/September
Levels: all
Min. age: 16
*Degree level teaching in drawing, painting, printmaking and sculpture with complementary lecture programme.*

# Painting

### Ardmiddle Enterprises          Centre 23
Location: Turriff
Duration: 7 days, October
Max. in group: 8
Levels: all
Min. age: 16

### Beaconhill East Kent
### Field Centre                   Centre 37
Location: Kent
Duration: 3 days, all year
Levels: all
Min. age: 7
*A variety of courses including landscape and flower painting using your own choice of media.*

### Cefn-y-Dre                     Centre 91
Location: Dyfed
Duration: varies, February-November
Max. in group: 6
Levels: all
Min. age: 16
*A relaxed atmosphere provided for visiting artists. Studio facilities, trips to painting locations and life drawing all available.*

### Cinderhill House              Centre 95
Location: Gloucestershire
Duration: 3 days, April-October
Max. in group: 10
Levels: all
Min. age: 18

### Colwall Park Hotel           Centre 101
Location: Worcestershire
Duration: 4 days, all year
Max. in group: 20
Levels: all
Min. age: 15
*Emphasis on relaxation to paint at your own pace, indoors and outdoors, receiving individual guided instruction.*

### Coombe Farm Studios          Centre 108
Location: Devon
Duration: 5 days, March-October
Max. in group: 12
Levels: all
Min. age: 14
*Beginner to advanced tuition in the studio or outdoors, using watercolour or oils as per programme.*

### Dale Fort Field Centre       Centre 121
Location: Pembrokeshire
Duration: 7 days, September
Levels: all
Min. age: 16
*Any medium used to develop individual interpretation of the Pembrokeshire coastline and countryside.*

### Dane Lodge Hotel             Centre 122
Location: Cheshire
Duration: 2-6 days, April-February
Max. in group: 20
Levels: all
Min. age: 16
*Courses to improve techniques and stimulate awareness within a landscape setting .*

## Painting continued

**Fellowship Afloat**
**Charitable Trust**          **Centre 164**
Location: Essex
Duration: 2 days, all year
Max. in group: 15
Levels: all
Min. age: 11
*Tuition and practice combined with community living on board light vessel.*

**Hazel Tree Farm**          **Centre 201**
Location: Kent
Duration: 2 days, May/June/October
Max. in group: 12
Levels: all
Min. age: 16
*A variety of courses in the studio, garden or surrounding area on landscape, still life, and flower painting in oil or watercolour.*

**Higham Hall Residential**
**Study Centre**          **Centre 214**
Location: Cumbria
Duration: 2-7 days, all year
Levels: all
Min. age: mostly 16
*Watercolour, pastel, and acrylics used in landscape, flower and miniature painting.*

**Higher Humber Farm**          **Centre 213**
Location: Devon
Duration: 2-3 days, February-April/July/August/October-November
Max. in group: 10
Levels: all
Min. age: 16
*Tuition in watercolour painting and other media, outdoors or in the studio.*

**Juniper Hall Field Centre**          **Centre 243**
Location: Surrey

Duration: 3-7 days, May-October
Levels: all
Min. age: 16
*A variety of courses in drawing and watercolour covering botanical illustration landscape and natural history.*

**Land Ends**          **Centre 256**
Location: Cumbria
Duration: 2-7 days, all year
Max. in group: 15
Levels: all
Min. age: 16
*A variety of courses in landscape and portraiture using watercolour, oils and pastels.*

**Learn at Leisure**          **Centre 260**
Location: Isle of Mull
Duration: 7 days, April-May
Max. in group: 25
Levels: all
Min. age: 16
*Landscape painting.*

**Malham Tarn Field Centre**          **Centre 278**
Location: Yorkshire
Duration: 7 days, July-August
Levels: all
Min. age: 16
*A variety of courses encouraging different techniques of pastel, oil and watercolour appropriate to chosen subjects.*

**Nairn Craft Holidays**          **Centre 311**
Location: Nairn
Duration: 5 days, May
Max. in group: 10
Levels: beginners intermediate
Min. age: 16
*During the course it is hoped that each student will complete a minimum of 3 paintings through a process of demonstrations and practical work.*

**Newlyn Workshops**          Centre 315
Location: Cornwall
Duration: 3 days, April-October
Max. in group: 8
Levels: all
Min. age: 16
*Course encourages creativity in a non-competitive atmosphere.*

**Old Vicarage (The)**          Centre 328
Location: Northumberland
Duration: 2-5 days, May-October
Max. in group: 10
Levels: all
Min. age: 18

**Shinafoot Fine Art Studios**     Centre 394
Location: Perthshire
Duration: 2/3/5 days, February-November
Max. in group: 12
Levels: all
Min. age: 15

**Snape Maltings**          Centre 411
Location: Suffolk
Duration: 2-4 days, May-September
Levels: all
*Courses include watercolour pastels and oils with emphasis on landscape painting. Studio work also undertaken with demonstration and discussion.*

**Summer Academy**          Centre 423
Location: Nationwide
Duration: 7 days, July-August
Levels: all
*Ring for details.*

**Talland Bay Hotel**          Centre 433
Location: Talland Bay
Duration: 4 days, April-October
Max. in group: 12
Levels: all
Min. age: 16

*Instruction on tone, space, expression, design and technique.*

**Taunton Summer School**      Centre 435
Location: Somerset
Duration: 5 days, July/August
Levels: all
Min. age: 8
*Ring for programme details.*

**University of Stirling**          Centre 459
Location: Stirling
Duration: 5 days, July
Max. in group: 20
Levels: all
Min. age: 16
*The course enables students to look at the special characteristics of the Scottish landscape in particular the effect of light and weather.*

**Watercolour Weeks at Weobley**          Centre 469
Location: Herefordshire
Duration: 6 days, March-October
Max. in group: 18
Levels: all
Min. age: 16
*A choice of nine courses which includes exercises to help painters overcome particular problems of the medium.*

**Waternish Workshop**          Centre 470
Location: Isle of Skye
Duration: 3 days, May-September
Max. in group: 8
Levels: all
Min. age: 12
*A choice of courses to equip students with basic techniques using different mediums with an emphasis on landscape painting.*

## Painting continued

**Wethersfield Arts**   **Centre 483**
Location: Essex
Duration: 3 days, February-December
Max. in group: 14
Levels: all
Min. age: 14
*Comprehensive individual tuition and group demonstrations in oil and watercolour technique.*

**Wiltshire Painting Holidays**   **Centre 495**
Location: Wiltshire
Duration: 2-5 days, all year
Max. in group: 16
Levels: all
Min. age: 18
*A structured course but loose style, outdoors or in the studio, using watercolour, pastel, pen & wash.*

# Painting & Drawing

**Acorn Activities**   **Centre 3**
Location: Herefordshire/Pembrokeshire
Duration: 2-7, all year
Levels: all
*Courses in drawing, oil painting, watercolours.*

**Alston Hall**
**Residential College**   **Centre 16**
Location: Cumbria
Duration: 2-6 days, April-July
Levels: all
Min. age: 16
*Courses in portrait, landscape, watercolour.*

**Artscape Painting**
**Holidays Ltd**   **Centre 26**
Location: nationwide
Duration: 7+ days, March-November

Max. in group: 15
Levels: all
*60 courses offered on portrait, flowers, landscape, marine, townscape etc. Full details in brochure.*

**Belstead House**   **Centre 39**
Location: Suffolk
Duration: 2 days, all year
Levels: all
*Courses on watercolour landscape, Chinese brush and miniature painting.*

**Braziers Adult College**   **Centre 53**
Location: Oxfordshire
Duration: 2 days, June/April
Levels: all
*Drawing and watercolour courses.*

**Broadlands Arts Centre**   **Centre 63**
Location: Norfolk
Duration: 2 days, March-August

Max. in group: 16
Levels: all
Min. age: 16
*A variety of courses in miniature painting, rural landscape, portraits in pastel, plus waterways and landscapes in watercolour.*

**British Universities**
**Accommodation Consortium    Centre 61**
Location: various universities in Britain
Duration: varies, June-September
*Ring for programme.*

**Burton Manor College        Centre 70**
Location: Cheshire
Duration: 1-5 days, all year
Max. in group: 16
Levels: all
Min. age: 14
*Courses in landscape, botanical, flower, portrait and life drawing. Also courses on art therapy.*

**Byre Yard                   Centre 72**
Location: Yorkshire
Duration: 3 days, July/August
Max. in group: 12
Levels: all
Min. age: 14
*Various courses available in drawing, watercolour, decorative paint finishes and china painting.*

**Cornwall Creative Activity Network**
**(CCAN)                     Centre 111**
Location: Cornwall
Duration: varies
Levels: all
*Many courses run by various artists on different mediums. Ring for brochure.*

**Coleg Harlech               Centre 100**
Location: Gwynedd
Duration: 7 days, August

Max. in group: 25
Levels: all
Min. age: 14
*Landscape painting in Snowdonia.*

**Countrywide Holidays        Centre 114**
Location: nationwide
Duration: 7 days, April-September
Levels: beginners
*Courses on drawing, watercolour, oil and landscape painting in the Lake District,*

**Dillington House            Centre 131**
Location: Somerset
Duration: 1-7 days, all year
Max. in group: varies
Levels: all
Min. age: 18
*Various courses throughout the year in calligraphy, portrait, painting, life drawing and chinese brush painting.*

**Drapers' Field Centre       Centre 137**
Location: Gwynedd
Duration: 7 days, May-August
Levels: all
Min. age: 16
*Landscape painting in Snowdonia using any preferred medium.*

**Earnley Concourse           Centre 141**
Location: Sussex
Duration: 2/4/7 days, all year
Max. in group: 16
Levels: all
Min. age: 16
*A variety of courses using acrylics, watercolours, oils in landscape, portrait, still life etc.*

**Please mention this guide when booking a course**

## Painting & Drawing continued

**Eden Centre (The)**  Centre 148
Location: Devon
Duration: 2-3 days, April-October
Max. in group: 12
Levels: all
Min. age: 17
*A course to explore ways of working in and with nature using relaxation and visualisation techniques.*

**Flatford Mill Field Centre**  Centre 169
Location: Essex/Suffolk
Duration: 3-7 days, February-November
Levels: all
Min. age: 16
*Various courses in oil, pastel, acrylics and watercolour of wildlife, landscape, portraiture, architecture and still life. Also courses on John Constable's paintings.*

**Gateway Education & Arts Centre**  Centre 183
Location: Shropshire
Duration: 2 days, all year
Levels: all
*Various courses. Ring for details.*

**Glanhelyg Painting Courses**  Centre 187
Location: Dyfed
Duration: 7 days, May-September
Max. in group: 8
Levels: all
Min. age: 16
*Courses on landscape painting and life drawing.*

**Hill Residential College**  Centre 218
Location: Gwent
Duration: 2-7 days, all year
Max. in group: 16
Levels: all
Min. age: 16

*A variety of courses in all mediums for all levels of competence from beginners to art foundation course level.*

**Inniemore School of Painting**  Centre 226
Location: Isle of Mull
Duration: 7 days, May-September
Max. in group: 20
Levels: all
Min. age: 15
*Tuition in the studio and on field trips to the Isle of Iona. Emphasis on landscape painting in all mediums.*

**Kindrogan Field Centre**  Centre 250
Location: Perthshire
Duration:7 days, August/September
Levels: all
*Landscape and botanical drawing plus painting in a variety of mediums.*

**Lancaster University Summer Programme**  Centre 255
Location: Lancashire
Duration: varies
Levels: all
*Various courses using different mediums as part of a multiactivity programme.*

**Logie Farm Riding Centre**  Centre 271
Location: Glenferness
Duration: 7 days, April-November
Max. in group: 8
Levels: all
*Instruction in painting and drawing with framing on site.*

**Summer University**  Centre 425
Location: Leicestershire
Duration: 5 days, July/August
Max. in group: 12
Levels: all
Min. age: 18

*Tuition to meet requirements of students. Brochure details give level of attainment necessary to pursue courses.*

**Lower Aston House**          Centre 273
Location: Worcestershire
Duration: 2/3/6 days, May-October
Max. in group: 10
Levels: all
Min. age: 12
*Courses cover still life, landscape and flower studies using drawing, pen and ink, pastels, watercolour, oil and acrylics.*

**Lyme Regis Painting
Workshops**          Centre 276
Location: Dorset
Duration: 2-7 days, all year
Max. in group: 9
Levels: all
Min. age: 9
*This course functions mainly as a comprehensive foundation or refresher course in painting and drawing.*

**Marlborough College
Summer School**          Centre 280
Location: Wiltshire
Duration: 5 days, July/August
Max. in group: 14
Levels: all
Min. age: 17
*A variety of courses in studio and landscape painting and drawing using mixed media techniques.*

**Maryland Residential College**    Centre 271
Location: Bedfordshire
Duration: 2 days, all year
Levels: all
Min. age: 18
*Various courses including life drawing, watercolour and still life.*

**Millfield School Village
of Education**          Centre 293
Location: Somerset
Duration: 5 days, July/August
Max. in group: 10
Levels: all
Min. age: 10
*Various courses including portraiture, watercolour and illustration.*

**Missenden Abbey**          Centre 296
Location: Buckinghamshire
Levels: all
Min. age: 18
*Various courses on landscape, flower, life drawing, miniature and watercolour.*

**Mounts Bay Art Centre**          Centre 307
Location: Cornwall
Duration: 7 days, May-October
Max. in group: 12
Levels: all
Min. age: 14
*Illustrated talks on the basics of landscape painting in all media with daily painting trips and individual tuition.*

**Nettlecombe Court**          Centre 314
Location: Somerset
Duration: 3-7 days, May-September
Levels: all
Min. age: 16
*Observation and composition techniques developed through painting and drawing landscapes and natural history subjects.*

**Orielton Field Centre**          Centre 329
Location: Pembrokeshire
Duration: 7 days, July
Levels: all
Min. age: 16
*Botanical and landscape painting and drawing working in a variety of mediums, with a spacious studio for evening lectures.*

## Painting & Drawing continued

**Peak National Park**
**Study Centre**                    Centre 340
Location: Derbyshire
Duration: 2-7 days, all year
Max. in group: 25
Levels: all
Min. age: 8
*Landscape painting and illustrating out in the field each day. Also courses on botanical illustration.*

**Preston Montford**
**Field Centre**                    Centre 357
Location: Shropshire
Duration: 3-7 days, March-October
Levels: all
Min. age: 16
*A variety of courses using different mediums and natural history subjects. Also courses on botanical illustration.*

**Rob Hastings Adventure**          Centre 370
Location: Wales
Duration: 2-7, July/August
Levels: all
Min. age: 8
*Course consists of figure drawing and landscape painting. Different drawing media and techniques will be introduced.*

**Sancreed School**
**of Painting**                     Centre 379
Location: Cornwall
Duration: 7 days, April-October
Max. in group: 8
Levels: all
Min. age: 16
*Emphasis on encouraging drawing as the basis for painting.*

**Shorelands**                      Centre 395
Location: Anglesey
Duration: 3 days, April
Max. in group: 6
Levels: all
Min. age: 16
*Tuition in all media for the sketching and painting of birds in the field.*

**Slapton Ley Field Centre**        Centre 406
Location: Devon
Duration: 7 days, July-August
Levels: all
Min. age: 16
*Landscape painting along the coast plus art and design exploration famous gardens in the area.*

**Smithy Art Studio**              Centre 409
Location: Devon
Duration: 1-7 days, all year
Max. in group: 5
Levels: all
Min. age: 16
*Tuition to teach new drawing and painting techniques and media.*

**Suffolk College**
**Summer School**                   Centre 422
Location: Suffolk
Duration: 5 days, July
Levels: all
Min. age: 16
*Many courses including landscape, flower, life and marine subjects in all mediums.*

**Summer Academy**                  Centre 423
Location: varies
Duration: 7 days, July/August
Max. in group: 40
Levels: all
Min. age: 16
*Landscape and nature painting.*

*West Dean College*

**Summer University**  Centre 425
Location: Loughborough
Duration: 5 days, July/August
Max. in group: 12
Levels: all
Min. age: 18

**Turret Art Holidays**  Centre 449
Location: Perthshire
Duration: 6-10 days, February-December
Max. in group: 12
Levels: all
Min. age: 14
*Skills and confidence encouraged in all
mediums.*

**Urchfont Manor College**  Centre 461
Location: Wiltshire
Duration: 3-6 days, June-August

Max. in group: 15
Levels: all
Min. age: 18
*Ring for brochure.*

**West Dean College**  Centre 481
Location: Sussex
Duration: 2-7 days
Levels: all
*Over 50 courses including landscape,
flowers, portraiture, watercolour, oils, life
drawing and painting, botanical illustra-
tion, miniature painting etc.*

**Ynys Hywel
Countryside Centre**  Centre 513
Location: Gwent
Duration: 5 days, August-September
Max. in group: 34
Levels: all
Min. age: 18
*A course in watercolour and drawing with
tuition by a well-known local artist.*

# Painting & Prayer

**Ammerdown Study Centre**  Centre 17
Location: Avon
Duration: 4-7 days, June/August
Max. in group: 40
Levels: all
*Painting at all levels with time for prayer
and quietness. Participants bring whatever
medium they use.*

**Carberry Tower**  Centre 88
Location: Midlothian
Duration: 7 days, September
Max. in group: 24
Levels: all
Min. age: 21
*A Christian retreat for those wishing to
paint and develop in spirit. Art therapy
courses also offered.*

# Painting on Silk

**Images On Silk**  Centre 225
Location: Cornwall
Duration: 1-2 days, all year
Max. in group: 2
Levels: beginners
Min. age: 13
*Basic theory and practice is taught. A second day achieves a finished piece of work whether it is fabric, cushions or pictures.*

**Millfield School Village of Education**  Centre 293
Location: Somerset
Duration: 5 days
Max. in group: 10
Levels: all
Min. age: 10

**Snape Maltings**  Centre 411
Location: Suffolk
Duration: 2 days, varies
Levels: all
*A course experimenting with a variety of silk painting techniques.*

# Printing

**Broadlands Arts Centre**  Centre 62
Location: Norfolk
Duration: 2 days, May
Max. in group: 12
Levels: all
Min. age: 16
*Designing, cutting and printing in colour.*

**Flatford Mill Field Centre**  Centre 169
Location: Essex
Duration: 7 days, July
Levels: all
Min. age: 16
*A course covering a variety of design and printing skills.*

**Malham Tarn Field Centre**  Centre 278
Location: Yorkshire
Duration: 7 days, August
Min. age: 16
*Landscape etching.*

**Byre Yard**  Centre 72
Location: Yorkshire
Duration: 3 days, July/August
Max. in group: 12
Levels: all
Min. age: 14
*Courses on etching and experimental printing.*

**Premier**  Centre 355
Location: Cambridgeshire
Duration: 1-4 days, April-October
Max. in group: 2
Levels: beginners
Min. age: 16
*Introduction to small offset litho printing, covering plate making and machine operation, plus small letterpress printing.*

**Slapton Ley Field Centre**  Centre 406
Location: Devon
Duration: 7 days, August
Min. age: 16
*Silk screen printing including line stencilling and photographic techniques.*

*West Dean College*

# Textile Crafts

## General Textile Crafts

**Burton Manor College**          Centre 70
Location: Cheshire
Duration: 1-7 days, all year
Max. in group: 16
Levels: all
Min. age: 14
*Embroidery, patchwork and quilting, printing on silk, screen printing.*

**Dillington House**          Centre 131
Location: Somerset
Duration: 1-7 days, all year
Max. in group: 70
Levels: all
Min age: 18
*Machine knitting, embroidery, lacemaking, patchwork and quilting.*

**Higher Humber Farm**          Centre 213
Location: Devon
Duration: 2-3 days, October-November/
February-Easter/July-August
Max. in group: 10
Levels: all
Min. age: 16

**Ladytrek - Ladytour**          Centre 253
Location: Wester Ross
Duration: 4 days, February/March/November
Max. in group: 6
Levels: beginners/intermediate
Min. age: 17

*Patchwork, knitting, sewing, rag rug making and papier mache covered, combined with walking.*

**Millfield School Village of
Education**          Centre 293
Location: Somerset
Duration: 5 days, July-August
Max. in group: 10
Levels: all
Min. age: 13

**Snape Maltings**          Centre 411
Location: Suffolk
Duration: 2 days, May-September
Levels: all
*Various courses in silk painting, lacemaking, patchwork and textile jewellery.*

**Styal Workshop**          Centre 421
Location: Cheshire
Duration: 2 days, October-August
Levels: all
Min. age: 16
*Varied programme of short courses on weaving and braiding, spinning, dyeing, printing and applied colour, 3D, constructed and experimental textiles, colour and design, knitting and crochet.*

## General Textile Crafts continued

**Suffolk College Summer
School**  **Centre 422**
Duration: 5 days, July
Levels: all
Min. age: 16
*Many courses including batik, embroidery,
patchwork, quilting, tapestry and upholstery.*

**Summer University**  **Centre 425**
Location: Leicestershire
Duration: 5 days, July-August
Max. in group: 12
Levels: all
Min. age: 18
*Ring for current programme.*

**West Dean College**  **Centre 481**
Location: Sussex
Duration: 3-5 days, all year
Levels: all
*Over 20 courses on lace making, embroi-
dery, knitting, tapestry, batik, silk painting,
weaving, and papermaking.*

# Batik & fabric painting

**Alston Hall Residential
College**  **Centre 16**
Location: Lancashire
Duration: 2 days, July
Levels: all
Min. age: 16

# Dyeing

**Byre Yard**  **Centre 72**
Location: Yorkshire
Duration: varies
Levels: all
*Hand-dyed textiles.*

*West Dean College*

**Snail Trail Handweavers**  **Centre 410**
Location: Dyfed
Duration: 7 days, April-October
Max. in group: 6
Levels: all
Min. age: 14
*Dyeing using natural and synthetic dyes, on
all types of fibre.*

# Embroidery

**Alston Hall Residential
College**  **Centre 16**
Location: Lancashire
Duration: 2/7 days, June/July
Min. age: 16
*Machine embroidery, fabric collage and
quilting.*

**Flatford Mill Field Centre**  **Centre 169**
Location: Suffolk
Duration: 2 days, September
Levels: all
Min. age: 16
*Wild flower and garden embroidery.*

**Icelandic Tapestry School**  **Centre 224**
Location: Somerset
Duration: 1-2 day, September-June
Max. in group: 20
Levels: all
Min. age: 6

**Juniper Hall Field Centre**    **Centre 243**
Location: Surrey
Duration: 3 days, May
Levels: beginners/intermediate
Min. age: 16

# Fabric Sculpture

**Acorn Activities**    **Centre 3**
Location: Herefordshire
Duration: varies, all year
Levels: all
*A course to create a period figurine from cotton fabric, wool and wire.*

# Handspinning

**Ardmiddle Enterprises**    **Centre 23**
Location: Aberdeenshire
Duration: June
Max. in group: 10
Levels: all
Min. age: 16
*Course concentrates on controlling the yarn for knitting and weaving.*

# Icelandic Embroidery

**Icelandic Tapestry School**    **Centre 224**
Location: Somerset
Duration: 1-2 days, September-June
Max. in group: 20
Levels: all
Min. age: 6
*Icelandic stitches with patterns taught without the use of a frame.*

# Japanese Ribbon Flower Making

**Grantley Hall**    **Centre 194**
Location: Yorkshire
Duration: 3 days, March
Levels: beginners/intermediate
*Flowers from ribbons imported from Japan.*

# Lacemaking

**Acorn Activities**    **Centre 3**
Location: Herefordshire
Duration: varies, all year
Levels: all

**Alston Hall Residential College**    **Centre 16**
Location: Lancashire
Duration: 2-6 days, April-September
Levels: all
Min. age: 16
*Bedfordshire, Honiton, Ruskin, bobbin and needle lacemaking.*

**Belstead House**    **Centre 39**
Location: Suffolk
Duration: 2 days, February
Levels: beginners/intermediate
*Needlepoint lacemaking.*

**Higham Hall Residential Study Centre**    **Centre 214**
Location: Cumbria
Duration: 2 days, June
Levels: all
Min. age: mostly 16
*Ruskin lacemaking.*

**Maryland Residential College**    **Centre 281**
Location: Bedfordshire
Duration: 2 days, April
Levels: all
Min. age: 18
*Courses for both practising lacemakers and newcomers. Individual tuition is provided in Bedfordshire, Bucks Point and Torchon Lace.*

## Lacemaking continued

**Nairn Craft Holidays**  **Centre 301**
Location: Inverness-shire
Duration: 5 days, May
Max. in group: 8
Levels: all
Min. age: 16
*A variety of laces are taught on an individual basis.*

**Robingarth Lace**  **Centre 361**
Location: Tweeddale
Duration: 2+ days, November-March
Max. in group: 4
Levels: beginners
Min. age: 10

# Machine Knitting

**Alston Hall Residential College**  **Centre 16**
Location: Lancashire
Duration: 3-7 days, April/September
Levels: all
Min. age: 16

**Ardmiddle Enterprises**  **Centre 23**
Location: Aberdeenshire
Duration: 7 days, June/October
Max. in group: 6
Levels: all
Min. age: 16
*Courses exploring the basic techniques, or more creative skills for experienced knitters.*

**Nairn Craft Holidays**  **Centre 311**
Location: Inverness-shire
Duration: 5 days, May
Max. in group: 8
Levels: beginners/intermediate
Min. age: 16

*West Dean College*

# Needlecraft

**Acorn Activities**  **Centre 3**
Location: Herefordshire
Duration: 2 days, all year
Levels: all
*Courses in tapestry, crochet, embroidery, tatting, rag rugs, machine knitting, dressmaking and soft furnishings.*

**Anne Justina Carhart**  **Centre 19**
Location: Yorkshire
Duration: 2 days, March-November
Max. in group: 8
Levels: all
Min. age: 14
*Courses include embroidery, patchwork, quilting, tatting and crochet.*

**Higham Hall Residential Study Centre**  **Centre 214**
Location: Cumbria
Duration: 2 days, June
Levels: all
Min. age: mostly 16

# Patchwork & Embroidery

**Grantley Hall**　　　　　**Centre 194**
Location: Yorkshire
Duration: 3 days, February
*A course exploring logcabin variations and shapes other than the traditional central square.*

**Ardmiddle Enterprises**　　**Centre 23**
Location: Aberdeenshire
Duration: 1/7 days, May/October
Max. in group: 6
Levels: all
Min. age: 16
*A variety of machine stitching techniques covered including log cabin, pineapple and appliqué.*

# Patchwork & Quilting

**Campions Crafts**　　　　**Centre 86**
Location: Devon
Duration: 2-5 days, all year
Max. in group: 6
Levels: all
Min. age: 12
*Introduces basic principles to novices and develops a wider knowledge of techniques and different traditions to those with experience.*

**Higham Hall Residential
Study Centre**　　　　　**Centre 214**
Location: Cumbria
Duration: 2 days, March
Levels: all
Min. age: 16
*American and Celtic patchwork.*

**Hill Residential College**　**Centre 218**
Location: Gwent
Duration: 2-7 days, all year
Max in group: 15

Levels: all
Min. age: 16

**Nairn Craft Holidays**　　**Centre 311**
Location: Inverness-shire
Duration: 5 days, May
Max. in group: 10
Levels: beginners/intermediate
Min age: 16

# Rag Dolls

**Marlborough College
Summer School**　　　　**Centre 280**
Location: Wiltshire
Duration: 5 days, late July-early August
Max. in group: 14
Levels: all
Min. age: 17

# Soft Furnishing

**Calluna Workshops**　　　**Centre 82**
Location: Somerset
Duration: 20 days, March/June/September
Max. in group: 6
Levels: all
Min. age: 16
*All handsewn soft furnishings covered*

# Spinning

**Acorn Activities**　　　　**Centre 3**
Location: Welsh Borders
Duration: 2 days, all year
*Courses cover sorting the fleece, carding, plying, skeining and dyeing. Equipment provided.*

**Please mention this guide when booking a course**

## Spinning continued

**Alston Hall Residential
College**                          **Centre 16**
Location: Lancashire
Duration: 2 days, April
Levels: all
Min. age: 16

**Fibrecrafts at Barnhowe**        **Centre 167**
Location: Cumbria
Duration: 1+ days, March-November
Max. in group: 4
Levels: all
Min. age: 8
*All aspects of spinning can be covered.*

**Snail Trail Handweavers**        **Centre 410**
Location: Dyfed
Duration: 7 days, April-October
Max. in group: 6
Levels: beginners
Min. age: 14
*An introduction to handspinning covering
fibre preparation, both long and short draw
spinning and plying.*

# Spinning, Weaving & Dyeing

**Anne Justina Carhart**           **Centre 19**
Location: Yorkshire
Duration: 2-5 days, January-November
Max. in group: 4
Levels: all
Min. age: 14
*A course with demonstrations and practical
sessions with trained tutors.*

**Braziers Adult College**         **Centre 53**
Location: Oxon
Duration: 2 days, March/April
Levels: all
*A variety of techniques and designs covered.*

**Eden Valley Woollen Mill**       **Centre 150**
Location: Cumbria
Duration: 1-5 days, varies
Max. in group: 10
Levels: all

**Laneside Weavers**               **Centre 257**
Location: Cumbria
Duration: 7 days, April-mid-October
Max. in group: 5
Levels: all
Min. age: 12
*Individual tuition given.*

**Tymawr Farm**                    **Centre 452**
Location: Gwent
Duration: 7 days, April-October
Max. in group: 3
Levels: all
Min. age: 13
*Equipment provided. Rag rug making
included.*

**Waternish Workshop**             **Centre 470**
Location: Isle of Skye
Duration: 2-3 days, May/July-September
Max. in group: 6
Min. age: 12

# Upholstery

**Fairhope Fine Furniture
Restoration Courses**              **Centre 160**
Location: Cornwall
Duration: 3/5 days, all year
Max. in group: 4
Levels: all
Min. age: 18

**Please refer to the Centres Index
for details about accommodation**

**Land Ends**      **Centre 256**
Location: Ullswater
Duration: 2 days, all year
Max. in group: 12
Levels: all
Min. age: 16
*The principles of upholstery are taught from beginning to advanced levels.*

# Weaving

**Ardmiddle Enterprises**      **Centre 23**
Location: Aberdeenshire
Duration: 7 days, June/September-October
Max. in group: 8
Levels: all
Min. age: 16
*Participants can tailor the course by selecting projects.*

**Snail Trail Handweavers**      **Centre 410**
Location: Dyfed
Duration: 7 days, April-October
Max. in group: 6
Levels: all
Min. age: 14
*Course provides a good foundation in handweaving for the beginner and extends and develops the craft for intermediate and advanced weavers.*

**Water Lily Weavers**      **Centre 468**
Location: Berwickshire
Duration: 5 days, all year
Max. in group: 3
Levels: all
Min. age: 8
*Course covers all aspects of the design and making of woven and tufted textiles.*

*Suffolk College Summer School*

# Ceramics, Pottery and Sculpture

## Calligraphy on Porcelain

**Broadland Arts Centre**　　Centre 62
Location: Essex
Duration: 2 days, March
Max. in group: 15
Levels: beginners/intermediate
Min. age: 16
*Demonstrations and practical tuition for china and porcelain artists. Slides and video presentations included.*

## Ceramics

**Blisland Porcelain**　　Centre 42
Location: Cornwall
Duration: 1 day, all year
Max. in group: 4
Levels: all
Min. age: 8
*Course covers handbuilding, china painting, jewellery making and slip casting.*

**Millfield School Village of Education**　　Centre 293
Location: Somerset
Duration: 5 days, July-August
Max. in group: 10
Levels: all
Min. age: 8
*Courses in china restoration, china painting and ceramic sculpture.*

## China Painting

**Acorn Activities**　　Centre 3
Location: Herefordshire
Duration: 2 days, all year
Levels: all
*Traditional handpainting on china.*

**Alston Hall Residential College**　　Centre 16
Location: Lancashire
Duration: 3 days, May
Levels: all
Min. age: 16
*Flower painting on bone china.*

## China Restoration

**Alston Hall Residential College**　　Centre 16
Location: Lancashire
Duration: 3 days, June
Levels: all
Min. age: 16

**Belstead House**　　Centre 39
Location: Suffolk
Duration: 2 days, various months
Levels: all
*Repairing, re-painting and glazing covered.*

**Burton Manor College**     **Centre 70**
Location: Cheshire
Duration: 2 days, April-September
Levels: all
Min. age: 14

**Dillington House**     **Centre 131**
Location: Somerset
Duration: 2 days, ring for months
Max. in group: varies
Levels: all
Min. age: 18

**Earnley Concourse**     **Centre 141**
Location: Sussex
Duration: 2/4 days, all year
Max in group: 12
Levels: all
Min age: 16
*China requiring repair should be brought along.*

**Hazel Tree Farm**     **Centre 201**
Location: Kent
Duration: 2 days, May-June/October
Max. in group: 12
Min. age: 16

**KLC Interior Design
Training**     **Centre 252**
Location: London
Duration: 3 days, January/July/September
Max. in group: 10
Levels: beginners
Min. age: 17

**Land Ends**     **Centre 256**
Location: Ullswater
Duration: 2/5 days, all year
Max. in group: 10
Levels: all
Min. age: 16
*Principles of china restoration from beginners to advanced levels.*

**Mowbray School of Porcelain
Restoration**     **Centre 308**
Location: Hertfordshire
Duration: 5-15 days, all year
Max. in group: 8
Levels: all
Min. age: 18
*Enables students to restore professionally or just for leisure. Broken porcelain objects may be brought along.*

**Mulberry House Studio**     **Centre 309**
Location: Oxfordshire
Duration: 5/10 days, June/September or by arrangement
Max. in group: 4
Levels: all
Min. age: none
*Courses in restoring ceramics, including dismantling old restoration, modelling, moulding and painting.*

# Clay Modelling

**Wethersfield Arts Centre**     **Centre 483**
Location: Essex
Duration: 2 days, September-December
Max. in group: 14
Levels: all
Min. age: 14
*A variety of studiesof the human form and animals.*

# Doll Making

**Recollect Doll Studios**     **Centre 366**
Location: Sussex
Duration: varies, March-October
Max. in group: 12
Levels: all
Min. age: 12
*A variety of doll related courses for collectors and restorers.*

# Pottery

**Acorn Activities**      **Centre 3**
Location: Herefordshire/Pembrokeshire
Duration: 2-5 days, various months
Levels: all
*Throwing and handbuilding in clay covered.*

**Alan Baxter Pottery
Workshop**      **Centre 13**
Location: Suffolk
Duration: 5 days, all year
Max. in group: 8
Levels: all
Min age: 16
*An extensive range of techniques working
with clay covered.*

**Blidworth Pottery**      **Centre 41**
Location: Nottinghamshire
Duration: 2 days, all year
Max. in group: 6
Levels: beginners/all
*A wide range of techniques are covered in a
relaxed atmosphere.*

**Brookhouse Pottery Workshop Centre 64**
Location: Clwyd
Duration: 7-14 days, April/July/September
Max. in group: 8
Levels: all
Min. age: 16
*All aspects of pottery making, plus firing,
glazing and decorating stoneware.*

**Coombe Farm Studios**      **Centre 108**
Location: Devon
Duration: 5 days, April-October
Max. in group: 6
Levels: all
Min. age: 8
*Instruction in throwing, handbuilding and
decoration of pottery.*

**Cornwall Creative Activity
Network**      **Centre 111**
Location: Cornwall
Duration: varies, all year
Levels: all
*Ring for details.*

**Lower Aston House
Pottery School**      **Centre 273**
Location: Worcestershire
Duration: 2/3/6 days, May-October
Max. in group: 10
Levels: all
Min. age: 12
*Covers throwing, handbuilding, turning and
firing of pots. Individual tuition given.*

**Nairn Craft Holidays**      **Centre 311**
Location: Inverness-shire
Duration: 5 days, May
Max. in group: 10
Min. age: 10

*Suffolk College Summer School*

**Suffolk College Summer School**     **Centre 422**
Location: Suffolk
Duration: varies
*Making and decorating terracotta tiles, enamelling and sculpture.*

**Summer University**     **Centre 425**
Location: Leicestershire
Duration: 5 days, July/August
Max. in group: 12
Levels: all
Min. age: 18

**Wenford Bridge Pottery**     **Centre 477**
Location: Cornwall
Duration: 6 days, various months
Max. in group: 5
Levels: all
Min. age: 15
*Course develops abilities in all stages of wheel thrown pottery.*

**West Dean College**     **Centre 481**
Location: Sussex
Duration: 2-5 days, all year
Levels: all
*Various courses covering throwing, turning, mosaic, handbuilding, modelling in clay and general pottery.*

**White Roding Pottery**     **Centre 489**
Location: Essex
Duration: 2-7 days, April-October
Max. in group: 9
Levels: all
Min. age: 14

**Wolfcastle Pottery**     **Centre 502**
Location: Pembrokeshire
Duration: 6 days, May-October
Max. in group: 7
Levels: all
Min. age: 16

*A variety of courses in pottery or pottery combined with aromatherapy and massage.*

# Saltglaze workshops

**Saltglaze Workshops**     **Centre 378**
Location: Sussex
Duration: 6 days, April/July/August
Max. in group: 6
Levels: intermediate/advanced
Min. age: 21
*Introduces the practice of saltglazing stoneware for pots or sculpture.*

# Sculpture

**Alston Hall**     **Centre 16**
Location: Lancashire
Duration: 2 days, June
Levels: all
*Course covers portraiture in clay*

**Blisland Porcelain**     **Centre 42**
Location: Cornwall
Duration: 1 day, all year
Max. in group: 4
Levels: all
Min. age: 15
*Courses tailored to the individual.*

**Brunel University Arts Centre**     **Centre 65**
Location: Middlesex
Duration: 5 days, July
Max. in group: 14
Levels: all
Min. age: 16

**Higham Hall Residential Study Centre**     **Centre 214**
Location: Cumbria
Duration: 2 days, June
Levels: all
*Ring for details.*

# Wood Crafts

## Basket Making

**Acorn Activities**                  Centre 3
Location: Herefordshire
Duration: 2 days, all year
Levels: all
*Course covers making cane shopping baskets, tablemats and basketware.*

**Welsh Woodland Skills**          Centre 476
Location: Powys
Duration: 3 days, April-October
Max in group: 10
Levels: all
Min age: 14
*Traditional Welsh baskets in oak, willow and hazel in a woodland workshop.*

**West Dean College**               Centre 481
Location: Sussex
Duration: 2-5 days, all year
Levels: all
*Willow and hedgerow basket making.*

## Cabinet Making

**Wynn Bishop**                       Centre 508
Location: Yorkshire
Duration: 2-5 days, all year
Max in group: 2
Levels: all
Min age: 16
*Introduces the student to the precise approach to woodwork of the cabinet maker.*

## Cane & Rush Seating

**Alston Hall Residential
College**                             Centre 16
Location: Lancashire
Duration: 3 days, June
Levels: all
Min. age: 16

**Fairhope Fine Furniture
Restoration Courses**              Centre 160
Location: Cornwall
Duration: 3+ days, all year
Max in group: 4
Levels: all
Min age: 18
*Traditional methods and patterns are taught to participants bringing their own furniture.*

**Nairn Craft Holidays**            Centre 311
Location: Inverness-shire
Duration: 5 days, May
Max in group: 8
Levels: all
Min age: 16
*Chair seating in split cane, using natural materials and traditional techniques.*

**West Dean College**               Centre 481
Location: Sussex
Duration: 2-5 days, all year
Levels: all
*Various courses. Ring for details.*

# Chair Making

**Welsh Woodland Skills**
**Centre**                    **Centre 476**
Location: Powys
Duration: 5/7 days, April-October
Max in group: 8
Levels: all
Min age: 14
*Chair making from green wood, turning the legs on a pole lathe, steam bending, etc.*

# Clog Making

**Welsh Woodland Skills**
**Centre**                    **Centre 476**
Location: Powys
Duration: 3 days, May-October
Max in group: 8
Levels: all
Min age: 14
*Traditional Welsh clogs are made using hand tools and green timber.*

# Coracle Building

**Welsh Woodland Skills**
**Centre**                    **Centre 476**
Location: Powys
Duration: 3 days, May-October
Max in group: 8
Levels: all
Min age: 14
*Welsh coracle building from green wood with an opportunity in learning to use it.*

# French Polishing

**Fairhope Fine Furniture**
**Restoration Courses**        **Centre 160**
Location: Cornwall
Duration: 3/5/6 days, all year
Max in group: 4
Levels: all
Min age: 18
*Course covers removal of rings, bruises, staining, graining and correct french polishing.*

*Coracle building with Welsh Woodland Skills Centre*

# Marquetry & Parquetry

**Fairhope Fine Furniture**
**Restoration Courses**          **Centre 160**
Location: Cornwall
Duration: 4 days, all year
Max in group: 4
Levels: all
Min age: 18
*Techniques taught in building a picture using a range of contrasting veneers.*

# Modeling

**Dillington House**          **Centre 131**
Location: Somerset
Duration: 2 days, March
Levels: all
Min age: 18
*A course on making dolls houses and miniatures.*

# Pyrography

**Waternish Workshop**          **Centre 470**
Location: Isle of Skye
Duration: 3 days, May-June/August-September
Max in group: 6
Min age: 12
*Participants are taught to develop their own designs based on natural forms and Celtic art styles.*

# Restoration

**Broadland Arts Centre**          **Centre 62**
Location: Essex
Duration: 2/4/6 days, October
Max in group: 15
Levels: all
Min age: 16
*Course covers design for painted furniture*

*and decorative finishes, upholstery restoration and repair.*

**Fairhope Fine Furniture**
**Restoration Courses**          **Centre 160**
Location: Cornwall
Duration: 3/5/6 days/1 month, all year
Max in group: 4
Levels: all
Min age: 18
*An introduction to antique furniture restoration working on own furniture.*

**Kelly's Antiques**          **Centre 246**
Location: Ayrshire
Duration: 2/5 days, all year
Max in group: 5
Levels: all
Min age: 12
*Participants bring their own furniture to restore, french polish, upholster, etc.*

**KLC Interior Design**
**Training**          **Centre 252**
Location: London
Duration: 3 days, January/July/September
Max. in group: 10
Levels: beginners
Min. age: 17
*Participants work on their own furniture.*

**West Dean College**          **Centre 481**
Location: Sussex
Duration: 2-5 days, all year
Levels: all
*Various courses in antique restoration, special finishes, care and repair.*

**Please mention this guide when booking courses**

*West Dean College*

# Timber Frame Building

**Welsh Woodland Skills Centre**     **Centre 476**
Location: Powys
Duration: 5 days, May-October
Max in group: 12
Levels: all
Min age: 14
*Course covers the building of an oak frame barn using traditional methods and tools.*

# Wood Carving

**Burton Manor College**     **Centre 70**
Location: Cheshire
Duration: 2 days, September
Max. in group: 16
Levels: all
Min. age: 14

**Campions Crafts**     **Centre 86**
Location: Devon
Duration: 2-5 days, all year
Max in group: 4
Levels: all
Min age: 16

*Introduces basic principles to novices and widens the skills of those with experience.*

**Higham Hall Residential Study Centre**     **Centre 214**
Location: Cumbria
Duration: 2 days, February
Levels: all
*Wildlife woodcarving.*

**Kirkbeag Craft**     **Centre 251**
Location: Inverness-shire
Duration: 2-5 days, all year
Max in group: 3
Levels: beginners/intermediate
Min age: 16
*Advice given on materials and necessary skills involved in tool handling and maintenance.*

**Jeremy Williams Wood Carving**     **Centre 239**
Location: Cornwall
Duration: 3-6 days, all year
Max in group: 3
Levels: beginners/intermediate
Min age: 20
*Introduction to woodcarving in either relief or 3-D technique.*

**Missenden Abbey**     **Centre 296**
Location: Buckinghamshire
Duration: 2 days, all year
Levels: beginners/intermediate
Min. age: 18
*Ring for details.*

**Zoë Gertner Wood Carving**     **Centre 519**
Location: Somerset
Duration: 1/2/5/6 days, all year
Max in group: 5
Levels: all
Min age: 9

# Woodcrafts

**Cornwall Creative Activity**
**Network (CCAN)**          **Centre 111**
Location: Cornwall
Duration: varies, all year
Levels: all
*Courses in wood carving and basket making.*

**Marlborough College Summer**
**School**                  **Centre 280**
Location: Wiltshire
Duration: 5 days, July-August
Max. in group: 14
Levels: all
Min. age: 17
*Covers woodwork, french polishing cabinet*
*making, repair, etc.*

**Millfield School Village of**
**Education**               **Centre 293**
Location: Somerset
Duration: 5 days, July-August
Max. in group: 10
Levels: all
Min. age: 13

**Suffolk College Summer**
**School**                  **Centre 422**
Location: Suffolk
Duration: varies
Levels: all
*Courses in cabinet making, furniture*
*restoration, stencilling, upholstery, picture*
*framing and boat restoration.*

**West Dean College**       **Centre 481**
Location: Sussex
Duration: 2-5 days, all year
Levels: all
*Courses include cabinet making, furniture*
*restoration, picture framing, woodturning,*
*general carpentry and clock case designs.*

# Woodland Skills

**Welsh Woodland Skills**
**Centre**                  **Centre 476**
Location: Powys
Duration: 3 days, April-October
Max. in group: 10
Levels: all
Min. age: 14
*Course covers making charcoal, tent pegs,*
*rakes and besoms in a woodland workshop.*

# Woodturning

**Acorn Activities**        **Centre 3**
Location: Pembrokeshire
Duration: 2 days, all year
Max in group: 3-4
Levels: all
*All equipment provided. Courses given by*
*an internationally acclaimed turner.*

**Campions Crafts**         **Centre 86**
Location: Devon
Duration: 2-5 days, all year
Max in group: 4
Levels: all
Min age: 16
*Introduces basic principles to novices and*
*widens the skills of those with experience.*

**Craft Supplies Ltd**      **Centre 115**
Location: Derbyshire
Duration: 2 days, all year
Max in group: 4
Levels: all
Min age: 12
*Courses vary according to experience. Ring*
*for details.*

**Devon Woodcrafts**        **Centre 129**
Location: Devon
Duration: 1-2 days, all year

Max in group: 4
Levels: all
Min age: 14
*Various courses including lace bobbin and stool woodturning, plus general woodturning for beginners to the advanced.*

### Kirkbeag Craft     Centre 251
Location: Inverness-shire
Duration: 2-5 days, all year
Max in group: 3
Levels: beginners/intermediate
Min age: 16
*Course to advise on materials and introduce necessary skills involved in tool handling and maintenance.*

### Michael O'Donnell     Centre 288
Location: Caithness
Duration: 5 days, June/September
Max in group: 4
Levels: all
*Course covers use of equipment with opportunities to develop special skills and ideas.*

# Woodwork

### Living Wood Training     Centre 267
Location: Avon
Duration: 5-9 days, April-September
Max in group: 8
Levels: all
Min age: 16
*Course includes turning trees into chairs, tools and utensils within a woodland workshop using hand tools and traditional person-powered devices.*

### Michael O'Donnell     Centre 288
Location: Caithness
Duration: 5 days, June/September
Max in group: 4
Levels: all
*This course, called 'turning green' works with fresh wood.*

*Suffolk College Summer School*

# Other Crafts

## Blacksmithing

**Nairn Craft Holidays**　　　**Centre 311**
Location: Inverness-shire
Duration: 5 days, May
Max in group: 8
Levels: all
Min. age: 16
*Blacksmithing and wrought ironwork.*

**West Dean College**　　　**Centre 481**
Location: Sussex
Duration: 2-5 days, all year
Levels: all
*Ironwork and metal sculpture courses.*

## Bookbinding & Repair

**Acorn Activities**　　　**Centre 3**
Location: Herefordshire
Duration: 2/5 days, all year
Levels: all
*Learn the basics of pamphlet and hardback book binding.*

**Flatford Mill Field Centre**　　　**Centre 169**
Location: Essex
Duration: 6 days, February/November
Levels: all
Min. age: 16
*Covers the foundations of hand binding. Equipment provided.*

**Gateway Education & Arts Centre**　　　**Centre 183**
Duration: 2 days, March
Levels: all
*Learn the repair of leather books.*

**Wansfell College**　　　**Centre 466**
Location: Essex
Duration: 2 days, May
Levels: intermediate

**West Dean College**　　　**Centre 481**
Location: Sussex
Duration: 2-5 days, various months
Levels: beginners
*Bookbinding and paper marbling covered.*

## Conservation & Craft

**St George's Island Craft Centre**　　　**Centre 414**
Location: Cornwall
Duration: 7 days, April-September
Max in group: 8
Levels: all
Min age: 16
*Enjoy conserving the island while doing your own craftwork.*

## Decorations

**Ardmiddle Enterprises**　　　**Centre 23**
Location: Aberdeenshire
Duration: 1-6 days, November

Max in group: 10
Levels: all
Min age: 16
*Various short courses making Christmas decorations and gifts.*

# Display Case Making

**Malham Tarn Field Centre**      **Centre 278**
Location: Yorkshire
Duration: 3 days, October
Levels: all
Min age: 16
*For any artist or collector who wishes to display collections to their best advantage.*

# Eggcraft

**Acorn Activities**      **Centre 3**
Location: Worcestershire
Duration: 2 days, all year
Levels: all
*Skills taught include cutting, hingeing and decorating goose eggs.*

**HF Holidays Ltd**      **Centre 207**
Location: nationwide
Duration: 3-7 days, all year
Max. in group: 20-30
Levels: all

# Flowercraft

**Higham Hall Residential Study Centre**      **Centre 214**
Location: Cumbria
Duration: 2 days, January/February/June
Levels: beginners
*Courses on pressed and dried flowers, and flower arranging*

# Glass Blowing

**Yeoldon Country House Hotel**      **Centre 511**
Location: Devon
Duration: 3 days, October-May
Max in group: 12
Levels: all
Min age: 15

# Interior Design

**Calluna Workshops**      **Centre 82**
Location: Somerset
Duration: 10-15 days, varies
Max in group: 10
Levels: all
Min age: 18
*Home furnishings.*

**KLC Interior Design Training**      **Centre 252**
Location: London
Duration: 1/20 days, all year
Max. in group: 20
Levels: beginners/intermediate
Min. age: 17
*Full course provides a basic grounding in interior decoration. Plus one-days courses on curtain making, headboards, decorative finishes, stencilling, gilding and decoupage.*

# Jewellery

**Coombe Farm Studios**      **Centre 108**
Location: Devon
Duration: 5 days, April-October
Max in group: 4
Levels: all
Min age: 15
*Translation of sketch ideas and design into finished pieces in silver or base metals. Stone setting included.*

## Jewellery continued

**Earnley Concourse**          Centre 141
Location: Sussex
Duration: 2 days, various months
Levels: all
*Designing and making jewellery. Enamelling also covered.*

**Higham Hall Residential
Study Centre**          Centre 214
Location: Cumbria
Duration: 6 days, April
Levels: beginners/intermediate
*Course covers working with silver.*

**Malham Tarn Field Centre**   Centre 278
Location: Yorkshire
Duration: 7 days, August
Levels: all
Min. age: 16
*Jewellery from objects found in the countryside discarded by humans, animals, and nature.*

**Missenden Abbey**          Centre 296
Location: Buckinghamshire
Duration: 2 days, various months
Levels: beginners
*Ring for details.*

**Silverweed**          Centre 397
Location: Dyfed
Duration: 2/5 days, all year
Max in group: 2
Levels: all
Min age: 15
*For women only.*

**West Dean College**          Centre 481
Location: Sussex
Duration: 2-5 days, all year
Levels: all

*West Dean College*

*Various courses on silversmithing, enamelling and gem setting.*

# Lapidary

**Kirkbeag Craft**          Centre 251
Location: Inverness-shire
Duration: 2-5 days, all year
Max in group: 3
Levels: beginners/intermediate
Min age: 16
*Introduces the skills required in cotting, shaping and polishing of semi-precious stones*

# Leatherwork

**Nairn Craft Holidays**          Centre 311
Location: Inverness-shire
Duration: 5 days, May
Max. in group: 6
Levels: beginners/intermediate
Min. age: 16

*Course gives a grounding in basic techniques (cutting, embossing, dyeing, polishing, and stitching) all on cow hide.*

**West Dean College**　　　**Centre 481**
Location: Sussex
Duration: 5 days, various months
Levels: beginners/intermediate

# Mixed crafts

**Higher Humber Farm**　　**Centre 213**
Location: Devon
Duration: 2-3 days, October-November/
February-April/July-August
Max. in group: 10
Levels: all
Min. age: 16
*Courses on bookbinding, copper and pewter work and jewellery making.*

**Millfield School Village of
Education**　　　**Centre 293**
Location: Somerset
Duration: 5 days, July-August
Max. in group: 10
Levels: all
Min. age: 13
*Courses on dried flowers, green crafts, stencilling, home decorating, crafts and cards for Christmas.*

**Suffolk College Summer
School**　　　**Centre 422**
Location: Suffolk
Duration: varies
Levels: all
*A variety of courses including book refurbishment, jewellery, stained glass, sugarcraft, handmade shoes, interior design, picture framing, ropework, saddlery and stencilling. Ring for details.*

# Paper Making & Sculpture

**Acorn Activities**　　　**Centre 3**
Location: Herefordshire
Duration: 2/3/5 days, April/August
Levels: all

**Alston Hall Residential
College**　　　**Centre 16**
Location: Lancashire
Duration: 2 days, June
Levels: all

**Plant Papers**　　　**Centre 350**
Location: Herefordshire
Duration: 2/3/5 days, April/August
Max. in group: 6
Levels: all
Min. age: 14

**Higham Hall Residential
Study Centre**　　　**Centre 214**
Location: Cumbria
Duration: 2 days, February
Levels: all
*Basic techniques of folding, scoring and cutting, plus a history of the art form.*

# Picture Framing

**Earnley Concourse**　　　**Centre 141**
Location: Sussex
Duration: 3 days, varies
Levels: all
*From mount cutting to mitre joint construction.*

**Flatford Mill Field Centre**　　**Centre 169**
Location: Essex
Duration: 6 days, February/November
Levels: all
Min. age: 16

## Picture Framing continued

**Higham Hall Residential
Study Centre**　　　　　**Centre 214**
Location: Cumbria
Duration: 2 days, February
Levels: beginners

**Missenden Abbey**　　　　**Centre 296**
Location: Buckinghamshire
Duration: 2 days, various months
Levels: all
*Ring for details.*

## Silversmithing

**Acorn Activities**　　　　**Centre 3**
Location: Pembrokeshire
Duration: 2 days, all year
Levels: all
*Skills taught include casting, raising,
forging, boxmaking and polishing.*

**Kirkbeag Craft**　　　　**Centre 251**
Location: Inverness-shire
Duration: 2-5 days, all year
Max in group: 3
Levels: beginners/intermediate
Min age: 16
*Advice given on materials and introduces
necessary techniques for the making of
small items in silver.*

**Wolds Silver**　　　　**Centre 501**
Location: Yorkshire
Duration: 2+ days, April-December
Max in group: 5
Levels: all
Min age: 15
*Silversmithing and jewellery. Anything from
rings to teapots.*

# Stained Glass & Engraving

**Chichester Interest Holidays**　**Centre 93**
Location: Cornwall
Duration: 3 days, all year
Levels: all
Min age: 18
*Production of stained glass articles using
lead. Tuition in pattern making, glass
cutting and soldering.*

**Flatford Mill Field Centre**　**Centre 169**
Location: Essex
Duration: 6 days, February/October
Levels: all
Min age: 16
*Course includes the making of windows and
panels and painting and firing of designs
onto glass.*

**Gateway Education &
Arts Centre**　　　　**Centre 183**
Location: Shropshire
Duration: 2 days, April
Levels: all

**Higham Hall Residential
Study Centre**　　　　**Centre 214**
Location: Cumbria
Duration: 2-4 days, January/May
Levels: all
*General techniques including stained glass
painting.*

**Preston Montford
Field Centre**　　　　**Centre 357**
Location: Shropshire
Duration: 2 days, May/June
Levels: beginners

**Missenden Abbey**　　　　**Centre 296**
Location: Buckinghamshire
Duration: 2 days, various months

Levels: all
*Stained glass and glass gilding.*

**Paul San Casciani Stained
Glass Activities          Centre 338**
Location: Oxfordshire
Duration: 4 days, August-September
Max. in group: 6
Levels: beginners/intermediate
Min. age: 16
*Basic training in traditional leading and
copperfoiling as well as glass painting.*

**Preston Montford
Field Centre          Centre 357**
Location: Shropshire
Duration: 3 days, May/June
Levels: all
Min. age: 16
*Covers design, cutting, leading-up, foil
work, soldering and finishing.*

**Starlight Studio          Centre 416**
Location: Gloucestershire
Duration: 4 days, all year
Max. in group: 4
Levels: all
Min. age: 15
*All stages of design and production are
covered.*

**West Dean College          Centre 481**
Location: Sussex
Duration: 2-5 days, all year
Levels: all
*Stained glass and glass engraving courses
offered.*

## Strawcraft

**Acorn Activities          Centre 3**
Location: Herefordshire
Duration: 2-5 days, all year
Levels: all
*Corn dollies, thatching and rick finials, lip
work for baskets, straw hats and marquetry.*

**Straw Craft Studios          Centre 419**
Location: Herefordshire
Duration: 1-6 days, all year
Max. in group: 8
Levels: all
Min. age: 8
*Corn dollies, straw lace, marquetry, simple
thatching for models, rick finials, lipwork
for furniture, and models.*

## West Country Crafts

**Taunton Summer School          Centre 435**
Location: Somerset
Duration: 5 days, July/August
Max. in group: 8-14
Levels: all

*Belstead Brook*
HOTEL

Belstead Rd, Ipswich, Suffolk, IP2 9HB
Tel: 0473 684241. Fax: 0473 681249

The eight acres of nature's artwork, in which the Belstead Brook Hotel is set, make it the ideal venue for social and business gatherings alike. True Suffolk hospitality in luxurious surroundings, the sound of our resident pianist and the warmth of roaring log fires combine to create the ambience of the real country house hotel.

Our oak-panelled restaurant is renowned for its classical English kitchen serving superb a la carte and table d'hote menus at very reasonable prices. Gluten-free, diabetic and vegetarian menus are served.

Private dining rooms are available overlooking our beautiful gardens.

# Photography, Film and Video

## Film Study

**University of Oxford**  Centre 458
Location: Oxford
Duration: 7 days, July-August
Max. in group: 12
Levels: all
Min. age: 18
*Seminars analysing a range of films. No practical courses.*

## Photography

**Acorn Activities**  Centre 3
Location: Herefordshire
Duration: 2 days, April-October
Levels: all
*A course on landscape, portrait and dramatic action photography in fully equipped studio with darkroom. Use of latest equipment.*

**Broadland Arts Centre**  Centre 63
Location: Essex
Duration: 2 days, October
Max. in group: 12
Levels: beginners/intermediate
Min. age: 16
*Nude photography in colour and black & white.*

**Burton Manor College**  Centre 70
Location: Cheshire
Duration: 1-5 days, April-August
Max. in group: 16
Levels: all
Min. age: 14
*Portrait, landscape, social and documentary, colour and black & white printing.*

**Coombe Farm Studios**  Centre 108
Location: Devon
Duration: 5 days, April-October
Max. in group: 4
Levels: all
Min. age: 14
*Composition, manual use of camera, shooting, processing, printing and retouching of photographs covered.*

**Countrywide Holidays**  Centre 114
Location: nationwide
Duration: 7 days, June
Levels: all
*Use of compact cameras taught. Photography combined with walking.*

**Dale Fort Field Centre**  Centre 121
Location: South Wales
Duration: 7 days, April-June
Levels: all
*Coastal scenery and wildlife are explored in the field and studio. Black & white and colour facilities available.*

*Inversnaid Photography*

**Inversnaid Photography**  Centre 234
Location: Stirlingshire
Duration: 3-6 days, March-November
Max. in group: 12
Levels: all
Min. age: 16
*A variety of courses offered from landscape and wildlife to studio and darkroom techniques.*

**Dillington House**  Centre 131
Location: Somerset
Duration: 1-7 days, varies
Max. in group: 70
Levels: all
Min. age: 18
*Portrait, landscape and travel photography covered.*

**Juniper Hall Field Centre**  Centre 243
Location: Surrey
Duration: 3-7 days, March-October
Levels: all
*Courses on landscape, wildflowers, nature and fungi in colour and black & white.*

**Kindrogan Field Centre**  Centre 250
Location: Perthshire
Duration: 7 days, August/October
Levels: all
*Close-up work in the field and studio.*

**Draper's Field Centre**  Centre 137
Location: Gwynedd
Duration: 3-7 days, February-May
Levels: all
*Emphasis on landscape and natural history subjects.*

**Lakeland Photographic
Holidays**  Centre 254
Location: Cumbria
Duration: any, February-December
Max. in group: 12
Levels: all
Min. age: 16
*Tuition in all aspects of black & white and colour.*

**Flatford Mill Field Centre**  Centre 169
Location: Essex/Suffolk
Duration: 3 days, February-November
Levels: all
*Colour techniques, close-up and winter landscapes covered.*

**Land Ends**  Centre 256
Location: Ullswater
Duration: 2-5 days, all year
Max. in group: 12
Levels: all
Min. age: 16
*Colour landscape photography.*

# Arts, Crafts, Photography and Video

## Photography continued

**Malham Tarn Field Centre**    **Centre 278**
Location: Yorkshire
Duration: 2-7 days, August/October
Levels: all
Min. age: 16
*Landscape and nature photography.*

**Missenden Abbey**    **Centre 296**
Location: Buckinghamshire
Duration: 2 days, all year
Levels: all
*Various courses available in black & white
and cibachrome colour.*

**Orielton Field Centre**    **Centre 329**
Location: Pembrokeshire
Duration: 7 days, July
Levels: all
Min. age: 16

**Ossian Guides**    **Centre 330**
Location: Inverness-shire
Duration: 7 days, June/October
Max. in group: 12
Min. age: 18
*Photographic tuition with evening clinics.*

**Peak National Park
Study Centre**    **Centre 340**
Location: Derbyshire
Duration: 2-7 days, all year
Max. in group: 25
Levels: all
Min. age: 8

**Photographer's Place (The)**    **Centre 348**
Location: Derbyshire
Duration: 2-5 days, April-October
Max. in group: 12
Levels: intermediate/advanced
Min. age: 18

*Seminars and practical intense sessions with
professional art photographers on all aspects.*

**Premier**    **Centre 355**
Location: Cambridgeshire
Duration: 1-2 days, April-October
Max. in group: 2
Levels: beginners
Min. age: 14
*Introduction to black & white and colour
printing.*

**Preston Montford
Field Centre**    **Centre 357**
Location: Shropshire
Duration: 3-7 days, February-October
Levels: all
*Courses in close-up, nature, wildlife and
landscape.*

**Slapton Ley Field Centre**    **Centre 406**
Location: Devon
Duration: 3-7 days, June-August
Levels: all
*Landscape and wildlife photography on
Dartmoor.*

**Taunton Summer School**    **Centre 435**
Location: Somerset
Duration: 5 days, July/August
Max. in group: 8-14
Levels: all
*Ring for details.*

**Wansfell College**    **Centre 466**
Location: Essex
Duration: 2 days, all year
Levels: all
Min. age: 18
*Various courses in black & white and
colour.*

**West Dean College**    **Centre 481**
Location: Sussex
Duration: 2-5 days, all year
Levels: all
*A variety of courses covering many aspects.*

# Photography & Video

**Coleg Harlech**    **Centre 100**
Location: Gwynedd
Duration: 7 days, August
Max. in group: 10
Levels: beginners/intermediate
Min. age: 14
*A practical course on using camcorders.*

**Earnley Concourse**    **Centre 141**
Location: Sussex
Duration: 3-7 days, all year
Max. in group: 16
Levels: all
Min. age: 16
*Various courses in black & white, colour and video.*

**HF Holidays Ltd**    **Centre 207**
Location: London
Duration: 3-7 days, March-September
Max. in group: 20
Levels: all

**Millfield School Village of Education**    **Centre 293**
Location: Somerset
Duration: 5 days, July/August
Max. in group: 10
Levels: beginners
Min. age: 13
*Photography and television workshops.*

**Y Neuadd Guest House & Photographic Holidays**    **Centre 509**
Location: Dyfed
Duration: 1+ day, February-October
Max. in group: 4
Levels: all
Min. age: 18
*Informal photographic and/or video instruction. Darkroom skills and video editing covered.*

*Millfield School Village of Education*

# Sports and Outdoor Activities

The emphasis now on a healthy lifestyle and personal fulfilment has attracted more and more people to holidays offering some kind of outdoor activity, whether it is as adventurous as parascending or as ordinary as cycling and walking. The following section provides an extensive list of holidays which cater for all ages, for both individuals and groups, many of which have special facilities for the disabled.

There is a vast range of watersports in Britain. You can try your hand at canoeing in North Wales, windsurfing in Cornwall, diving in Devon, or sailing at almost any offshore location. Many of the courses are affiliated to the Royal Yachting Association (RYA) or the British Canoe Union (BCU) and lead to recognised certificates, even for complete beginners. If you want a quieter life on the other hand, there are holidays available on board narrowboats on inland waterways or yachting around spectacular isles and lochs in Scotland.

There are numerous airsports to choose from for those people who would prefer to be in the driving seat of a flying machine. You may wish to experience the exhilaration of hang gliding, the challenge of parachute jumping or the gentle soaring of gliding.

If however, watersports or airsports do not appeal, there are a wealth of land based courses and holidays available, from walking in the Lake District, cycling in Norfolk or horseriding in Wales. These, of course, do not have to be soft options. Try mountain biking in the Forest of Dean, abseiling in the Peak District or mountaineering on Ben Nevis.

Whether you want to improve your golf handicap, brush up your tennis for next summer, fulfill a lifelong ambition or simply want to be fitter, the courses in the following section will give you plenty of options from which to choose.

# Water Sports and Holidays Afloat

## Canal Cruising

**Acorn Activities**                    Centre 3
Duration: 2 days, all year
Max. in group: 4
Levels: all
*Breaks in 25' steel narrow boats.*

**Calder Valley Cruising**          Centre 81
Location: Yorkshire
Duration: 2 days, April-October
Max. in group: 20
Levels: all
Min. age: 16
*Includes excursions and talks.*

**English County Cruises**      Centre 156
Location: Cheshire
Levels: all
*Free instruction given on request.*

**Middlewich Narrowboats**      Centre 289
Location: Cheshire
Duration: 7 days, March-December
Max. in group: 12
Levels: all
Min. age: 18
*Free tuition in boat steering and lock operation.*

**Rose Narrowboats**            Centre 374
Location: Warwickshire
Duration: 1-14 days, March-November
Max. in group: 12
Levels: all
*Instruction on handling craft.*

## Canoeing

**Acorn Activities**                    Centre 3
Location: River Wye
Duration: 2-5 days, all year
Levels: all
*Canadian canoes and kayaks available, plus white water canoeing during the winter.*

**Allenheads Lodge**
**Outdoor Centre**                  Centre 15
Location: Northumberland
Duration: 2/5/7 days, all year
Max. in group: 20
Levels: all
Min. age: 8
*River trips in 2 person Canadian canoes.*

## Canoeing continued

**Ardeonaig Outdoor Centre**      **Centre 22**
Location: Perthshire
Duration: 7 days, July-August
Max. in group: 32
Levels: all
Min. age: 14
*Course develops skills in kayaking and open
canoeing while exploring lochs and rivers
of Highland Perthshire.*

**Bowles Outdoor Centre**      **Centre 50**
Location: Sussex
Duration: 2 days, April-September
Max. in group: 12
Levels: all
Min. age: 16

**C.A.C Watersports**      **Centre 75**
Location: Cornwall
Duration: 5 days, April-October
Max. in group: 10
Levels: beginners/intermediate
Min. age: 10
*River trips and sea canoeing. Various
courses available.*

**Cumbrae - Scottish National Sports
Centre**      **Centre 117**
Location: Ayrshire
Duration: 2 days, April-October
Levels: all
Min age: 14
*Introductory course.*

**Felpham Sailing & Sports
School**      **Centre 165**
Location: Sussex
Duration: 2 days, all year
Levels: all
*River canoeing with overnight camp*

*Bearsports Outdoor Centres*

**Highlander Mountaineering**      **Centre 217**
Location: Aberdeenshire
Duration: 5 days, June-September
Levels: beginners
Min. age: 16
*Courses in flat or moving water and surf to
cover a variety of techniques.*

**Linguisport Sailing
School**      **Centre 264**
Location: Suffolk
Duration: 2-6 days, April-October
Max. in group: 15
Levels: all
Min. age: 8
*Teaching in six varieties of craft on inland
water.*

**Monmouth Canoe Hire &
Activities Centre**      **Centre 297**
Location: River Wye
Duration: 1-7 days, March-October
Max. in group: 15
Levels: all
Min. age: 8
*Canadian canoes or single kayaks with
instruction in basic or advanced techniques.*

**Mountain Stream Activities    Centre 305**
Location: Devon
Duration: 2 days, September-March
Max. in group: 34
Levels: all
Min. age: 16
*Various courses including whitewater rescue.*

**North York Moors**
**Adventure Centre             Centre 320**
Location: Yorkshire
Duration: 2 days, April-October
Max. in group: 12
Levels: intermediate/advanced
Min. age: 12
*Whitewater canoeing on lakes and sea.*

**Plas Menai National**
**Watersports Centre           Centre 351**
Location: Gwynedd
Duration: 2-5 days, all year
Max. in group: 6
Levels: all
Min. age: 14
*Canoeing in pool bats, whitewater kayaks, sea tourers and Canadian canoes.*

**Port Edgar Sailing**
**School                       Centre 353**
Location: West Lothian
Duration: 2-4 days, May-September
Max. in group: 6
Levels: beginners
Min. age: 12
*Basic courses using sea kayaks, open Canadian and slalem canoes in sheltered harbours or exposed estuaries.*

**R & L Adventures            Centre 362**
Location: Cumbria
Duration: 1 day
Levels: all
*Ring for details.*

**Rob Hastings**
**Adventure                    Centre 370**
Location: North Wales
Duration: 1-3 days, July-August
Levels: all
Min. age: 14

**Skern Lodge                 Centre 401**
Location: Devon
Duration: 6 days, July-September
Levels: beginners/intermediate
Min. age: 9

**Surface Watersports         Centre 427**
Location: Leicestershire
Duration: 1 day, all year
Levels: beginners
*Instruction to BCU standard on Rutland Water.*

**Twy-y-Felin Outdoor Centre  Centre 451**
Location: Pembrokeshire
Duration: 2-6 days, all year
Max. in group: 30
Levels: all
Min. age: 8

**U.K. Sailing Centre         Centre 453**
Location: Isle of Wight
Duration: 2-7 days, March-October
Max. in group: varies
Levels: all

**Wyedean Canoe &**
**Adventure Centre             Centre 507**
Location: Gloucestershire
Duration: 1-6 days, March-November
Max. in group: 60
Levels: all
Min. age: 8
*Tuition for beginners to senior instructor level in kayaks and Canadian canoes.*

## Canoeing continued

**YMCA National Centre**　　**Centre 512**
Location: Cumbria
Duration: 2 days, March-November
Levels: all
*Introduction to whitewater kayaking
techniques on Lake District rivers, plus
courses for instructors.*

# Catamaran Sailing

**C.A.C. Watersports**　　**Centre 75**
Location: Cornwall
Duration: 5 days, all year
Max. in group: 12
Levels: all
Min. age: 16
*RYA recognised courses for beginners and
advanced sailors.*

**Laser School and Cat. Clinic**　**Centre 258**
Location: Cambridgeshire
Duration: 1-5 days, all year
Max. in group: 10
Levels: all
Min. age: 16
*Instruction in catamaran sailing for
beginners to advanced sailors.*

# Chartwork & Navigation

**Fort Bovisand Underwater
Centre**　　**Centre 173**
Location: Devon
Duration: 2 days, all year
Max. in group: 16
Levels: intermediate
Min. age: 16
*Introduction to charts and navigation
enabling divers to locate their own sites..*

# Coastal Skipper Training

**East Anglian
School of Sailing**　　**Centre 143**
Location: Suffolk
Duration: 5 days, January-November
Max. in group: 5
Levels: all
Min. age: 17
*Covers RYA competence courses. Also
advanced practical courses available for
day/night coastal passages.*

# Cruising

**Cumbrae - The Scottish National
Sports Centre**　　**Centre 117**
Location: Ayrshire
Duration: 2-5 days, March-October
Max. in group: 6
Levels: all
Min. age: 14
*Full RYA syllabus from beginner to
yachtmaster.*

**Fowey Cruising School**　　**Centre 175**
Location: Cornwall
Duration: 6 days, April-October
Max. in group: 15
Levels: all
Min. age: 18
*RYA courses at all levels of practical
cruiser sailing.*

**Mylor Sailing School**　　**Centre 310**
Location: Cornwall
Duration: 1-7 days, all year
Max. in group: 6
Levels: beginners/intermediate
Min. age: 18

**Please refer to the Centres Index
for details about accommodation**

# Dinghy Sailing

## C.A.C. Watersports     Centre 75
Location: Cornwall
Duration: 5 days, all year
Max. in group: 16
Levels: all
Min. age: 8
*RYA recognised courses offered.*

## Calshot Activities Centre     Centre 83
Location: Hampshire
Duration: 6 days, July/August
Levels: all
Min. age: 13
*Dinghy sailing using toppers and wayfarers with an expedition to the Isle of Wight.*

## Chichester Sailing Centre     Centre 94
Location: Sussex
Duration: any, April-October
Max. in group: 50
Levels: all
Min. age: 7
*RYA courses levels 1-5 for beginners to dinghy instructors. Also level 4 racing.*

## Cumbrae - The Scottish National Sports Centre     Centre 117
Location: Ayrshire
Duration: 2-5 days, April-October
Levels: all
Min. age: 14
*RYA syllabuses covered in 470's, lasers, wayfarers and pipers.*

## Emsworth Sailing School     Centre 154
Location: Hampshire
Duration: 2/3/6 days, March-October
Max. in group: 50-100
Levels: all
Min. age: 10
*Familiarisation with dinghies and the basics of sailing taught.*

## Fellowship Afloat Charitable Trust     Centre 164
Location: Essex
Duration: 2-7 days, April-October
Max. in group: 36
Levels: all
Min. age: 16
*Full range of RYA courses up to instructor level combined with community living on board light vessels.*

## Galloway Sailing Centre     Centre 181
Location: Kirkcudbrightshire
Duration: 5 days, April-October
Max. in group: 2
Levels: all
Min. age: 12
*A range of courses in dinghy sailing and racing.*

## Hamble Dinghy Sailing     Centre 197
Location: Hampshire
Duration: 2/5 days, March-November
Max. in group: 50
Levels: all
Min. age: 7
*RYA levels 1-3 courses.*

## John Sharp Sailing     Centre 241
Location: Cornwall
Duration: 1-5 days, April-October
Max. in group: 20
Levels: all
Min. age: 8
*Sailing to RYA certificate levels.*

## Laser School and Cat. Clinic     Centre 258
Location: Cambridgeshire
Duration: 1-5 days, all year
Max. in group: 20
Levels: all
Min. age: 8
*Group or individual tuition.*

## Dinghy Sailing continued

**Mylor Sailing School**    Centre 310
Location: Cornwall
Duration: 1-7 days, April-November
Max. in group: 20
Levels: beginners/intermediate
Min. age: 8
*Teaching for beginners to RYA level 3.*

**Port Edgar Sailing School**    Centre 353
Location: West Lothian
Duration: 2-5 days, April-October
Max. in group: 12
Level: all
Min. age: 12
*Instruction at all levels including assessment for RYA levels 1-5.*

**Queen Mary Sailsports**    Centre 361
Location: Middlesex
Duration: 5 days, April/May/July/August
Max. in group: 15
Levels: all
Min. age: 14

**Surface Watersports**    Centre 427
Location: Leicestershire
Duration: 1-5 days, all year
Levels: all
*Courses giving instruction in boat handling.*

**Tignabruaich Sailing School**    Centre 439
Location: Argyll
Duration: 6 days, May-September
Max. in group: 60
Levels: all
Min. age: 8
*Tuition for all RYA courses.*

**UK Sailing Centre**    Centre 453
Location: Isle of Wight
Duration: 2-7 days, March-October

Max. in group: 134
Levels: all
Min. age: 8

**YMCA National Centre**    Centre 512
Location: Cumbria
Duration: 7 days, July/August
Levels: all
*RYA levels 1-3 covered.*

# Diving

**Acorn Activities**    Centre 3
Location: Pembrokeshire/Herefordshire
Duration: 5 days, all year
Levels: all
*Novice Diver and Sports Diver courses in pools or open water with accompanying lectures.*

**Diver Training School**    Centre 133
Location: Devon
Duration: 5 days, all year
Max. in group: 12
Levels: all
Min. age: 12
*Training courses to BSAC or PADI standards.*

**Diving Leisure Ltd**    Centre 134
Location: Dorset
Duration: 2-5 days, all year
Max. in group: 6-12
Levels: beginners/advanced
Min. age: 12
*Scuba diving courses for beginners to instructor level.*

**Fort Bovisand**
**Underwater Centre**    Centre 173
Location: Devon
Duration: 2 days, April-September
Max. in group: 12
Levels: beginners
Min. age: 15

*Theoretical and practical instruction in scuba diving.*

**Fort Bovisand
Underwater Centre**     **Centre 173**
Location: Devon
Duration: 5 days, July-September
Max. in group: 20
Levels: intermediate/advanced
Min. age: 18
*Provides qualified divers with a range of interesting dives and visits to centres of maritime interest.*

**Seaways - Truro Diving
Services**     **Centre 391**
Location: Cornwall
Duration: 5 days, all year
Levels: all
*A full range of BSAC and PADI courses.*

# Multiwatersports

**Adventure Sports**     **Centre 10**
Location: Cornwall
Duration: 5 days, April-October
Max. in group: 20
Levels: all
Min. age: 16
*Waterskiing, windsurfing, sailing, surfing, and snorkelling offered daily.*

**Bearsports Outdoor Centres**     **Centre 38**
Location: Northumberland
Duration: any, all year
Max. in group: 40
Levels: all
Min. age: 9
*Kayaking, canoeing, sailing, surfing and windsurfing approved by RYA and BCU.*

---

**Please refer to the Centres Index
for details about accommodation**

---

**C.A.C. Watersports**     **Centre 75**
Location: Cornwall
Duration: 1-5 days, April-October
Max. in group: 40
Levels: all
Min. age: 8
*Sailing, windsurfing, canoeing, surfing, water skiing and yachting.*

**Calshot Activities Centre**     **Centre 83**
Location: Hampshire
Duration: 2 days, April-October
Levels: all
Min. age: 13
*A choice of sailing, canoeing and windsurfing.*

**Cumbrae - Scottish National
Sports Centre**     **Centre 117**
Location: Ayrshire
Duration: 2-5 days, April-September
Levels: beginners
Min age: 14

**Devon & Dorset
Activities Centre**     **Centre 128**
Location: Devon/Dorset
Duration: 2-7 days, March-October
Max. in group: 350
Levels: all
Min. age: 7
*Waterskiing, raft building and lake crossing, canoeing, dinghy sailing, windsurfing and waterskiing.*

**Eastbourne Marine**     **Centre 145**
Location: Sussex
Duration: 5 days, April-October
Max. in group: 10
Levels: all
Min. age: 15
*A choice of sailing, windsurfing, canoeing and powerboating.*

## Multiwatersports continued

**Eclipse Outdoor Discovery**     **Centre 146**
Location: Cumbria
Duration: 2-6 days, all year
Max. in group: 30
Levels: all
Min. age: 8
*Canoeing, sailing, scuba diving, river snorkelling and river tubbing.*

**Felpham Sailing &**
**Sports School**     **Centre 165**
Location: Sussex
Duration: 2-7 days, April-October
Levels: all
*Courses in windsurfing, sailing and canoeing.*

**Freetime Holidays**     **Centre 176**
Location: Cornwall
Duration: 7 days, June-Sept
Max. in group: 50
Levels: beginners/intermediate
Min. age: 16
*A range of activities including surfing, windsurfing, surfski-ing and sailing.*

**Galloway Sailing Centre**     **Centre 181**
Location: Kirkcudbrightshire
Duration: 1-5 days, April-October
Levels: all
Min. age: 8

**Grafham Water Centre**     **Centre 193**
Location: Cambridgeshire
Duration: 2 days, May-October
Max. in group: 40
Levels: all
Min. age: 10
*Sailing, windsurfing, canoeing and power boating for all RYA and BCU qualifications.*

**Loch Insh Watersports &**
**Skiing Centre**     **Centre 269**
Location: Inverness-shire
Duration: 2-14 days, May-October
Max. in group: 60
Levels: all
Min. age: 7
*Windsurfing, sailing, canoeing and raft building.*

**Rock Lea Activity Centre**     **Centre 372**
Location: Derbyshire
Duration: 2 days, all year
Max. in group: varies
Levels: beginners
Min. age: 18
*Sailing, canoeing, windsurfing and water skiing.*

**Stubbers Outdoor Centre**     **Centre 420**
Location: Essex
Duration: 2-7 days, all year
Max. in group: 40
Min. age: 11
*Full range of adventure activities including canoeing and windsurfing.*

**Wayford Watersports**     **Centre 472**
Location: Norfolk
Duration: 5 days, June-August
Max. in group: 30
Levels: all
Min. age: 8

**Wight Water Adventure**
**Sports**     **Centre 491**
Location: Isle of Wight
Duration: 2-5 days, April-October
Max. in group: 40
Levels: beginners/intermediate
Min. age: 8
*An introduction to a range of watersports - catamaran sailing, windsurfing, canoeing, surfing, wave skiing and body boarding.*

*Acorn Activities*

# Power Boating

**Acorn Activities**                 Centre 3
Location: Pembrokeshire
Duration: 2 days, all year
Levels: all
*Courses to learn to drive small speedboats, 10-40hp.*

**Chichester Sailing Centre**        Centre 94
Location: Sussex
Duration: 2 days, March-October
Max. in group: 8
Levels: all
Min. age: 14
*RYA levels 1 or 2 covered, coxswains certificate plus advanced fleet training.*

**Cumbrae - The Scottish National
Sports Centre**                      Centre 117
Location: Ayrshire
Duration: 2 days, March-November
Levels: all
Min. age: 14
*RYA courses, plus more advanced rescue boat courses.*

**Fellowship Afloat
Charitable Trust**                   Centre 164
Location: Essex
Duration: 2 days, February-November

> ## Please mention this guide
> ## when booking courses

Max. in group: 8
Levels: all
Min. age: 16
*Full range of courses up to rescue level combined with community living on board light vessel.*

**Fort Bovisand
Underwater Centre**                  Centre 173
Location: Devon
Duration: 2 days, all year
Max. in group: 16
Levels: beginners/intermediate
Min. age: 18
*Basic knowledge and training for RYA National Powerboat Certificate.*

**Plas Menai National
Watersports Centre**                 Centre 351
Location: Gwynedd
Duration: 2-5 days, all year
Levels: all
*RYA levels covered plus courses for instructors.*

# Sailing

**Abernethy Outdoor Centre**         Centre 1
Location: Inverness-shire
Duration: 7 days, August
Max. in group: 14
Levels: beginner/intermediate
Min. age: 16

**Acorn Activities**                 Centre 3
Location: Pembrokeshire
Duration: 2/5 days, April-October
Levels: all
*Sailing in Wayfarers and Toppers to RYA levels 1-5.*

## Sailing continued

**Anvil Yacht Charters**     **Centre 20**
Location: Dorset
Duration: 7-14 days, March-November
Max. in group: 12
Levels: all
Min. age: 14

**British Offshore Sailing
School**     **Centre 59**
Location: Hampshire
Duration: 2/5 days, all year
Levels: all
Min. age: 16
*RYA courses in Competent Crew, Day
Skipper, Coastal Skipper, and Yachtmaster,
plus long distance cruise courses.*

**Bulldog Sailing Centre**     **Centre 68**
Location: Hampshire
Duration: 5 days, all year
Max. in group: 5
Levels: all
Min. age: 16
*RYA courses from beginner to yachtmaster.*

**C-Charters Sea School**     **Centre 73**
Location: Hampshire
Duration: 5 days, all year
Max. in group: 5
Levels: all
Min. age: 16
*Offshore sailing techniques covered, enabling
participants to become effective crew members.*

**C.A.C. Watersports**     **Centre 75**
Location: Cornwall
Duration: 1-5 days, March-October
Max. in group: 40
Levels: all
Min. age: 8
*Sailing tuition in dinghies and catamarans.*

**Chichester Sailing Centre**     **Centre 94**
Location: Sussex
Duration: any, all year
Max. in group: 50
Levels: all
Min. age: 7

**Clyde Offshore Sailing Centre**   **Centre 98**
Location: Renfrewshire
Duration: 5/10/28 days, all year
Max. in group: 7
Levels: all
Min. age: 16
*Day/night skipper courses, covering astro
navigation and seamanship skills.*

**Compass Ventures**     **Centre 104**
Location: Loch Lomond
Duration: 2-7 days, April-September
Max. in group: 8
Levels: all
Min. age: 16

**Felpham Sailing &Sports
School**     **Centre 165**
Location: Sussex
Max. in group: varies
Duration: varies, all year
Levels: all

**Fowey Cruising School**     **Centre 175**
Location: Cornwall
Duration: 6 days, March-October
Max. in group: 15
Levels: all
Min. age: 10
*RYA courses at all levels of cruiser sailing.*

**Great Glen School of Adventure**   **Centre 195**
Location: Inverness-shire
Duration: 2,5 days, April-October
Max. in group: 6
Levels: beginners,intermediate
Min. age: 6

*Acorn Activities*

**High Adventure Holidays**     **Centre 208**
Location: Isle of Wight
Duration: 1-7 days, all year
Max. in group: 6
Levels: beginners/intermediate
Min. age: 6
*One to one tuition suitable for all ages .*

**Instow Sailing Tuition Centre  Centre 230**
Location: Devon
Duration: 4/6 days, May-September
Max. in group: 15
Levels: all
Min. age: 10
*Sailing tuition to RYA certificate standard.*

**Island Cruising Club**     **Centre 237**
Location: Devon
Duration: 2+ days, March-November
Max. in group: 60
Levels: all
Min. age: 10
*RYA courses offered.*

**Linguisport Sailing School**     **Centre 264**
Location: Suffolk
Duration: 2-6 days, April-October

Max. in group: 15
Levels: all
Min. age: 8

**Linnhe Marine Boating Centre Centre 265**
Location: Argyllshire
Duration: 2/5 days, May-October
Max. in group: 4
Levels: beginners/intermediate
Min. age: 10

**Millfield  School Village of
Education**                    **Centre 293**
Location: Somerset
Duration: 5 days, July-August
Max. in group: 15
Levels: beginners
Min. age: 14

**Mylor Sailing School**     **Centre 310**
Location: Cornwall
Duration: 1-7 days, April-November
Max. in group: 6
Levels: beginners/intermediate
Min. age: 18

**Newton Ferrers Sailing
School**                      **Centre 316**
Location: Devon
Duration: 6 days, April-September
Max. in group: 28
Levels: all
Min. age: 8
*RYA recognised tuition in dayboats and
Toppers in estuary open sea and river.*

**Ocean Youth Club**     **Centre 327**
Location: Hampshire
Duration: March-October
Max. in group: 12
Levels: all
Min. age: 12

## Sailing continued

**Oystercat Cruises**          **Centre 333**
Location: Dorset
Duration: 2-14 days, April-October
Max. in group: 4
Levels: all
Min. age: 16
*Live aboard ocean-going catamaran with tuition in boat-handling, seamanship and navigation.*

**P & Q Sailing Centre**          **Centre 334**
Location: Suffolk
Duration: 2/5 days, May-October
Max. in group: 5
Levels: all
*RYA recognised instruction in seamanship and navigation from Competent Crew to Yacht Master.*

**Plas Menai National
Watersports Centre**          **Centre 351**
Location: Gwynedd
Duration: 2-5 days, all year
Max. in group: 6
Levels: all
Min. age: 14
*Training in crewed and single handed sailing.*

**Queen Mary Sailsports**          **Centre 361**
Location: Middlesex
Duration: 5 days, April-November
Max. in group: 5
Levels: beginners/intermediate
Min. age: 15
*Tuition to RYA level 2.*

**Rob Hastings Adventure**          **Centre 370**
Location: North Wales
Duration: 1-3 days, July-August
Levels: all
*Ring for details.*

**Rockley Point Sailing School   Centre 373**
Location: Dorset
Duration: 2/5/6 days, March-November
Max. in group: 80
Levels: all
Min. age: 8
*RYA or NFSS recognised tuition at all levels.*

**Sail Training Association**          **Centre 377**
Location: Hampshire
Duration: 2-13 days, March-December
Max. in group: 39
Levels: all
Min. age: 16
*Adventure voyages on board 150' schooners.*

**Sinbad Charters**          **Centre 398**
Location: Dunbarton
Duration: 6 days, April-October
Max. in group: 5
Levels: all
Min. age: 17
*Informal tuition or formal RYA sailing courses*

**Skyes'l Charters**          **Centre 404**
Location: Isle of Skye
Duration: 6/9/12 days, April-September
Max. in group: 6
Levels: all
Min. age: 16
*Traditional sailing skills are learnt whilst living aboard this 60' yacht.*

**Sleat Marine Services**          **Centre 408**
Location: Isle of Skye
Duration: 7 days, April-October
Max. in group: 6-8
Levels: all
Min. age: 24

**Solent Coastal & Offshore
Sailing School**          **Centre 412**
Location: Hampshire
Duration: 5 days, all year

Max. in group: 5
Levels: all
Min. age: 14
*RYA sailing, navigation and metreology courses.*

**Suffolk College
Summer School** Centre 422
Location: Suffolk
Duration: 5 days, July
Max. in group: varies
Levels: all
Min. age: 16
*RYA levels covered.*

**Tama Sailing** Centre 434
Location: Norfolk
Duration: 2-14 days, May-Sept
Max. in group: 5
Levels: all
Min. age: 12

**Wave Yacht Charters** Centre 471
Location: Perthshire
Duration: 6-12 days, April-October
Max. in group: 7
Levels: all
Min. age: 12
*Exploration of isles and lochs.*

**Whizz-Kid Sailing** Centre 490
Location: Cornwall
Duration: 7 days, April-October
Max. in group: 4
Levels: beginners/intermediate
Min. age: 7
*Introduction to boat handling, fishing, exploring and safety procedures.*

**Windermere Lake
Holidays Afloat** Centre 496
Location: Cumbria
Duration: 3-7 days, all year

Max. in group: varies
Levels: all
*An introduction to basic sailing skills.*

**Yacht Corryvreckan** Centre 510
Location: Island of Kerrera
Duration: 6/9/12 days, April-October
Max. in group: 10
Levels: all
Min. age: 12

**YMCA National Centre** Centre 512
Location: Cumbria
Duration: 7 days, July/August
Levels: beginners
Min. age: 16
*RYA levels 1-3 covered.*

# Sea Kayaking

**Preseli Mountain Bikes
& Sea Kayaking** Centre 356
Location: Pembrokeshire
Duration: 2-5 days, all year
Max. in group: 10
Levels: all
Min. age: 10
*Participants learn the sport through a variety of courses while exploring spectacular coastlines.*

# Skipper Training

**East Anglian
School of Sailing** Centre 143
Location: Suffolk
Duration: 5 days, January-December
Max. in group: 5
Min. age: 17
*Course covers coastal navigation, meteorology and seamanship.*

## Skipper Training continued

**Fowey Cruising School**     Centre 175
Location: Cornwall
Duration: 8 days, all year
Max. in group: 5
Levels: intermediate
Min. age: 16
*Iintensive RYA course on sailing in open water.*

# Surfing

**Freetime Holidays**     Centre 176
Location: Cornwall
Duration: 4 days, April-June,September
Max. in group: 10
Levels: beginners,intermediate
Min. age: 15
*BSA single fin proficiency course offered.*

**Surfrider Activity Holidays**     Centre 428
Location: Devon
Duration: 2-7 days, all year
Max. in group: 30
Levels: all
Min. age: 15
*BSA approved coaching from beginner to
competition standard.*

# Swimming

**Acorn Activities**     Centre 3
Location: Herefordshire
Duration: 5 days, all year
Levels: all
*Intensive individual tuition.*

**G & C Holidays Ltd**     Centre 180
Location: Devon
Duration: 7 days, all year
Levels: all
Min. age: 6
*Learn to swim in 7 days or money back
guarantee.*

# Underwater Explosives

**Fort Bovisand
Underwater Centre**     Centre 173
Location: Devon
Duration: 2 days, all year
Max. in group: 18
Min. age: 18
*Introduction to the safe use of underwater
explosives.*

# Waterskiing

**Acorn Activities**     Centre 3
Location: Pembrokeshire
Duration: 2 days, all year
Levels: all
*Tuition from basic introduction to mono-ski
standard.*

**Apollo Water-Ski School**     Centre 21
Location: Norfolk
Duration: 2 days, May-September
Max. in group: 6
Levels: beginners
Min. age: 14

# Wildlife Cruise

**Pointdrake Ltd**     Centre 352
Location: Hebrides
Duration: 4-10 days, April-October
Max. in group: 12
Levels: all
Min. age: 25

# Windsurfing

**Abernethy Outdoor Centre**     Centre 1
Location: Inverness-shire
Duration: 7 days, August
Max. in group: 12
Levels: beginners/intermediate
Min. age: 16

*Acorn Activities*

**Acorn Activities**                    Centre 3
Location: Pembrokeshire
Duration: 2/5 days, April-October
Levels: all
*Courses to RYA levels 1-5.*

**C.A.C. Watersports**                  Centre 75
Location: Cornwall
Duration: 5 days, April-October
Max. in group: 10
Levels: beginners,intermediate
Min. age: 12
*A range of courses offered.*

**Chichester Sailing Centre**           Centre 94
Location: Sussex
Duration: 2 days, June-September
Max. in group: 8
Levels: beginners/intermediate
Min. age: 8
*RYA levels 1 and 2 covered.*

**Cumbrae - The Scottish National
Sports Centre**                         Centre 117
Location: Ayrshire
Duration: 2-3 days, April-October
Levels: all
Min. age: 14
*RYA syllabuses covered on most courses.*

**Felpham Sailing
& Sports School**                       Centre 165
Location: Sussex
Duration: varies, all year
Levels: all

**Freetime Holidays**                   Centre 176
Location: Cornwall
Duration: 7 days, July/August
Max. in group: 50
Levels: beginners
Min. age: 16

**Galloway Sailing Centre**             Centre 181
Location: Kirkcudbrightshire
Duration: 5 days, April-October
Max. in group: 4
Levels: beginners
Min. age: 10

**Great Glen School
of Adventure**                          Centre 195
Location: Inverness-shire
Duration: 3 days, May-October
Max. in group: 6
Levels: beginners
Min. age: 12

**Harbour Sports
Windsurfing Centre**                    Centre 198
Location: Devon
Duration: 1 day, April-October
Max. in group: 6
Levels: beginners/intermediate
Min. age: 12
*RYA levels 1 and 2 covered.*

**Linnhe Marine
Watersports Centre**                    Centre 265
Location: Argyllshire
Duration: 2/5 days, May-October
Max. in group: 4
Levels: beginners/intermediate
Min. age: 10

## Windsurfing continued

**Millfield School Village of
Education**                  **Centre 293**
Location: Somerset
Duration: 5 days, July-August
Max. in group: 15
Levels: beginners
Min. age: 14

**Outdoor Adventure**        **Centre 331**
Location: Cornwall
Duration: 1-6 days, March-November
Max. in group: 25
Levels: all
Min. age: 16
*RYA levels 1-5 covered.*

**Plas Menai National
Watersports Centre**         **Centre 351**
Location: Gwynedd
Duration: 2-5 days, all year
Max. in group: 6
Levels: all
Min. age: 14
*RYA levels 1-5, plus courses for instructors.*

**Port Edgar Sailing School**   **Centre 353**
Location: West Lothian
Duration: 2/3 days, May-September
Max. in group: 6
Levels: beginners/intermediate
Min. age: 12
*RYA levels 1 and 2 covered.*

**Queen Mary Sailsports**    **Centre 361**
Location: Middlesex
Duration: 2 days, April- October
Max. in group: 15
Levels: beginners
Min. age: 15
*RYA level 1 covered.*

**Surface Watersports**      **Centre 427**
Location: Leicestershire
Duration: 2 days, all year
Levels: beginners
*Introductory course leading to RYA level 1.*

**Tignabruaich Sailing School**   **Centre 439**
Location: Argyll
Duration: 6 days, May-September
Max. in group: 20
Levels: beginners/intermediate
Min. age: 8
*Tuition for all RYA courses.*

**Torquay Boardsailing
Centre &School**             **Centre 441**
Location: Devon
Duration: 1 day, May-September
Levels: all
Min. age: 11

**UK Sailing Centre**        **Centre 453**
Location: Isle of Wight
Duration: 2-7 days, March-October
Max. in group: varies
Levels: all
Min. age: 8

**Windsurfing Worcester**    **Centre 499**
Location: Worcestershire
Duration: 1 day, April-October
Max. in group: 6
Levels: beginners/intermediate
Min. age: 10
*RYA courses offered.*

# Yachting

**Argyll and Isles Cruising
Tuition**                    **Centre 25**
Location: Argyll
Duration: 5 days, May-September
Max. in group: 5
Levels: all

Min. age: 18
*RYA practical courses at Competent Crew; Day Skipper and Coastal Skipper levels.*

**Chichester Sailing Centre          Centre 94**
Location: Sussex
Duration: 2-14 days, all year
Max. in group: 6
Levels: all
Min. age: 14
*RYA courses in Competent Crew to Yachtmaster Ocean.*

**Clyde Offshore
Sailing Centre          Centre 98**
Location: Renfrewshire
Duration: 10 days, April-September
Max. in group: 6
Levels: intermediate/advanced
Min. age: 16
*Tuition in racing.*

**East Anglian School of
Sailing          Centre 143**
Location: Suffolk
Duration: 5 days, March-November
Min. age: 17
*Competent Crew, Day Skipper, Coastal Skipper and Yachtmaster courses offered.*

**EME Yacht Charter          Centre 153**
Location: Cornwall
Duration: varies, all year
Levels: all

**Emsworth Sailing School          Centre 154**
Location: Hampshire
Duration: 2-7 days, all year
Max. in group: 100
Levels: all
Min. age: 14
*Tuition in basic sailing and yacht handling.*

**Medway Sea School          Centre 282**
Location: Kent
Duration: 2-14 days, all year
Max. in group: 5
Levels: all
Min. age: 10
*Training in yachting theory and handling.*

# Yachtmaster Training

**Chichester Sailing Centre          Centre 94**
Location: Sussex
Duration: any, all year
Max. in group: 15
Levels: all
Min. age: 14
*VHF radio courses, plus Day skipper, Yachtmaster, Coastal Skipper and Ocean Yachtmaster courses covered.*

**East Anglian School
of Sailing          Centre 143**
Location: Suffolk
Duration: 5 days, March-November
Max. in group: 5
Min. age: 20
*Practical brush up for candidates intending to take their Yachtmaster (Offshore) exam*

**East Down Centre          Centre 144**
Location: Devon
Duration: 7-8 days, September-April
Max. in group: 8
Min. age: 16
*RYA shorebased courses at every level for individual yachtsmen.*

**Fowey Cruising School          Centre 175**
Location: Cornwall
Duration: 5 days, March-October
Levels: advanced
Min. age: 18
*Preparation course and examination for RYA/Yachtmaster (Offshore).*

# Air Sports

## Ballooning

**Acorn Activities**               **Centre 3**
Location: Herefordshire
Duration: 1 day, all year
Levels: all

**Balloon Base**                  **Centre 33**
Location: Avon
Duration: varies during Summer.
Levels: all

**Headland Hotel**               **Centre 204**
Location: Cornwall
Duration: any, March-November
Max. in group: 4-5
Levels: all
Min. age: 7

**Hilton Hotels**                 **Centre 220**
Location: nationwide
Duration: 1 day, all year
Levels: all

**Millfield School Villge of
Education**                       **Centre 293**
Location: Somerset
Duration: 5 days, July-August
Levels: all
Min age: 16

## Flight Training

**Acorn Activities**               **Centre 3**
Location: Herefordshire/Pembrokeshire
Duration: all year
Levels: all
*Assessment course including theory and
practical work.*

**Cabair Group Ltd**             **Centre 76**
Location: Hertfordshire
Duration: varies, all year
Max. in group: various
Levels: all
Min. age: 16
*Flight training courses in aircraft and
helicopters, from introductory lessons to
Private Pilots Licence.*

**Headland Hotel**               **Centre 204**
Location: Cornwall
Duration: any, March-November
Max in group: 2
Levels: beginners
Min age: 18
*Tuition in flying a light aircraft.*

**Hilton Hotels**                 **Centre 220**
Location: nationwide
Duration: 1/2-1 day, all year
Levels: beginners
Min. age: 18
*Introductory course.*

# Gliding

**Acorn Activities**      **Centre 3**
Location: Herefordshire/Wales
Duration: 2/5 days, all year
Levels: all

**Booker Gliding Club**      **Centre 46**
Location: Buckinghamshire
Duration: 1-10 days, all year
Max. in group: 10
Levels: all
Min. age: 12

**Bristol & Gloucestershire
Gliding Club**      **Centre 57**
Location: Gloucestershire
Duration: 5 days, April-October
Max. in group: 10
Levels: all
Min. age: 15
*Training for beginners, plus soaring and
cross-country training for more experienced
pilots.*

**Derbyshire & Lancashire
Gliding Club**      **Centre 125**
Location: Derbyshire
Duration: 5 days, April-September
Max. in group: 12
Levels: all
Min. age: 14
*Basic gliding training, plus further courses
for those with more experience.*

**Hilton Hotels**      **Centre 220**
Location: nationwide
Duration: 2 days, all year
Levels: beginners
Min. age: 18
*Introductory course.*

*Acorn Activities*

**Lasham Gliding**      **Centre 259**
Location: Hampshire
Duration: 2/5 days, March-October/all year
Max. in group: 4/15
Levels: beginners/intermediate
Min. age: 16

**London Gliding Club**      **Centre 272**
Location: Bedfordshire
Duration: 1/2/5 days, all year
Max. in group: 4-12
Levels: beginners/intermediate
Min. age: 14

**Mendip Gliding Club**      **Centre 283**
Location: Avon
Duration: 5/10 days, June-August
Max. in group: 4
Levels: all
Min. age: 14
*Tuition at all levels to BGA standards.*

**Midland Gliding Club**      **Centre 290**
Location: Shropshire
Duration: 5 days, March-October
Max. in group: 10
Levels: all
Min. age: 16
*Introduces beginners to the sport of soaring,
plus advanced courses.*

# Hang Gliding

**Acorn Activities**      **Centre 3**
Location: Wales
Duration: 2/6 days, all year
Levels: all
*Elementary Pilot Certificate courses.*

**Adventure Sky Sports UK**      **Centre 9**
Location: nationwide
Duration: 2/3 days, all year
Levels: all
Min. age: 16

**Airborne Hang Gliding &**
**Paragliding Centre**      **Centre 12**
Location: Yorkshire
Duration: 1-4 days, March-November
Max. in group: 15
Levels: all
Min. age: 14
*Various courses in basic theory, Student
Pilot course, solo flight course.*

**Cairnwell Hang Gliding**
**School**      **Centre 80**
Location: Aberdeenshire
Duration: 2/3/5-10 days, May-September/
November
Max. in group: 6
Levels: all
Min. age: 16
*Introductory, advanced, basic Elementary
Pilot and Club Pilot courses.*

**Fly High Parascending/**
**Paragliding**      **Centre 170**
Location: Kent
Duration: 1 day, all year
Max in group: 8
Levels: all
Min age: 16
*Basic introduction.*

**High Adventure**      **Centre 208**
Location: Isle of Wight
Duration: 1-7 days, all year
Max. in group: 20
Levels: all
Min. age: 16

**Hilton Hotels**      **Centre 220**
Location: nationwide
Duration: 2 days, all year
Max. in group: 8-12
Levels: beginners
Min. age: 16
*Introductory course.*

**Lejair Ltd**      **Centre 261**
Location: Norfolk
Duration: 1/5/9 days, March-December
Max. in group: 15
Levels: all
Min. age: 16

**Peak Hang Gliding Ltd**      **Centre 339**
Location: Staffordshire
Duration: 1-7 days, all year
Max. in group: 25
Levels: beginners/intermediate
Min. age: 16
*Training to Club Pilot standard.*

**Peak School of Hang Gliding**   **Centre 341**
Location: Derbyshire
Duration: 2/5 days, all year
Max. in group: 30
Levels: beginners/intermediate
Min. age: 16
*Introductory 2 day course or 5 day Elementary Pilot course at BHGA level.*

**Please mention this guide when
booking courses**

*Acorn Activities*

**Pennine Hang Gliding
Centre**        Centre 344
Location: Yorkshire
Duration: 1-5 days, all year
Max. in group: 24
Levels: all
Min. age: 16
*Courses to BHGA elementary pilots
certificate standard and above.*

**Skysports**        Centre 405
Location: Gwent
Duration: 2/5/6/8 days, all year
Max. in group: 12
Levels: beginners/intermediate
Min. age: 16
*Courses leading to Elementary Pilot or
Club Pilot certificate standard.*

**Sussex College of Hang Gliding
& Paragliding**        Centre 429
Location: Sussex
Duration: 3 days, all year
Max. in group: 12
Levels: all
Min. age: 14

**Welsh Hang Gliding Centre**    Centre 474
Location: Gwent
Duration: varies, April-December
Max. in group: 16

Levels: all
Min. age: 16
*Courses from Ab-initio to Club Pilot level.*

**Wiltshire Hang Gliding, Paragliding
& Microlight Centre**        Centre 494
Location: Wiltshire
Duration: any, all year
Max. in group: 12
Levels: all
Min. age: 16
*Basic introduction or training to pilot's
licence standard.*

# Helicopter Flying

**Hilton Hotels**        Centre 220
Location: nationwide
Duration: all year
Levels: beginners
Min. age: 18
*Introductory course.*

# Microlighting

**Acorn Activities**        Centre 3
Location: Herefordshire/Pembrokeshire
Duration: 1/3/5 days, all year
Levels: all

**Hilton Hotels**        Centre 220
Location: nationwide
Duration: 1 day, all year
Max. in group: 1
Levels: beginners
Min. age: 15

**Northern Microlight School**    Centre 321
Location: Lancashire
Duration: any, all year
Max. in group: 2
Levels: all
Min. age: 17
*Training for private pilot's licence.*

## Microlighting continued

**Wiltshire Hang Gliding, Paragliding & Microlight Centre    Centre 494**
Location: Wiltshire
Duration: any, all year
Max. in group: 12
Levels: all
Min. age: 16
*Basic introduction or training to pilot's licence standard.*

**Windsports Centre    Centre 498**
Location: Yorkshire
Duration: 1/4 days, all year
Max. in group: 3
Levels: all
Min. age: 17
*Basic introduction to flying in both fixed wing and flexwing aircrafts. Solo flying can be achieved after four days.*

# Parachuting

**Acorn Activities    Centre 3**
Location: Gloucestershire
Duration: 2 days, all year
Levels: all
*Static line courses and/or tandem jumps.*

**Blue Skies Parachute Training School    Centre 43**
Location: Devon
Duration: 2 days, all year
Max. in group: 12
Levels: beginners
Min. age: 16
*Parachuting for beginners progressing to freefalling.*

**Border Parachute Centre    Centre 47**
Location: Northumberland
Duration: 2 days, all year

Max. in group: 24
Levels: beginners

**Eaglescott Parachute Centre    Centre 140**
Location: Devon
Duration: 2 days, all year
Max. in group: 24
Levels: beginners
Min. age: 16
*Introduction to parachuting. Further instruction in skydiving is available.*

**Headcorn Parachute Club    Centre 203**
Location: Kent
Duration: varies, all year
Max. in group: various
Levels: beginners
Min. age: 16
*Courses in basic parachute jumping, static line, tandem jumping and freefall.*

**Hilton Hotels    Centre 220**
Location: East Midlands
Duration: 2 days, all year
Max. in group: 8-12
Levels: beginners
Min. age: 16
*Courses in both round and square para-chuting plus tandem skydiving.*

**Merlin Parachute Centre    Centre 286**
Location: Yorkshire
Duration: 1/2 days, all year
Max. in group: 36
Levels: all
Min. age: 16
*Various courses in static line, freefall and tandem jumping.*

**Please refer to the Centres Index for details about accommodation**

**Scottish Parachute Club**    **Centre 387**
Location: Perthshire
Duration: 1 day, all year
Max. in group: 40
Levels: all
Min. age: 16

**Swansea Parachute Club**    **Centre 431**
Location: West Glamorgan
Duration: 1 day, January-November
Max. in group: 6
Levels: all
Min. age: 16

# Paragliding

**Acorn Activities**    **Centre 3**
Location: varies
Duration: 2/5 days, all year
Levels: all
*Student Pilot courses offered.*

**Active Edge Paragliding**    **Centre 5**
Location: Yorkshire
Duration: 1/2/4/7 days, all year
Max. in group: 14
Levels: all
Min. age: 16
*Basic, Student Pilot, Club Pilot and advanced courses.*

**Adventure Sky Sports UK**    **Centre 9**
Location: nationwide
Duration: any, all year
Levels: all
Min. age: 16

**Adventure Sports**    **Centre 10**
Location: Cornwall
Duration: varies, all year
Max. in group: 20
Levels: all
Min. age: 14
*Pilot rated courses to all levels.*

**Airborne Hang Gliding & Paragliding Centre**    **Centre 12**
Location: Yorkshire
Duration: 2/4 days, March-November
Max. in group: 15
Levels: all
Min. age: 14

**Countrywide Holidays**    **Centre 114**
Location: nationwide
Duration: 7 days, April/September
Levels: beginners
*Basic introductory course.*

**Fly High Parascending/ Paragliding**    **Centre 170**
Location: Kent
Duration: 1/2/7 days, all year
Max. in group: 8
Levels: all
Min. age: 14
*Basic introduction, Student Pilot, and advanced courses.*

**HF Holidays Ltd**    **Centre 207**
Location: nationwide
Duration: 7 days, August-September
Max. in group: 20
Levels: all

**High Adventure**    **Centre 208**
Location: Isle of Wight
Duration: 1-7 days, all year
Max. in group: 20
Levels: all
Min. age: 16
*Flying from basics to advanced level.*

**Hilton Hotels**    **Centre 220**
Location: nationwide
Duration: 2 days, all year
Max. in group: 8-12
Levels: beginners
Min. age: 16

## Paragliding continued

**Skydragons Paragliding**          Centre 403
Location: Clwyd
Duration: 1/2/4 days, all year
Max. in group: 15-20
Levels: all
Min. age: 14

**Sussex College of Hang Gliding
& Paragliding**          Centre 429
Location: Sussex
Duration: 3 days, all year
Max. in group: 12
Levels: all
Min. age: 14

**Welsh Hang Gliding Centre    Centre 474**
Location: Gwent
Duration: varies, April-December
Max. in group: 16
Levels: all
Min. age: 16
*Courses from Ab-initio to Club Pilot level.*

**Wiltshire Hang Gliding, Paragliding
& Microlight Centre          Centre 494**
Location: Wiltshire
Duration: any, all year
Max. in group: 12
Levels: all
Min. age: 16
*Basic introduction or training to pilot's
licence standard.*

# Powerchuting

**Acorn Activities          Centre 3**
Location: varies. Ring for details
Duration: 2/5 days, all year
Levels: all
*Course consists of flying a microlight with a
specially designed parachute.*

*Acorn Activities*

# Winter Sports

## Dry Skiing

**Lyncombe Lodge**  **Centre 277**
Location: Avon
Duration: 2-20 days, all year
Max. in group: 30
Levels: all
Min. age: 7
*A complete learn-to-ski course particularly suitable for those who have never ventured onto snow.*

## Mountaineering

**Compass Christian Centre**  **Centre 103**
Location: Perthshire
Duration: 4-5 days, February-March
Max. in group: 6
Levels: all
Min. age: 16

**Merlin Mountain Activities**  **Centre 285**
Location: Gwynedd
Duration: 6 days, January-March
Max. in group: 20
Levels: all
Min. age: 16
*Tuition in the skills required for the safe pursuit of winter mountaineering.*

**Mountain Adventure Guides**  **Centre 303**
Location: nationwide
Duration: 1-5 days, varies

> **Abbreviations used in this section:**
> **BASI  British Association of Ski Instructors**

Max. in group: 6
Levels: all
Min. age: 16
*Various courses in winter climbing, alpine climbing and ski mountaineering.*

**Mountain Craft**  **Centre 304**
Location: Inverness-shire
Duration: 2-5 days, January-April
Max. in group: 5
Levels: all
Min. age: 18
*Instruction in winter hillwalking and snow and ice climbing.*

**Professional Mountaineering Services**  **Centre 359**
Location: Inverness-shire
Duration: 2+ days, all year
Max. in group: 12
Levels: all
Min. age: 16
*All aspects taught.*

## Ski Touring and Walking

**Barry Skinner**  **Centre 35**
Location: Gwynedd
Duration: 1-7 days, in season
Max. in group: 6
Levels: all

Min. age: 18
*Cross-country ski instruction and winter walking skills.*

**Bearsports Outdoor Centres**    Centre 38
Location: Northumberland
Duration: varies, November-April
Max. in group: 40
Levels: all
Min. age: 14

# Skiing

**Abernethy Outdoor Centre**    Centre 1
Location: Inverness-shire
Duration: 7 days, January-April
Max. in group: 76
Levels: all
Min. age: 10
*Instruction and in-course transport provided. Equipment hire included.*

**Allenheads Lodge
Outdoor Centre**    Centre 15
Location: Northumberland
Duration: 2/5/7 days, February
Max. in group: 20
Levels: all
Min. age: 8
*Downhill skiing taught.*

**Aviemore Ski School**    Centre 29
Location: Inverness-shire
Duration: 5 days, January-April
Max. in group: 300
Levels: all
Min. age: 9

**Bobsport (Scotland) Ltd**    Centre 44
Location: Scotland
Duration: 1/3/6/10 days, January-November
Max. in group: varies
Levels: all
Min. age: 8

**Bowles Outdoor Centre**    Centre 50
Location: Kent
Duration: 1 day, October-March
Max. in group: 12
Levels: all
Min. age: 8

**Cairnwell Ski School**    Centre 80
Location: Aberdeenshire
Duration: 5 days, December-April
Max. in group: 12
Levels: all
Min. age: 6

**Calshot Activities Centre**    Centre 83
Location: various
Duration: 2 days, October-February
Max. in group: varies
Levels: all
*Courses from basic to instructor level.*

**Compass Christian Centre**    Centre 103
Location: Perthshire
Duration: 2-6 days, January-March
Max. in group: 8
Levels: all
Min. age: 10
*Alpine skiing.*

**Craigower Lodge
Outdoor Centre**    Centre 116
Location: Inverness-shire
Duration: 5 day, January-March
Max. in group: 50
Levels: all
Min. age: 10
*Instruction by the BASI method.*

**Derbyshire Ski Action**    Centre 127
Location: Derbyshire
Duration: varies, in season
Levels: beginners
*Instruction especially suitable for novices, and as a pre-introduction to ski holidays.*

**Eclipse Outdoor Discovery**   Centre 146
Location: Cumbria
Duration: 6 days, February-May
Max. in group: 12
Levels: intermediate/advanced
Min. age: 18
*Alpine ski touring and off-piste skiing with guide.*

**Glencoe Outdoor Centre**   Centre 188
Location: Argyllshire
Duration: varies, January-April
Levels: all
Min. age: 6
*Ski holidays based at Glencoe and Nevis Range, with skills awareness clinics.*

**Glenmulliach Nordic Ski Centre**   Centre 190
Location: Banffshire
Duration: varies, November-May
Max. in group: varies
Levels: beginners/intermediate
Min. age: 5

**High Force Training Centre**   Centre 209
Location: Co. Durham
Duration: varies, December-March
Max. in group: 30
Levels: all
Min. age: 7

**John Bull School of Adventure**   Centre 240
Location: Yorkshire
Duration: 1-5 days, all year
Max. in group: 20
Levels: all
Min. age: 8

**Loch Insh Watersports & Skiing Centre**   Centre 269
Location: Inverness-shire

Duration: 2-14 days, December-April
Max. in group: 60+
Levels: all
Min. age: 7
*Cross-country or downhill.*

**Mountain Adventure Guides**   Centre 303
Location: nationwide
Duration: 1-5 days, varies
Max. in group: 6
Levels: all
Min. age: 16

**Scottish-Norwegian Ski School**   Centre 389
Location: Inverness-shire
Duration: 1-7 days, December-April
Max. in group: 12
Levels: all
Min. age: 7
*Nordic, Alpine, and telemarking skills taught.*

**Ski Wildcountry**   Centre 402
Location: Inverness-shire
Duration: 2-5 days, January-April
Max. in group: 12
Levels: all
Min. age: 16
*Instruction in Nordic ski touring, ski mountaineering and telemarking.*

# Snow & Ice Climbing

**Highlander Mountaineering**   Centre 217
Location: Banffshire
Duration: 5 days, January-April
Levels: beginners
Min. age: 16
*Instruction in ice axe work, crampon technique, ropework, leading, gully and buttress climbing, multi-pitch routes with one night spent out in the mountains.*

# Winter Hillwalking

**Ardeonaig Outdoor Centre**     Centre 22
Location: Perthshire
Duration: 5 days, January-March
Max. in group: varies
Levels: all
Min. age: 14
*Develops the necessary skills to traverse hills using specialist equipment. Small groups.*

**Compass Ventures**     Centre 104
Location: Dunbartonshire
Duration: 2-7 days, January-April
Max. in group: 8
Levels: beginners/intermediate
Min. age: 16
*Exploration of Scottish mountains with instruction in snow techniques and use of ice axes.*

**Discover**     Centre 132
Location: Ross-shire
Duration: 3-6 days, January-March
Max. in group: 4
Levels: all
Min. age: 18
*Basic instruction in winter skills.*

**Highlander Mountaineering**   Centre 217
Location: Banffshire
Duration: 5 days, January-April
Max. in group: 4
Levels: beginners
Min. age: 16
*A course covering the basic skills with one night spent out in the mountains.*

**High Trek Snowdonia**     Centre 212
Location: Gwynedd
Duration: 3 days, January-March
Max. in group: 7
Levels: beginners/intermediate
Min. age: 18
*Teaches winter hill walking skills to those already experienced in summer hill walking.*

# Winter skills

**Glencoe Outdoor Centre**     Centre 188
Location: Argyllshire
Duration: varies, January-April
Levels: all
Min. age: 15
*Avalanche hazards, use of ice axe and crampons, navigation, emergency shelters and rope work.*

**Helvellyn Youth Hostel**     Centre 206
Location: Cumbria
Duration: 2 days, January-March
Max. in group: 16
Levels: beginners
Min. age: 16
*Ice axe breaking, crampon work and survival shelters.*

**Motherby House Activities**     Centre 300
Location: Cumbria
Duration: 2 days, January-March
Max. in group: 12
Levels: beginners/intermediate
Min. age: 16
*Ice axe braking, use of crampons and navigation.*

**Ossian Guides**     Centre 330
Location: Inverness-shire
Duration: 7 days, January-October
Max. in group: 8
Min. age: 18
*Crampon technique, ice axe and navigation taught.*

**YMCA National Centre**     Centre 512
Location: Cumbria
Duration: 2 days, February/March
Levels: all
*Instruction in navigation, rope work, use of ice axe and crampons.*

# Other Sports

## Archery

**Budleigh Farm Target
Shooting Centre**     Centre 67
Location: Devon
Duration: 1-4 days, all year
Max. in group: 18
Levels: all
Min. age: 8
*Coaching from beginner to expert level.*

## Bowls & Croquet

**Moonfleet Manor Hotel &
Sports Resort**     Centre 298
Location: Dorset
Duration: 2-4 days, all year
Max. in group: 1
Levels: all
Min. age: 14

**HF Holidays Ltd**     Centre 207
Location: nationwide
Duration: 7 days, May-October
Max. in group: 20-30
Levels: all

## Clay Pigeon Shooting

**Bobsport (Scotland) Ltd**     Centre 44
Location: Edinburgh
Duration: 1/3/6/10 days, 15th January-end
November
Max. in group: varies
Levels: all
Min. age: 8
*Tuition in shooting.*

**Redfern Hotel (The)**     Centre 367
Location: Shropshire
Duration: 2 days, March-November
Max. in group: 12
Levels: all
Min. age: 17
*Sessions include all clays and instruction as
necessary.*

**Clay Farm - Sporting Heights**   Centre 96
Location: Worcestershire
Duration: 1 day, all year
Max. in group: 20
Levels: all
Min. age: 14

> **Please refer to the Centres
> Index for details about
> accommodation**

## Clay Pigeon Shooting continued

*Acorn Activities*

**Wharton Lodge**                 **Centre 484**
Location: Herefordshire
Duration: 1 day, all year
Max. in group: 10
Levels: all
*Tuition using single or multiple traps to create a simulated game shoot.*

# Falconry & Hawking

**British School of Falconry**     **Centre 60**
Location: Kent
Duration: 5 days, February-November
Max. in group: 8
Levels: beginners
Min. age: 12
*Course covers handling, training and maintaining of birds of prey.*

**Traditional School of
Falconry**                         **Centre 443**
Location: West Midlands
Duration: 5 days, all year
Max. in group: 4
Levels: all
Min. age: 14
*Introduction to the art of falconry: its history,*

*culture and modern day aproach to hunting and conservation activities.*

**Wharton Lodge**                 **Centre 484**
Location: Herefordshire
Duration: 2 days, September-April
Max. in group: 16
Levels: all
Min. age: 7
*Introductory course.*

# Fishing

**Bobsport (Scotland) Ltd**        **Centre 44**
Location: Edinburgh
Duration: 1/3/6/10 days, 15th January-end November
Max. in group: varies
Levels: all
Min. age: 8

**Clay Farm - Sporting Heights   Centre 96**
Location: Worcestershire
Duration: 1 day, all year
Max. in group: 10
Levels: beginners/all
Min. age: 14
*Tuition in fly fishing.*

**Pitlochry Angling**              **Centre 349**
Location: Perthshire
Duration: 1-5 days, May-September
Max. in group: 8
Levels: all
Min. age: 13
*Various courses available covering all aspects of fly fishing.*

**School of Casting Salmon & Trout
Fishing**                          **Centre 381**
Location: Selkirkshire
Duration: 6 days, April-October
Max. in group: 8-10

Levels: all
Min age: 8
*Wet fly and dry fly fishing on rivers and lochs. Courses also covers all methods of fly casting, entymology and knot tying.*

**Tufton Arm Hotel (The)**     **Centre 448**
Location: Cumbria
Duration: 4 days, March-September
Max. in group: 4
Levels: all
Min. age: 12
*Course covers casting, fishing locations, night fishing and wading.*

**Tweed Valley Hotel**     **Centre 450**
Location: Peebles-shire
Duration: varies, May-October
Levels: all
*A variety of courses at different fishing venues. Courses in casting, fishing, knot tying and fly dressing.*

## Fishing & Shooting

**East Down Centre**     **Centre 144**
Location: Devon
Duration: 2-6 days, March-October
Max. in group: 16
Levels: all
Min. age: 15
*A combination of trout fishing and clay pigeon shooting for family or club groups.*

## Go Karts

**Acorn Activities**     **Centre 3**
Location: Welsh Borders
Duration: any, all year
Levels: all
*Rally Karts and Super Karts on half mile circuit.*

*Acorn Activities*

## Golf

**Bobsport (Scotland) Ltd**     **Centre 44**
Location: Edinburgh
Duration: 1/3/6/10 days, January-November
Max. in group: varies
Levels: all
Min. age: 8
*Tuition in fishing for salmon and trout, golf and shooting.*

**Countrywide Holidays**     **Centre 114**
Location: nationwide
Duration: 7 days, May-June/September
*Players must produce a handicap certificate.*

**Forest of Arden Hotel**     **Centre 172**
Location: Warwickshire
Duration: 2 days, July-September
Max. in group: 16
Levels: all
Min. age: 18
*Tuition is tailored to individual needs.*

**HF Holidays Ltd**     **Centre 207**
Location: nationwide
Duration: 7 days, April-October
Max. in group: 20-30
Levels: all

## Golf continued

**Inverclyde - Scottish National
Sports Centre**     **Centre 233**
Location: Ayrshire
Duration: 2-4 days, February-October
Max in group: 24
Levels: all
Min age: No
*Course includes tuition by teaching professionals and rounds at local courses.*

**Park Grove Hotel (The)**     **Centre 337**
Location: Cornwall
Duration: 7 days, May-October
Max in group: 10
Levels: all
Min age: 12-15
*Course offers a range of teaching facilities for beginners to advanced level.*

**Scottish Youth Hostels**     **Centre 388**
Location: Ayrshire
Duration: 7 days, June-August
Max in group: 10
Levels: beginners
Min age: 15
*Basic tuition or development of existing skills.*

**Summer University**     **Centre 425**
Location: Leicestershire
Duration: 5 mornings, July-August
Max in group: 10
Levels: beginners
Min age: 18

**Terrick Hall Country
Hotel (The)**     **Centre 438**
Location: Shropshire
Duration: any, all year
Max in group: 24
Levels: all
Min age: 12

*Golf tuition and playing on Hill Valley golf course.*

**Wharton Lodge**     **Centre 484**
Location: Herefordshire
Duration: 1 day, all year
Levels: all
*Ring for details.*

# Grass Skiing

**Devon & Dorset Activities**     **Centre 128**
Location: Devon/Dorset
Duration: 2-7 day, March-October
Max in group: 350
Levels: all
Min age: 7

# Motor Cycle Training

**Acorn Activities**     **Centre 3**
Location: Herefordshire
Duration: 2/3 days, all year
Levels: all
*Two day basic training course for driving on the public highway. Optional extra day for those wishing to take their motorcycle test. Also courses in four wheel all terrain bikes cross-country.*

*Acorn Activities*

# Motor Sports

**Acorn Activities**       **Centre 3**
Location: Welsh Borders
Duration: any
Levels: all
*Introductory rally driving course in fully prepared Fords.*

**Hilton Hotels**       **Centre 220**
Location: nationwide
Duration: 2 days, all year
Max. in group: 20
Levels: all
Min. age: 17
*Introductory courses in motor racing, rallying, go karting, 4 x 4 off-road driving.*

# Multisports

**HF Holidays Ltd**       **Centre 207**
Location: nationwide
Duration: 7 days, May-August
Max. in group: 20-30
Levels: all
*Choices include tennis, swimming, riding, cycling, watersports, and keep fit.*

**Iris-Activity Breaks**       **Centre 235**
Location: nationwide
Duration: 1-2 days, all year
Levels: all
*Many courses including golf, watersports, driving, airsports, tennis, fishing and archery.*

**Millfield School Village of
Education**       **Centre 293**
Location: Somerset
Duration: 5 days, July-August
Max. in group: 10
Levels: all
Min. age: 8
*Tuition in badminton, bowls, cricket, golf, squash and tennis.*

*Acorn Activities*

# Shooting

**Budleigh Farm Target
Shooting Centre**       **Centre 67**
Location: Devon
Duration: 1-4 days, all year
Max. in group: 20
Levels: all
Min. age: 14
*Target rifle and pistol coaching from beginner to expert level.*

# Soccer

**ISCA Children's Holidays**       **Centre 236**
Location: Devon
Levels: all
Min. age: 7

# Tennis

**Braeside Sports**       **Centre 55**
Location: Tyne & Wear
Duration: 7 days, all year
Max. in group: 25
Levels: intermediate/advanced

## Tennis continued

**Felpham Sailing & Sports School**                Centre 165
Location: Sussex
Duration: 7 days
Max. in group: 10
Levels: all
Min. age: 9
*Coaching and free-play sessions under the guidance of a qualified tennis coach.*

**ISCA Children's Holidays**      Centre 236
Location: Devon
Duration: August
Levels: all
Min. age: 7

**Sunnybanks Tennis Farm**      Centre 426
Location: Cornwall
Duration: 7 days, April-October
Max. in group: 20

Levels: all
Min. age: 8
*Coaching for beginners to experts with qualified coaches.*

**Tennis Coaching International   Centre 437**
Location: Bedfordshire
Duration: any, March-October
Max. in group: 36
Levels: all
Min. age: 9
*Coaching from beginner to champion level with qualified coaches.*

**Wetherby**                Centre 482
Location: Berkshire
Duration: all year
Max. in group: 6
Levels: all
Min. age: 6
*Coaching to improve basic strokes and match play.*

*Millfield School Village of Education*

# Cycling, Walking and Outdoor Pursuits

| Abbreviations used in this section: |
| --- |
| **MLTB** Mountain Leaders Training Board |

## Cycling

**Achanalt House Guided Mountain
Bike Holidays**      **Centre 2**
Location: North West Scotland
Duration: 6 days, all year
Max. in group: 6
Levels: all
Min. age: 14
*Off-road exploration of the northern Highlands.*

**Acorn Activities**      **Centre 3**
Location: Herefordshire
Duration: 2-5 days, all year
Levels: all
*Tourer and mountain bikes with guides if
required.*

**Adventure Cycles**      **Centre 7**
Location: Devon
Duration: 1-14 days, all year
Max. in group: 10
Levels: all
Min. age: 10
*A range of self-led or guided holidays on
mountain bikes, tourers and tandems using
detailed route maps.*

**Anglia Cycling Holidays**      **Centre 18**
Location: East Anglia
Duration: various, all year
Max. in group: 25
Levels: all
Min. age: 9

**Bicycle Beano**      **Centre 40**
Location: Wales
Duration: 7 days, April-September
Max. in group: 30
Levels: all
Min. age: 18
*Guided cycling holidays.*

**Clive Powell Mountain
Bikes**      **Centre 97**
Location: Wales
Duration: 2-6 days, May-October
Max. in group: 16
Levels: all
Min. age: 12
*Emphasis on enjoyment, fitness, safety and
environmental awareness.*

**Combe Lodge Hotel**      **Centre 102**
Location: Devon
Duration: various, all year
Max. in group: 10
Levels: intermediate/advanced
Min. age: 16
*Self-led cycling tours with route maps and
transport provided.*

## Cycling continued

**Countrywide Holidays**            Centre 114
Location: nationwide
Duration: 7 days, May
Levels: all
*Various courses. Ring for details.*

**Cycle Tracks**            Centre 119
Location: Scotland
Duration: varies, April-October
Max. in group: 6
Levels: all
Min. age: 11
*Tailor-made, self-led touring on mountain bikes.*

**Cyclists' Touring Club**            Centre 120
Location: nationwide
Duration: 3-15 days, March-October
Levels: all
*Many courses throughout Britain. Ring for programme.*

**Flatford Mill Field Centre**            Centre 169
Location: Essex/Suffolk
Duration: 3 days, May-October
Levels: all
Min. age: 16
*Instructive short courses exploring the terrain around Flatford with regular stops to discuss the landscape, local history and wildlife.*

**Further Afield**            Centre 179
Location: Northumbria
Duration: various, all year
Max. in group: 12
Levels: all
Min. age: 9
*Touring or centre based holiday.*

**Garden of England
Cycling Holidays**            Centre 182
Location: Kent
Duration: 7 days, April-October
Max. in group: 6
Levels: all
Min. age: 15
*Cycling tour taking in castles or following the Pilgrims' route.*

**Gloucestershire Mountain
Bike Tours**            Centre 191
Location: West Country
Duration: 3-5 days, April-October
Max. in group: 8
Levels: beginners/intermediate
Min. age: 15
*Guided mountain bike tours of the Cotswolds, Severn Vale and Forest of Dean.*

**High Adventure**            Centre 208
Location: Isle of Wight
Duration: 1-7 days, all year
Max. in group: 20
Levels: all
Min. age: 12
*Organised or self-led mountain bike tours along trails.*

**Holmhead Guest House**            Centre 221
Location: Northumberland
Duration: varies, December/January
Max. in group: 12
Levels: all
Min. age: 7
*Maps and instructions for self led groups with collection and delivery. Guided tours if required.*

**Just Pedalling**            Centre 244
Location: Norfolk/Suffolk
Duration: 3/7/14 days, all year
Max. in group: no limit
Levels: all

**Millnain**                          **Centre 294**
Location: Ross-shire
Duration: 2-7 days, all year
Max. in group: 6
Levels: all
Min. age: 12

**Norfolk Cycling Holidays**    **Centre 317**
Location: Norfolk/East Anglia
Duration: 2/8/15 days, all year
Max. in group: 16
Levels: all
Min. age: 3
*Self-led holidays including route map and
equipment, B&B accommodation arranged in
advance.*

**North York Moors Adventure
Centre**                               **Centre 320**
Location: Yorkshire
Duration: 2 days, April-October
Max. in group: 12
Levels: all
Min. age: 18
*Coastal and moorland mountain biking in
North York Moors National Park.*

**Pedalaway**                          **Centre 342**
Location: Herefordshire
Duration: varies, all year
Max. in group: 10
Levels: all
*Routes and tours planned on request.*

**PGL Adventure Holidays**    **Centre 345**
Location: Welsh Borders
Duration: 7 days, July/August
Levels: all
Min. age: 12-16
*Mountain biking through the Wye Valley
and Forest of Dean.*

**Preseli Mountain Bikes &
Sea Kayaking**                        **Centre 356**
Location: Pembrokeshire
Duration: 2-5 days, all year
Max. in group: 12
Levels: all
Min. age: 7
*Mountain bike riding techniques and
mechanics taught while cycling in the
Pembrokeshire Coast National Park.*

**Scottish Cycling Holidays**    **Centre 386**
Location: Perthshire
Duration: varies, all year
Max. in group: 35
Levels: all
Min. age: 9

**Scottish Youth Hostels**      **Centre 388**
Location: Isles of Mull/Oban/Skye/Raasay
Duration: 7 days, June-September
Max. in group: 15
Levels: all
Min. age: 12
*Island hopping with tour leader.*

**Slapton Ley Field Centre**    **Centre 406**
Location: Devon
Duration: 7 days, July
Levels: all
Min. age: 16
*Emphasis on exploring scenery, landforms
and wildlife.*

**Windmill Ways**                    **Centre 497**
Location: Norfolk
Duration: various, March-November
Levels: all
Min. age: 10

---

**Please refer to the Centres Index
for details about accommodation**

---

# Hillwalking

**Ardeonaig Outdoor Centre**     **Centre 22**
Location: Perthshire
Duration: varies, April/July/August
Max. in group: 32
Levels: all
Min. age: 14
*Series of walks with instruction in the appropriate skills to enjoy Highland Perthshire.*

**Cader Ventures**     **Centre 77**
Location: Snowdonia
Duration: 5 days, April-October
Max. in group: 8
Levels: all
Min. age: 16
*A basic hillwalking course covering skills in navigation, route-finding and first aid.*

**Glencoe Outdoor Centre**     **Centre 188**
Location: Argyllshire
Duration: 2/5/7 days, April-October
Levels: all
Min. age: 15
*Guided hill and ridge walking for different levels of ability.*

**Glenmore Lodge - Scottish National Sports Centre**     **Centre 189**
Location: Inverness-shire
Duration: 5-6 days, June-September
Levels: beginners
Min. age: 15
*Introduction to travelling in the mountains, and the basic skills for summer conditions.*

**Highlander Mountaineering**     **Centre 217**
Location: Scotland
Duration: 5 days, June-September
Max. in group: 8
Levels: beginners
Min. age: 16
*Course covers summer hillwalking techniques: navigation, river crossing, scrambling, with one night spent out in the mountains.*

**Kevin Walker Mountain Activities**     **Centre 248**
Location: Wales
Duration: 2 days, all year
Max. in group: 16
Levels: all
Min. age: 16
*An introduction to the techniques required for the safe enjoyment of hillwalking.*

**Ski Wildcountry**     **Centre 402**
Location: Scotland
Duration: 7 days, May-October
Max. in group: 8
Levels: all
Min. age: 16
*Techniques to improve navigation skills and safety on the hills.*

# Map & Compass Skills

**Compass Ventures**     **Centre 104**
Location: North West Scotland
Duration: 2 days, April/October
Max. in group: 8
Levels: beginners/intermediate
Min. age: 16
*Instruction in navigating in mountain country using map and compass.*

**Freetime Activities**     **Centre 176**
Location: Yorkshire
Duration: 1 day, all year
Max. in group: 10
Levels: beginners/intermediate
Min. age: 12
*Practical route finding with tuition for navigation on hills.*

*Bearsports Outdoor Centre*

### High Trek Snowdonia     Centre 212
Location: Snowdonia
Duration: 3 days, June-October
Max. in group: 7
Levels: beginners/intermediate
Min. age: 14

### Preston Montford Field
### Centre     Centre 357
Location: Shropshire
Duration: 7 days, July/September
Levels: all
Min. age: 16
*Instruction to develop the skill and confidence to devise your own routes.*

### Wildquest     Centre 493
Location: Peak District
Duration: 3 days, May-September
Max. in group: 16
Levels: all
Min. age: 10
*Skills required for coping confidently in bad weather conditions.*

# Mountain Craft

### Cader Ventures     Centre 77
Location: Snowdonia
Duration: 5 days, May-October
Max. in group: 4
Levels: intermediate/advanced
Min. age: 16
*A course for those wanting to try more ambitious ascents.*

### Dartmoor Expedition Centre     Centre 123
Location: Devon
Duration: 6 days, March-December
Max. in group: 32
Levels: advanced
Min. age: 18
*Course leading to qualifications for those wishing to lead groups on hills and mountains.*

### Glenmore Lodge - Scottish National
### Sports Centre     Centre 189
Location: Inverness-shire
Duration: 5-6 days, June-September
Levels: intermediate
Min. age: 15
*MLTB course designed for those wanting to develop their skills on longer expeditions and demanding terrain.*

### Kevin Walker Mountain
### Activities     Centre 248
Location: Wales
Duration: 6 days, Spring/Autumn
Max. in group: 16
Levels: all
Min. age: 18
*MLTB course in the basic techniques necessary to lead others safely in the mountains in summer conditions. Maximum 4 people per instructor.*

### Mountain Craft     Centre 304
Location: Scotland
Duration: 5 days, May-September
Max. in group: 5
Levels: intermediate/advanced
Min. age: 18
*An intensive course for experienced hillwalkers wanting to develop their skills in complex mountain terrain.*

# Mountain walking

**Highlander Mountaineering   Centre 217**
Location: Scotland
Duration: 5 days, June-September
Max. in group: 4
Levels: beginners
Min. age: 16
*A variety of topics covered and many routes ascended giving participants a fine grounding in mountain scrambling.*

**Kindrogan  Field Centre     Centre 250**
Location: Scottish Highlands
Duration: 7 days, June-September
Levels: intermediate/advanced
Min. age: 16
*A course for fit walkers who wish to understand the structure and ecology of well known and less well known mountains.*

**Merlin Mountain Activities   Centre 285**
Location: Snowdonia/Lake District
Duration: 1-10 days, April-October
Max. in group: 50
Levels: all
Min. age: 16
*A course covering the skills required for for safe enjoyment of mountain walking.*

**Mountain Craft              Centre 304**
Location: Scotland
Duration: 5 days, May-September
Max. in group: 10
Levels: beginners/intermediate
Min. age: 18
*Introduces walkers to the Scottish mountains and the techniques required for safe travel.*

**Wasdale Mountain Walking
Holidays                     Centre 467**
Location: Cumbria
Duration: 7 days, July/August

Max. in group: 4
Levels: all
Min. age: 10
*Guided walks to the highest peaks for children aged 10-14.*

# Mountaineering

**Keswick Mountaineering
School                       Centre 247**
Location: Cumbria
Duration: 2-4 days, all year
Max. in group: 3
Levels: all

**Professional Mountaineering
Services                     Centre 359**
Location: Inverness-shire
Duration: 2+ days, all year
Max. in group: 12
Levels: all
Min. age: 16
*All aspects of mountaineering skills taught.*

### See Winter Sports section for Winter Mountaineering courses

*Bearsports Outdoor Centres*

*The Lutterworth Guide to* Activity and Study Holidays

*Rock Lea Activity Centre*

# Outdoor Activities

**Acorn Activities**               **Centre 3**
Location: Herefordshire/Pembrokeshire
Duration: 2-5 days
Levels: all
*Choice of abseiling, caving and climbing.*

**Allenheads Lodge
Outdoor Centre**               **Centre 15**
Location: Northumberland
Duration: 2/5/7 days, all year
Max. in group: 20
Levels: all
Min. age: 8
*A range of guided walking, mountain biking
and outdoor pursuits.*

**Bearsports Outdoor Centres**   **Centre 38**
Location: Northumberland
Duration: varies, all year
Max. in group: 80
Levels: all
Min. age: 9
*Rockclimbing, hillwalking, orienteering,
mountain biking, bivouacing/camp craft and
cliff jumping available. Training courses
with instruction also provided.*

**Compass Christian Centre**     **Centre 103**
Location: Perthshire
Duration: 2-6 days, April-December
Max. in group: 42
Levels: all
Min. age: 8
*Combined options of walking, orienteering
and various sports with instruction.*

**Country Venture Activities**   **Centre 113**
Location: Cumbria
Duration: 1-7 days, February-December
Max. in group: 40
Levels: all
Min. age: 5

**Cwm Uchaf**                    **Centre 118**
Location: Brecon Beacons
Duration: 3-5+ days, all year
Max. in group: 18-40
Levels: all
Min. age: 10
*Guided or self-led coastal walks of different
levels as required with cycling and other
sports.*

**East Down Centre**             **Centre 144**
Location: Devon
Duration: 2-6 days, all year
Max. in group: 16
Levels: beginners/intermediate
Min. age: 10
*Introduction to a variety of activities for
families or club groups.*

**Eclipse Outdoor Discovery**    **Centre 146**
Location: Cumbria
Duration: 2-6 days, all year
Max. in group: 60
Levels: all
Min. age: 8
*Mountain biking, fell walking, rockclimbing,
mountain and gorge scrambling.*

## Outdoor Activities continued

**Edale YHA Activity Centre    Centre 147**
Location: Yorkshire
Duration: 2 days, all year
Levels: all
*Courses on climbing and caving.*

**Freetime Activities    Centre 177**
Location: Yorkshire
Duration: 2 day, all year
Max. in group: 12/16
Levels: all
Min. age: 12/16
*Abseiling and caving available.*

**High Trek Snowdonia    Centre 212**
Location: Snowdonia
Duration: 3 days, June-October
Max. in group: 6
Levels: beginners/intermediate
Min. age: 14
*Scrambling skills covered including rope use, safety and route finding.*

**Kevin Walker Mountain
Activities    Centre 248**
Location: Brecon Beacons
Duration: 2 days, all year
Max. in group: 4
Levels: all
Min. age: 16
*An introduction to the techniques of caving.*

**Minerva Training    Centre 295**
Location: Dyfed
Duration: 2-5 days, all year
Max. in group: 30-40
Levels: all
Min. age: 10
*Caving, walking and abseiling as part of an activity programme.*

**Outward Bound Trust    Centre 332**
Location: nationwide
Duration: 8/12/20 days, all year
Levels: all
Min. age: 14
*Outdoor activity challenges, problem solving and expeditions as part of a variety of courses. Ring for details.*

**PGL Adventure Holidays    Centre 345**
Location: Herefordshire
Duration: 7 days, July/August
Max. in group: 12
Levels: all
Min. age: 13-17
*Hiking, climbing, canoeing and caving.*

**R & L Adventures    Centre 362**
Location: Cumbria
Duration: varies
Levels: all
*Abseiling, rock climbing, orienteering and pot holing.*

**Rock Lea Activity Centre    Centre 372**
Location: Derbyshire
Duration: 2 days, all year
Levels: all
Min. age: 18
*Climbing and caving courses.*

**Transcotland Holiday
Expeditions    Centre 445**
Location: Scotland
Duration: 6 days, May-October
Levels: all
Min. age: 12
*Walking, cycling, rock climbing and canoeing whilst on the coast-to-coast route.*

**Please mention this guide when booking a course**

**Worlds End Lodge**                 **Centre 505**
Location: Herefordshire
Duration: 2-5 days, all year
Max. in group: 70
Levels: all
Min. age: 10
*Outdoor activities and education courses*
*for organised groups only. No individuals.*

# Rambling

**Hill Residential College**        **Centre 218**
Location: Gwent
Duration: 2-7 days, all year
Max. in group: 25-30
Levels: all
Min. age: 16
*Emphasis on enjoyment and safety.*

**Kindrogan Field Centre**          **Centre 250**
Location: Scottish Highlands
Duration: 7 days, June-October
Levels: all
Min. age: 16
*Walks of varying degrees of length with*
*wildlife, history and geology discussed en route.*

**Malham Tarn Field Centre**        **Centre 278**
Location: Yorkshire
Duration: 7 days, August
Levels: all
Min. age: 16
*Rambling through Limestone Dales with an*
*introduction to the landscape local history*
*and wildlife of the Yorkshire Dales.*

# Rockclimbing

**Abernethy Outdoor Centre**        **Centre 1**
Location: Inverness-shire
Duration: 7 days, August
Max. in group: 16
Levels: beginners/intermediate
Min. age: 16

**Bowles Outdoor Centre**           **Centre 50**
Location: Sussex
Duration: 2 days, April-September
Max. in group: 12
Levels: all
Min. age: 16

**Cader Ventures**                  **Centre 77**
Location: Snowdonia
Duration: 5 days, May-September
Max. in group: 6
Levels: beginners/intermediate
Min. age: 16
*Thorough grounding in basic techniques.*

**Canopy Training**                 **Centre 87**
Location: Peak District
Duration: 2 days, April-October
Max. in group: 6
Levels: all
Min. age: 18
*For women only, with beginners in mind but*
*all levels welcome.*

**Compass West - International School of**
**Rockclimbing**                    **Centre 105**
Location: Cornwall/Scotland
Duration: 2/6 days, April-October
Max. in group: 15
Levels: all
Min. age: 16
*Various courses providing a sound knowl-*
*edge of use of equipment, rock movement*
*and training methods.*

**Glenmore Lodge - Scottish National**
**Sports Centre**                   **Centre 189**
Location: Inverness-shire
Duration: 5-6 days, May-October
Levels: all
Min. age: 15
*A range of instructional courses aimed to*
*build on strengths and abilities of each*
*individual.*

## Rockclimbing continued

**Great Glen School of
Adventure**      **Centre 195**
Location: Inverness-shire
Duration: 2 days, all year
Max. in group: 4
Levels: beginners
Min. age: 12

**Highlander Mountaineering**   **Centre 217**
Location: Scotland
Duration: 5 days, June-September
Max. in group: 4
Levels: beginners/intermediate
Min. age: 16
*Courses for beginners or leaders.*

**Kevin Walker Mountain
Activities**      **Centre 248**
Location: Wales
Duration: 2 days, all year
Max. in group: 4
Levels: all
Min. age: 16

**Merlin Mountain Activities**   **Centre 285**
Location: Snowdonia/Lake District
Duration: 1-10 days, April-October
Max. in group: 50
Levels: all
Min. age: 16
*A course covering the skills required for the
safe enjoyment of rockclimbing.*

**Motherby House Activities**   **Centre 300**
Location: Cumbria
Duration: 2/6 days, March-October
Max. in group: 12
Levels: beginners
Min. age: 14
*Course covers rope work, abseiling and use
of specialist equipment.*

*Rock Lea Activity Centre*

**Mountain Adventure Guides**   **Centre 303**
Location: Cumbria
Duration: 1-5 days, May-October
Max. in group: 6
Levels: all
Min. age: 16
*Both basic introduction and advanced rope
skills for leading offered.*

**Towers Adventure Centre**      **Centre 442**
Location: Snowdonia
Duration: 2-5 days, May-September
Max. in group: 20
Levels: all
Min. age: 8
*A range of courses for beginners to leader
level.*

**Twr-y-Felin Outdoor Centre**   **Centre 451**
Location: Dyfed
Duration: 2-6 days, March-October
Max. in group: 30
Levels: all
Min. age: 8
*Rope work and safety skills taught.*

# Survival

**Acorn Activities**          Centre 3
Location: Herefordshire
Duration: 2 days
Levels: all
*Survival skills for living outdoors, and coping under stress in dangerous situations.*

**Breakaway Survival School**    Centre 54
Location: Wales
Duration: 2/5 days, all year
Max. in group: 30
Levels: all
Min. age: 14
*All aspects of survival and mountaincraft for individuals or organised groups.*

**Canopy Training**          Centre 87
Location: Peak District
Duration: 2 days, March-October
Max. in group: 14
Levels: all
Min. age: 18
*Activities for women only, including walking, abseiling, problem-solving exercises, climbing and orienteering.*

# Walking

**Acorn Activities**          Centre 3
Location: Herefordshire/Wales
Duration: varies, all year
Levels: all
*Easy to energetic options with guides and many local anecdotes.*

**Please refer to the Centres Index for details about accommodation**

**Adventureline**          Centre 11
Location: Cornwall
Duration: 7 days, April-October
Max. in group: 10
Levels: all
Min. age: 8
*Walking and appreciation of natural history, geology and local archaeology.*

**Avalon Trekking Scotland**    Centre 28
Location: nationwide
Duration: 6-15 days, April-October
Max. in group: 10
Levels: intermediate/advanced
Min. age: 20
*A variety of long distance walks throughout Britain.*

**Barry Skinner**          Centre 35
Location: Snowdonia
Duration: up to 7 days, all year
Max. in group: 6
Levels: all
Min. age: 18

**Beaconhill - East Kent
Field Centre**          Centre 37
Location: Kent
Duration: 3 days, October-April
Levels: all
Min. age: 7
*A range of gentle or more vigorous walks incorporating many aspects of Kent life and wildlife, some taking in evening theatre or concert visits.*

**C-n-Do Scotland Ltd**          Centre 74
Location: Scotland
Duration: 1-15 days, all year
Max. in group: 13
Levels: all
Min. age: 16
*Holidays throughout Scottish mainland and Western Isles.*

## Walking continued

**Chichester Interest Holidays**    **Centre 93**
Location: Cornwall
Duration: 7 days, March-October
Max. in group: 7
Levels: all
Min. age: 18
*Easy walking on coastal and countryside paths.*

**Cold Keld Guided Walking
Holidays**    **Centre 99**
Location: Cumbria
Duration: 7 days, April-October
Max. in group: 10
Levels: all
Min. age: 18
*Guided walking holidays in small groups. Active blind people welcome.*

**Combe Lodge Hotel**    **Centre 102**
Location: Devon
Duration: varies, all year
Max. in group: 20
Levels: all
Min. age: 16
*Self-led walks with route maps and transport provided.*

**Compass Ventures**    **Centre 104**
Location: Scotland
Duration: 2-7 days, April-October
Max. in group: 8
Levels: all
Min. age: 16
*Walking in the West Highlands, Arrochar Alps and Munros.*

**Countrywide Holidays**    **Centre 114**
Location: nationwide
Duration: 7 days, all year
Levels: all

*A range of guided walks for different levels of fitness.*

**Dale Fort Field Centre**    **Centre 121**
Location: Pembrokeshire
Duration: 7 days, June-September
Levels: all
Min. age: 16
*Emphasis on geology scenery and natural history of Pembrokeshire Coast Path.*

**Discover**    **Centre 132**
Location: Ross-shire
Duration: 6 days, December-October
Max. in group: 8
Levels: all
Min. age: 16
*Guided walking progressing from easy to rougher higher ground and ridge scrambling.*

**Drapers' Field Centre**    **Centre 137**
Location: Gwynedd
Duration: 3-7 days, February-October
Levels: all
Min. age: 16
*Easy rambles exploring the flora, castles, and environment of Snowdonia or long distance walking through the wilder eastern margins of the National Park.*

**Earnley Concourse**    **Centre 141**
Location: Sussex
Duration: 2-7 days, April-September
Levels: all
*The South Downs, Arun Valley and The Wayfarers' Way are incorporated with wildlife walks.*

**English Wanderer**    **Centre 158**
Location: nationwide
Duration: 2-17 days, all year
Max. in group: 15
Levels: all

Min. age: 12
*Many options throughout the UK. Ring for programme.*

**Flatford Mill Field Centre**   **Centre 169**
Location: Essex/Suffolk
Duration: 3 days, March-October
Levels: all
Min. age: 16
*Walking in Constable country during different seasons learning about the landscape, history and wildlife.*

**Focus Holidays**   **Centre 171**
Location:Wales
Duration: 1-6 days, all year except November
Max. in group : 10
Levels: beginners/intermediate
Min. age: 12

**Fortify the Spirit**   **Centre 174**
Location: Lake District
Duration: 2+ days, June-September/December
Max. in group: 12
Levels: all
Min. age: 16

**Further Afield**   **Centre 179**
Location: Northumbria
Duration: varies, all year
Max. in group: 12
Levels: all
Min. age: 8
*Self-led walks with route guide.*

**Gidleigh Park**   **Centre  186**
Location: Dartmoor
Duration: 3-5 days, December-March
Max. in group: 10
Levels: all
Min. age: 10
*Guided walks on Dartmoor.*

**Greenholme Holidays**   **Centre 196**
Location: Northern England/Scotland
Duration: 3-8 days, May-November
Max. in group: 16
Levels: all
Min. age: 18
*Walking on trails and hills with sightseeing en-route in Britain's National Parks and Border Country.*

**Head for the Hills**   **Centre 202**
Location: Powys
Duration: 4-10 days, April-October
Max. in group: 12
Levels: beginners
Min. age: 11
*Gentle tours off the beaten track.*

**Heathfield House**   **Centre 205**
Location: Devon
Duration: 2-7 days, March-November
Max. in group: 8
Levels: all
Min. age: 16

**Helvellyn Youth Hostel**   **Centre 206**
Location: Cumbria
Duration: 2 days, May/August/September
Max. in group 24
Levels: all
Min. age: 16

**HF Holidays Ltd**   **Centre 207**
Location: nationwide
Duration: 2-7 days, all year
Levels: all
*Guided walking with experienced leaders on a choice of walks available to suit all standards.*

**Please refer to the Centres Index for details about accommodation**

## Walking continued

**High Force Training Centre**    **Centre 209**
Location: Co. Durham
Duration: varies, all year
Max. in group: 30
Levels: all
Min. age: 7
*Courses to suit requirements of clients.*

**High Trek Snowdonia**    **Centre 212**
Location: Snowdonia
Duration: 3-7, April-October
Max. in group: 7
Levels: all
Min. age: 14
*Various options from trekking to summiting all 14 Welsh peaks over 3000' in a long weekend.*

**Higham Hall Residential
Study Centre**    **Centre 214**
Location: Cumbria
Duration: 2-6 days, all year
Levels: all
*Low level lakeland walks, walking with poetry themes, or basic orienteering courses offered.*

**Hillscape Walking Holidays**    **Centre 219**
Location: Mid-Wales
Duration: 6 days, March-November
Max. in group: 8
Levels: all
Min. age: 11
*Route descriptions and maps of 5-20 miles, with easy to mountainous terrain.*

**Hilton Hotels**    **Centre 220**
Location: nationwide
Duration: 2 days, June-September
Max. in group: 30
Levels: all

Min. age: 12
*Rambling with leader up to 12 miles covering the history, geography and environment of the area.*

**Holmhead Guest House**    **Centre 221**
Location: Northumberland
Duration: varies, December/January
Max. in group: 12
Levels: all
Min. age: 7
*Maps and instructions for self-led groups with collection and delivery. Guided tours if required.*

**Instep Linear
Walking Holidays**    **Centre 228**
Location: England/Wales
Duration: 5-15 days, May-September
Max. in group: 16
Levels: all
Min. age: 16
*Long distance walking - Coast to Coast, Offa's Dyke, Henney - Avon Canal, Brecon - Abergavenny Canal.*

**Juniper Hall Field Centre**    **Centre 243**
Location: Surrey
Duration: 3-7 days, June-September
Levels: all
Min. age: 16
*Landscapes, history and natural history are explored along the North Downs Way.*

**Lightfoot**    **Centre 262**
Location: Cornwall
Duration: 2-30 days, all year
Max. in group: 30
Levels: all
*Coastal walking at your own pace. Luggage goes ahead.*

**Millnain**     Centre 294
Location: Ross-shire
Duration: 2-7 days, all year
Max. in group: 6
Levels: all
Min. age: 12

**Motherby House Activities**     Centre 300
Location: Cumbria
Duration: 2/6 days, March-November
Max. in group: 12
Levels: all
Min. age: 14

**Nettlecombe Court**     Centre 314
Location: Somerset
Duration 7 days, July
Levels: all
Min. age: 16
*A natural history exploration of the Brendon Hills Quantocks and the Somerset Coast.*

**North York Moors Adventure Centre**     Centre 320
Location: Yorkshire
Duration: 5 days, April-October
Max. in group: 15
Levels: all
Min. age: 16
*Coastal and moorland walks in North York Moors National Park.*

**North-West Frontiers**     Centre 318
Location: Scottish Highlands
Duration: 7 days, May-October
Max. in group: 8
Levels: intermediate/advanced
Min. age: 15
*Graded walking from moderate to strenuous up to 12 miles daily.*

**Northumbria Experience (The)**     Centre 323
Location: Northumberland
Duration: 7 days, August/September
Max. in group: 50
Levels: beginners/intermediate
Min. age: 16
*A series of guided walks of 6-8 miles designed to appeal to the 'average rambler'.*

**Orielton Field Centre**     Centre 329
Location: Dyfed
Duration: 7 days, August
Levels: all
*Walks along Pembrokeshire coastal paths and Preseli Hills.*

**Peak National Park Study Centre**     Centre 340
Location: Peak District
Duration: 2-7 days, all year
Max. in group: 25
Levels: all
Min. age: 18
*Various guided walks of 8-12 miles covering different skills.*

**Pencerrig Walking Holidays**     Centre 343
Location: Mid Wales
Duration: 3-7 days, all year
Max. in group: 12
Levels: beginners/intermediate
Min. age: 14
*Guidance in the skills of map reading, plus walking in countryside at a leisurely pace.*

**Preston Montford Field Centre**     Centre 357
Location: Shropshire
Duration: 7 days, May-October
Levels: all
Min. age: 16
*A range of different walks exploring the geology, natural history, local history and legend.*

## Walking continued

**Ramblers Holidays Ltd**          Centre 364
Location: nationwide
Duration: 7 days, April-October
Max. in group: 20
Levels: all
Min. age: 16
*Many options. Ring for programme.*

**Rob Hastings Adventure**          Centre 370
Location: North Wales
Duration: 3 days, July/August
Levels: all
Min. age: 8
*Walking on Offa's Dyke and Brenig forest trails or more strenuous ridge walking in Snowdonia as part of a tailored adventure programme.*

**Scottish Youth Hostels**          Centre 388
Location: Scotland
Duration: various, May-September
Max. in group: varies
Levels: all
Min. age: 15
*A range of classic walking tours.*

**Shoreline Leisure**          Centre 396
Location: Cornwall
Duration: 7 days, April/September/October
Max. in group: 40
Levels: beginners
*Geology, archaeology, history and natural history introduced along route.*

**SKADI - Women's Walking Holidays**          Centre 399
Location: Lake District/Yorkshire
Duration: 4-6 days, April-October
Max. in group: 6
Levels: all
Min. age: 11

*Walking for women, map and compass courses and black women's walking holidays.*

**Slapton Ley Field Centre**          Centre 406
Location: Devon
Duration: 3-7 days, May-August
Levels: all
Min. age: 16
*Walking through remote Dartmoor or rambling through lanes and hidden paths of Devon with an emphasis on exploring natural and local history.*

**Step by Step Walking**          Centre 417
Location: Isle of Wight
Duration: 2-7 days, all year
Max. in group: 30
Levels: all
Min. age: 14

**Sussex Seen**          Centre 430
Location: Sussex
Duration: 2/3 days, March/May/July/October
Max. in group: 20
Levels: all
Min. age: 12
*Guided walks exploring Sussex countryside, 12-14 miles a day.*

**Temewalk**          Centre 436
Location: Wales
Duration: 1-7 days, all year
Max. in group: 8
Levels: all
Min. age: 16

**Wales Wildlife Holidays**          Centre 464
Location: Wales
Duration: 7 days, March-November
Max. in group: 6
Levels: all
Min. age: 12

**Walkers' Britain**     **Centre 465**
Location: Scotland/Wales and England
Duration: 4/7/14 day, May-October
Levels: all
Min. age: 12
*Nine well-known British walks escorted or unescorted.*

**Wharton Lodge**     **Centre 484**
Location: Welsh borders
Duration: varies, all year
Levels: all
*Walking in the Wye Valley and Forest of Dean with guides and transport if required.*

**Windmill Ways**     **Centre 497**
Location: Norfolk
Duration: varies, March-November
Levels: all
Min. age: 10
Youth Hostel Association Centre
:Location:

**Ynys Hywel Countryside
Centre**     **Centre 513**
Location: Gwent
Duration: 2 days, August-October
Max. in group: 34
Levels: all
Min. age: 18

## Walking & Writing

**Malham Tarn Field Centre**     **Centre 278**
Location: Yorkshire
Duration: 7 days, August
Levels: all
Min. age: 16
*Daily walks with written responses to the landscape and to experiences thus gained, with advice on writing skills.*

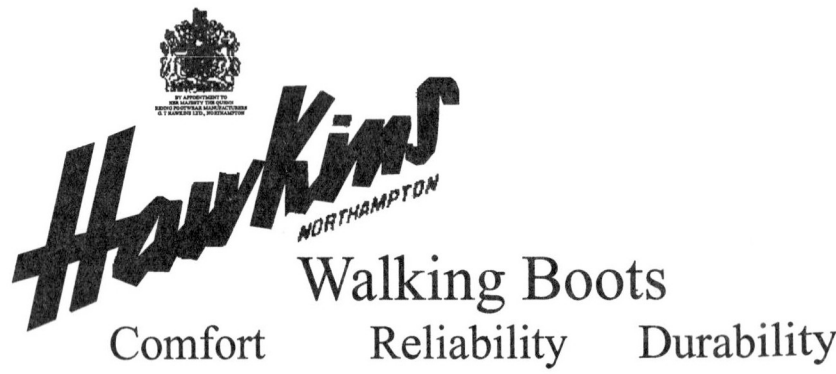

# Horses

## Horse Drawn Caravans

**Acorn Activities**                    **Centre 3**
Location: Welsh Borders
Duration: 7 days, all year
Max. in group: 4
Levels: all

**Northumbria Horse Holidays  Centre 324**
Location: Northumberland
Duration: 7 days, April-October
Max. in group: 50
Levels: all
Min. age: none
*Self-catering caravans for up to 5 people.*

**Welsh Horse Drawn Holidays Centre 475**
Location: South Wales
Duration: 7 days, May-October
Max. in group: 4
Levels: intermediate
Min. age: one person over 18

## Pony Camp

**White Horse Riding Centre    Centre 487**
Location: Wiltshire
Duration: 5 days, August
Max. in group: 12
Levels: all
Min. age: 10

*Pony care and safe riding taught, camping on organic farms, lectures, picnics and carriage driving.*

## Riding

**Adventure & Computer
Holidays**                          **Centre 6**
Location: Cornwall
Duration: 7 days, July/August
Max. in group: 10
Levels: all
Min. age: 6
*Tuition for 6-14 year olds including stable management.*

**Albion Rides**                    **Centre 14**
Location: Norfolk
Duration: 2-6 days, all year
Max. in group: 6
Levels: intermediate/advanced
Min. age: 18
*Riding at varied paces visiting places of interest.*

**Ayrshire Equitation Centre    Centre 31**
Location: Ayrshire
Duration: 2+ days, all year
Max. in group: 15
Levels: all
Min. age: none

**Barend Properties Ltd**  **Centre 34**
Location: Kirkcudbrightshire
Duration: 1-5 days, April-October
Max. in group: 6
Levels: all
Min. age: 6
*Emphasis on improving ability, confidence in riding and knowledge of horse/pony care.*

**Broadlands Riding Centre**  **Centre 63**
Location: Hampshire
Duration: 5 days, April/July/August
Max. in group: 7
Levels: all
Min. age: 10
*Dressage, show jumping, cross country riding, games and horse care are covered.*

**Bryn Ffynnon Farm
Riding Centre**  **Centre 66**
Location: North Wales
Duration: varies, all year
Max. in group: 10
Levels: all
Min. age: 8

**Contessa Riding Centre**  **Centre 106**
Location: Hertfordshire
Duration: varies, all year
Max. in group: 10
Levels: all
Min. age: 15
*Riding, stable management and horsecare instruction.*

**Copley Stables**  **Centre 109**
Location: South Wales
Duration: 5-14 days, May-November
Max. in group: 8
Levels: all
Min. age: 8
*Tuition in riding, trekking and stable management to BHS Tests 1 & 2.*

**Devon & Dorset Activities**  **Centre 128**
Location: Devon/Dorset
Duration: 2-7 days, March-October
Levels: all
Min age: 7

**Drywell Farm Riding Centre**  **Centre 138**
Location: Devon
Duration: 7 days, May-October
Max. in group: 10
Levels: intermediate/advanced
Min. age: 14
*Riding over open moorland.*

**Elvaston Castle Riding
Centre**  **Centre 152**
Location: Derbyshire
Duration: 6 days, April-November
Max. in group: varies
Levels: all
Min. age: 9
*Instruction to suit aims of individuals. BHS exams and training also offered.*

**Farsyde Stud & Riding
Centre**  **Centre 163**
Location: Yorkshire
Duration varies, all year
Max. in group: 8
Levels: intermediate/advanced
Min. age: 8

**Highland Riding Centre**  **Centre 216**
Location: Inverness-shire
Duration: varies, all year
Levels: all

**Please refer to the
Centres Index
for details about
accommodation**

## Riding continued

**International Warwick School of Riding**　　Centre 232
Location: Warwickshire
Duration: 5 days, April-August/October
Max. in group: 35
Levels: all
Min. age: 5
*Emphasis on improving horsemanship including gymkhana and jumping.*

**Limes Farm Holiday Centre**　　Centre 263
Location: Kent
Duration: 3 days-4 weeks, all year
Max. in group: 12
Levels: all
Min. age: 10
*Emphasis on improving all aspects of equitation.*

**Llangorse Riding Centre**　　Centre 268
Location: Brecon Beacons
Duration: varies, all year
Levels: all
*Guides available if required. Cross country routes for the more experienced.*

**Logie Farm Riding Centre**　　Centre 271
Location: Nairnshire
Duration: varies, all year
Max. in group: 6-8
Levels: all
Min. age: 8
*Riding holidays with instruction, plus long or short hacks as required.*

**Lydford House & Riding Stables**　　Centre 275
Location: Devon
Duration: any, all year
Max. in group: varies
Levels: all
Min. age: 5
*Riding over Dartmoor in small escorted groups.*

**Lyncombe Lodge**　　Centre 277
Location: Avon
Duration: 2-20 days, all year
Max. in group: 35
Levels: all
Min. age: 5

**Mill Farm Riding Centre**　　Centre 291
Location: Shropshire
Duration: 5 days, all year
Max. in group: varies
Levels: all
*Riding holidays for individuals, small groups and families with instruction.*

**Millfield School Village of Education**　　Centre 293
Location: Sussex
Duration: 5 days, July/August
Max. in group: 10
Levels: all
Min. age: 8
*Riding and jumping tuition.*

**Moss Farm Riding**　　Centre 299
Location: Cornwall
Duration: 1-14 days, all year
Max. in group: 6
Levels: intermediate/advanced
Min. age: 18
*Riding and hunting on Bodmin Moor. Instruction on stable management also available.*

**North Wheddon Farm Riding Holidays**　　Centre 319
Location: Somerset
Duration: 6 days, April-November
Max. in group: 8
Levels: intermediate/advanced
Min. age: 16

*Riding at all paces over Exmoor. Tour riding from hotel to hotel.*

**Northumbria Horse Holidays  Centre 324**
Location: Northumberland
Duration: 5 days, March-November
Max. in group: 50
Levels: all
Min. age: 6
*Complete tuition in horse riding with qualified instructors. Intensive courses also offered.*

**Oathill Farm Riding Centre   Centre 326**
Location: Kent
Duration: 2-28 days, all year
Max in group: 18
Levels: all
Min age: 10
*Riding and horse management skills covered.*

**Parc-le-Breos Riding & Holiday Centre            Centre 335**
Location: South Wales
Duration: 2 days, all year
Levels: all
Min. age: ring for details
*Trekking and stable management covered.*

**Pound Cottage Riding Centre   Centre 354**
Location: Dorset
Duration: 7 days, all year
Max. in group: 4
Levels: all
Min. age: 8
*A mixture of instruction, hacking, stable management and competition for unaccompanied children.*

**Rhiwiau Riding Centre         Centre 368**
Location: Gwynedd
Duration: 7 days, all year
Max. in group: 25
Levels: all

Min. age: 9
*Instructional rides and cross country jumping covered.*

**Rob Hastings Adventure         Centre 370**
Location: North Wales
Duration: 2-7 days, July-August
Levels: all
Min. age: 8

**Rosebrook Equestrian Centre                    Centre 375**
Location: Norfolk
Duration: varies, all year
Levels: all
Min. age: 16
*Instructional holidays to improve skills.*

**Scope Sport Redesdale Riding Centre             Centre 382**
Location: Northumberland
Duration: varies, all year
Levels: all
Min. age: 9
*Tuition in hacking, dressage, jumping and cross-country riding.*

**Skaigh Stables Farm            Centre 400**
Location: Devon
Duration: 2-8 days, April-October
Max. in group: 10
Levels: intermediate/advanced
Min. age: 12
*Riding on Dartmoor.*

**Slate Hall Riding Centre       Centre 407**
Location: Northumberland
Duration: 2 days, all year
Max. in group: 6
Levels: all
Min. age: 10

# Riding & Horsecare

**TM International School of
Horsemanship**     **Centre 440**
Location: Cornwall
Duration: 2+ days, all year
Max. in group: 20
Levels: all
Min. age: 7
*Tuition in riding skills, jumping, horsecare
and stable management. BHS Progressive
Riding Tests also available.*

**Urchinwood Manor Equitation
Centre**     **Centre 462**
Location: Avon
Duration: 7 days, all year
Max. in group: 10
Levels: all
Min. age: no minimum
*Holiday includes hacking, stable management,
dressage, show-jumping and cross-country.*

**Wellington Riding**     **Centre 473**
Location: Hampshire
Duration: 6 days, all year
Max. in group: 8
Levels: all
Min. age: 8

**Wheal Buller Riding School**     **Centre 485**
Location: Cornwall
Duration: 6 days, all year
Max. in group: 24
Levels: all
Min. age: 7

**Yorkshire Riding Centre**     **Centre 515**
Location: Yorkshire
Duration: 6 days, all year
Levels: all
Min. age: 13

**Zara Training Centre**     **Centre 518**
Location: Sussex
Duration: varies, all year
Max. in group: 5
Levels: all
Min. age: 12
*Improvement courses in English and
Western style riding to national show
standard.*

# Trail Riding

**Acorn Activities**     **Centre 3**
Location: Herefordshire/Wales
Duration: 2-5 days, all year
Levels: beginners/intermediate

**Northfield Farm Riding
Centre**     **Centre 322**
Location: Derbyshire
Duration: 2 days, June-September
Max. in group: 12
Levels: intermediate/advanced
Min. age: 14
*Riding through Derbyshire Dales and high
peak trails.*

**Trans-Wales Trails**     **Centre 444**
Location: Powys
Duration: 2-7 days, all year
Levels: intermediate
*Trail riding in the Black Mountains.*

**Trewysgoed Riding Centre**     **Centre 447**
Location: Gwent
Duration: varies, all year
Max. in group: 15
Levels: all
Min. age: 9
*Trail rides and mountain hacks. Career
courses also offered.*

**White Horse Trail Rides**  **Centre 488**
Location: Wiltshire/Berkshire
Duration: 2-7 days, all year
Max. in group: 6
Levels: intermediate/advanced
Min. age: 16
*Long distance trail riding on Spanish horses through unspoilt remote country. Accommodation en-route.*

# Trekking

**Freewheeling Trekking
Expeditions**  **Centre 178**
Location: Sussex
Duration: 1-7 days, April-October
Max. in group: 5
Levels: intermediate
Min. age: 14

**Northumbria Horse Holidays**  **Centre 324**
Location: Northumberland
Duration: 7/14 days, March-November
Max. in group: 50
Levels: all
Min. age: 6
*Trekking across Northumbria. All types of horses from ponies to thoroughbreds for different levels of ability.*

**White Horse Riding Centre**  **Centre 487**
Location: Wiltshire
Duration: 3 days, May-October
Max. in group: 8
Levels: intermediate/advanced
Min. age: 12
*Trekking over the Ridgeway and Lambourne Downs.*

*Acorn Activities*

# Multiactivity and Holidays for Children

Multiactivity holidays are fast becoming a growth industry within the leisure trade, and are essentially geared towards having immense fun while having a go at a wide range of activities in an action-packed weekend, week or even longer. These holidays are an ideal way of beginning a new skill or hobby while improving an existing one. Many of the activities are outdoor pursuits, such as canoeing, waterskiing, windsurfing and sailing but some combine arts and crafts with sports to offer an all round choice. Often they are aimed at complete beginners, assuring participants of expert tuition, a helping hand and lots of encouragement.

With an emphasis on group activities and participation, single people are as welcome as couples or families. Whatever your age and level of ability, holidays can be tailored to suit your individual needs. Most of the following Centres offer on-site accommodation often in spectacular parts of Britain, so whatever your inclination, the following pages will give you ideas for a varied and enjoyable holiday.

On the other hand, the organisations in the 'Holidays for Children' section provide perfect breaks especially designed for those parents who would like to have a holiday 'away from it all', allowing children the chance to get away on their own.

Most of the organisations offer dormitory accommodation providing a suitable environment for children to meet new friends and to develop their independence and self confidence. The daytime activities are usually multiactivities offering a 'taster' session of arts, crafts or sports and often providing the basis for a newly found interest. These holidays do not necessarily have to be confined to the summer months either. Many organisations offer Easter as well as other holiday breaks. The minimum recommended age varies so it is always advisable to ring individual Centres for more information and a brochure.

Safety is of course the top priority for these organisations and as such many belong to the BAHA (British Activity Holidays Association) and have expert tutors and administrators on hand at all times to look after the children, giving parents the ideal opportunity for a relaxing break and peace of mind.

# Multiactivity

**Abernethy Outdoor Centre**    **Centre 1**
Location: Inverness-shire
Duration: 7 days, August
Max. in group: 76
Levels: beginners/intermediate
Min. age: 10

**Acorn Activities**    **Centre 3**
Location: Herefordshire
Duration: 7 days
Max. in group: varies
*Courses designed for families, singles and unaccompanied teenagers, including abseiling, climbing, caving, canoeing, orienteering and cycling.*

**Adventure & Computer Holidays**    **Centre 6**
Location: Cornwall
Duration: 2-7+ days, July-September
Max. in group: 30
Levels: all
Min. age: 5
*Canoeing, surfing, sea fishing and cycling available for families or unaccompanied children.*

**Adventure International**    **Centre 8**
Location: Cornwall
Duration: 6 days, April-October
Max. in group: 360
Levels: all
Min. age: 8

*An action packed activity week designed to develop self awareness through challenging activities in the outdoors.*

**Adventure Sports**    **Centre 10**
Location: Cornwall
Duration: 5 days, April-October
Max. in group: 20
Levels: beginners/all
Min. age: 16
*Watersports, airsports, climbing and abseiling available.*

**Allenheads Lodge Outdoor Centre**    **Centre 15**
Location: Northumberland
Duration: 2/5/7 days, all year
Max. in group: 20
Levels: all
Min. age: 8
*A full range of outdoor activities, from climbing to gorge walking with an emphasis on fun.*

**Ardmore Adventures Ltd**    **Centre 24**
Location: Buckinghamshire
Duration: 5 days-6 weeks, all year
Levels: all
Min. age: 6

---

**Please refer the the Centres Index for details about accommodation**

---

**Bearsports Outdoor Centres**    Centre 38
Location: Northumberland
Duration: varies, all year
Max. in group: 80
Levels: all
Min. age: 9
*Flexible programme to suit requirements and levels of ability.*

**Bowles Outdoor Centre**    Centre 50
Location: Sussex
Duration: 4-7 days, July-August
Max. in group: 48
Levels: beginners
Min. age: 10
*Rockclimbing, canoeing and skiing available.*

**Butterfields**    Centre 71
Location: Clwyd
Duration: 5 days, all year
Max. in group: 12
Levels: beginners/intermediate
Min. age: 5
*Activity courses for young people with or without hearing impairment.*

**Calshot Activities Centre**    Centre 83
Location: Hampshire
Duration: 6 days, July-August
Max. in group: 30
Levels: beginners
Min. age: 10
*Canoeing, sailing, rockclimbing, skiing and orienteering available.*

**Calvert Trust Kielder**    Centre 84
Location: Northumberland
Duration: 7 days, all year
Max. in group: 50
Levels: all
Min. age: 16
*Physical, mental and sensory disabilities catered for. Able bodied family and groups also welcome.*

**Canopy Training**    Centre 87
Location: Yorkshire
Duration: 2 days, March-October
Max. in group: 14
Levels: all
Min. age: 18
*Walking, abseiling, problem solving and orienteering for women of all ages.*

**Chatsworth & Purbeck Activity Centres**    Centre 92
Location: Dorset
Duration: 5 days, all year
Max. in group: 100
Levels: beginners
Min. age: 7
*An introduction to outdoor activities to boost self confidence and generate environmental awareness and appreciation.*

**Compass Christian Centre**    Centre 103
Location: Perthshire
Duration: 2-6 days, April/August-December
Max. in group: 42
Levels: all
Min. age: 8

**Compass Ventures**    Centre 104
Location: Dunbartonshire
Duration: 7 days, April-October
Max. in group: 8
Levels: all
Min. age: Adults
*Course includes walks along the West Highland Way, skippered sailing on Loch Lomond, the ascent of Ben Lomond and Cobblers and mountain biking on forest roads.*

**Country Venture Activities**    Centre 113
Location: Cumbria
Duration: 7+ days, February-December
Max. in group: 40
Levels: all
Min. age: 5

**Craigower Lodge Outdoor
Centre**                    **Centre 116**
Location: Inverness-shire
Duration: 6 days, July-September
Max. in group: 25
Levels: all
Min. age: 8
*Includes an overnight expedition.*

**Cwm Uchaf**              **Centre 118**
Location: Powys
Duration: 3-5+ days, all year
Max. in group: 40
Levels: all
Min. age: 10

**Dartmoor Expedition Centre**  **Centre 123**
Location: Devon
Duration: 2-6 days, March-October
Max. in group: 32
Levels: all
Min. age: 11

**Derbyshire Action Holidays**  **Centre 126**
Location: Derbyshire
Duration: varies, all year
Levels: all
*Many activites to choose from.*

**Devon & Dorset Activities**   **Centre 128**
Location: Devon/Dorset
Duration: 2-7 days, March-October
Max. in group: 350
Levels: all
Min. age: 7
*2-3 activities available each day, including evening activities.*

**Dunolly House Activity
Centre**                    **Centre 139**
Location: Perthshire
Duration: 4-6 days, March-October
Max. in group: 60
Levels: all

Min. age: 8
*Activity courses aimed at young people.*

**East Down Centre**       **Centre 144**
Location: Devon
Duration: 2-6 days, all year
Max. in group: 16
Levels: beginners/intermediate
Min. age: 10
*For family or club groups only. Introduction to canoeing, climbing, caving, riding, sailing, fishing and walking.*

**Eclipse Outdoor Discovery**   **Centre 146**
Location: Cumbria
Duration: 2-5 days, all year
Max. in group: 60
Levels: all
Min. age: 8
*Fell walking, mountain scrambling, caving, climbing, abseiling, canoeing, orienteering and raft building available.*

**Edale YHA Activity Centre**   **Centre 147**
Location: Yorkshire
Duration: 2 day courses all year, 2/4/7 days, July-August
Max. in group: 10
Levels: all
Min. age: 12
*Climbing, caving, abseiling, orienteering, archery and cycling available.*

**Eden Valley Centre**     **Centre 149**
Location: Cumbria
Duration: 1-7 days, all year
Max. in group: 40
Levels: all
Min. age: 8

---

**Please mention this guide when
booking courses**

---

**First Ascent**  **Centre 168**
Location: Derbyshire
Duration: 2-28 days, February-December
Max. in group: 8-12
Levels: all
Min. age: 18
*Introduces people to outdoor activities in a safe and supportive environment. Women's courses also available.*

**Glencoe Outdoor Centre**  **Centre 188**
Location: Argyllshire
Duration: 2/5/7 days, April-October
Max. in group: varies
Levels: beginners/intermediate
Min. age: 10
*A variety of activities including sailing, canoeing, windsurfing, hillwalking, climbing, abseiling and orienteering.*

**High Adventure**  **Centre 208**
Location: Isle of Wight
Duration: 5 days, all year
Max. in group: 25
Levels: all
Min. age: 16

**High Force Training Centre**  **Centre 209**
Location: Co. Durham
Duration: varies, all year
Max. in group: 30
Levels: all
Min. age: 7
*Multiactivity courses arranged to suit the requirements of the clients.*

**High Plains Adventure
Centre**  **Centre 211**
Location: Cumbria
Duration: 1-14 days, all year
Max. in group: 46
Levels: all
Min. age: 8
*Courses in canoeing, climbing, cycling,*

*caving, skiing, orienteering, gorge walking and problem solving.*

**Highlander Mountaineering**  **Centre 217**
Location: Banffshire
Duration: 5 days, June-September
Max. in group: 6
Levels: beginners
Min. age: 14
*A week of various activities including rock climbing, kayaking, mountain biking, abseiling, hillwalking and gorge walking.*

**Iris-Activity Breaks**  **Centre 235**
Location: Middlesex
Duration: varies, all year
Levels: all

**ISCA Childrens Holidays**  **Centre 236**
Location: Devon
Duration: 7 days, August
Levels: all
Min. age: 7

**John Bull School of
Adventure**  **Centre 240**
Location: Yorkshire
Duration: 1-5 days, all year
Max. in group: 20
Levels: all
Min. age: 8
*Day courses and adventure holidays designed to suit all levels of ability.*

**Loch Morar Adventure
Centre**  **Centre 270**
Location: Inverness-shire
Duration: 3+ days, May-September
Max. in group: 10
Levels: all
Min. age: 6
*Tuition in sailing, canoeing, fishing, painting and photography to suit the ability of each individual.*

**Lyncombe Lodge**     Centre 277
Location: Avon
Duration: 2-20 days, all year
Max. in group: 35
Levels: all
Min. age: 5
*Instruction in horse riding, skiing, swimming, caving, archery, pistol shooting, mountain biking and canoeing.*

**Marlborough College Summer School**     Centre 280
Location: Wiltshire
Duration: 5 days, July-August
Max. in group: 14
Levels: all
Min. age: 17
*Courses in art, language, sport and special interests.*

**Mendip Outdoor Pursuits**     Centre 284
Location: Avon
Duration: 7+ days, all year
Max. in group: 100
Levels: all
Min. age: 8
*10-20 courses for individuals each year. Tailor made courses for groups of 4+. Activities include caving, climbing, abseiling, canoeing, orienteering, mountain biking, speedsailing, windsurfing, skiing and riding.*

**Mill on the Brue Activity Centre**     Centre 292
Location: Somerset
Duration: 2-6 days, February-November
Max. in group: 50
Levels: all
Min. age: 8

**Millfield School Village of Education**     Centre 293
Location: Somerset

Duration: 5 days, July-August
Levels: all
Min. age: 5-12
*Many activities. Ring for brochure.*

**Motherby House Activities**     Centre 300
Location: Cumbria
Duration: 6 days, June-September
Max. in group: 12
Levels: beginners
Min. age: 11

**Mountain & Water**     Centre 302
Location: Powys
Duration: 2-7 days, all year
Max. in group: 12
Levels: beginners/intermediate
Min. age: 8
*Taster or tuition sessions in one or more activities with BCU testing in canoeing and kayak courses where required.*

**Mountain Stream Activities**     Centre 305
Location: Devon
Duration: 2 days, varies
Max. in group: 34
Levels: beginners
Min. age: 6
*Canoeing, caving, hillwalking, climbing and abseiling.*

**Mountain Ventures Ltd**     Centre 306
Location: nationwide
Duration: 2/5-7 days, all year
Max. in group: 100+
Levels: all
Min. age: 7

**Please refer to the Centres Index for details about accommodation**

*Millfield School Village of Education*

**North York Moors**
**Adventure Centre**                 **Centre 320**
Location: Yorkshire
Duration: 2-7 days, April-October
Max in group: 24
Levels: all
Min age: 12
*Canoeing, caving, mountain biking, climbing, abseiling, pony trekking and orienteering.*

**Outdoor Adventure**            **Centre 331**
Location: Cornwall
Duration: 1/2/5/6 days, March-November
Max. in group: 25
Levels: all
Min. age: 16

**Plas Menai National Watersports**
**Centre**                             **Centre 351**
Location: Gwynedd
Duration: 5 days, all year

Max. in group: varies
Levels: beginners
Min. age: 8
*Sailing, canoeing, windsurfing and hillwalking.*

**R & L Adventures**             **Centre 362**
Location: Cumbria
Duration: 1+ day
Levels: all
*Courses for individuals or groups to suit requirements.*

**Raasay Outdoor Centre**        **Centre 363**
Location: Isle of Raasay
Duration: 7 days, July-August
Max. in group: 64
Levels: all
Min. age: 9
*Family, group or individual multiactivity holidays including sailing, windsurfing, canoeing, climbing, abseiling, expeditions, fishing, orienteering and archery.*

**Ranch Adventure**            Centre 365
Location: Gwynedd
Duration: 5 days, all year
Max. in group: 90
Levels: beginners
Min. age: 8

**Rob Hastings Adventure**     Centre 370
Location: North Wales
Duration: 2-7 days, July-August
Max. in group: varies
Levels: all
Min. age: 8

**Rock Lea Activity Centre**   Centre 372
Location: Yorkshire
Duration: 2-6 days, all year
Max. in group: varies
Levels: beginners
Min. age: 18
*Climbing, caving, mountain biking, sailing,*
*canoeing, windsurfing, horse riding,*
*orienteering and abseiling.*

**Rua Fiola Island**
**Exploration Centre**         Centre 376
Location: Argyllshire
Duration: 8 days, April-September
Max. in group: 40
Levels: all
Min. age: 9

**Scope Sport - Redesdale**
**Riding Centre**              Centre 382
Location: Northumberland
Duration: 7 days, July-September
Max. in group: 8
Levels: beginners/intermediate
Min. age: 9
*Brief introduction to climbing, abseiling,·*
*canoeing, sailing, orienteering, cycling and*
*navigation.*

**Scottish Centres**           Centre 385
Location: Lanarkshire
Duration: varies, March-October
Max. in group: 10-250
Levels: beginners/intermediate
Min. age: 8
*Outdoor activities for groups of 10 minimum.*

**Scottish Youth Hostels**     Centre 388
Location: Loch Lomond
Duration: 7 days, May-September
Max. in group: Varies
Levels: all
Min. age: 12
*Activities including canoeing, touring,*
*windsurfing, archery and orienteering.*

**Sealyham Activity Centre**   Centre 390
Location: Pembrokeshire
Duration: any, March-November
Max. in group: 100
Levels: all
Min. age: 9
*Canoeing, sailing, rockclimbing and pony*
*trekking.*

**Shaftesbury Homes Venture**
**Centre**                     Centre 393
Location: Kent
Duration: 5 days, all year
Max. in group: 80
Levels: all
Min. age: 6
*Courses including climbing, canoeing,*
*orienteering, dry-slope skiing and horse riding.*

**Shoreline Leisure**          Centre 396
Location: Cornwall
Duration: 7 days, July-August
Max. in group: 30
Levels: beginners
Min. age: 8
*Introduction to kayak, Canadian canoeing,*
*surfing, abseiling, climbing and archery.*

**Skern Lodge**      **Centre 401**
Location: Devon
Duration: 6 days, July-September
Max. in group: 100
Levels: all
Min. age: 9
*A choice of ten activities.*

**SPICE**      **Centre 413**
Location: Essex
Duration: varies, all year
Levels: beginners
Min. age: 18
*Many activites with instruction for beginners.*

**Stubbers Outdoor Centre**      **Centre 420**
Location: Essex
Duration: 2-7 days, all year
Max. in group: 40
Levels: all
Min. age: 11
*Organised adventure activities on lake, climbing wall and other outdoor facilities.*

**Surfrider Activity Holidays**      **Centre 428**
Location: Devon
Duration: 2-7 days, March-October
Max. in group: 30
Levels: all
Min. age: 15
*Surfing, waterskiing, climbing, abseiling, mountain biking, tennis and volleyball.*

**Towers Adventure Centre**      **Centre 442**
Location: Gwynedd
Duration: 2/5 days, April-October
Max. in group: 20
Levels: all
Min. age: 8
*Walking, canoeing, climbing, abseiling and caving.*

**Twr-y-Felin Outdoor Centre**      **Centre 451**
Location: Dyfed
Duration: 2-6 days, all year
Max. in group: 30
Levels: all
Min. age: 8

**Uist Outdoor Centre**      **Centre 454**
Location: Outer Hebrides
Duration: 7 days, all year
Max. in group: 50
Levels: all
Min. age: 8

**White Hall Centre**      **Centre 486**
Location: Derbyshire
Duration: 2-7 days, all year
Levels: all
Min. age:14
*Personal development and outdoor activities.*

**Wyedean Canoe & Adventure Centre**      **Centre 507**
Location: Gloucestershire
Duration: 1-6 days, March-November
Max. in group: 60
Levels: all
Min. age: 8
*Adventurous challenges to promote confidence and self-esteem.*

**Youth Hostels Association**      **Centre 517**
Location: nationwide
Duration: 2-7 days, all year
Levels: all
Min. age: 8
Climbing, abseiling, canoeing, orienteering and archery offered at different locations.

**YMCA National Centre**      **Centre 512**
Location: Cumbria
Duration: 5 days, July-August
Max. in group: varies
Levels: all

# Holidays for Children

**Adventure & Computer Holidays**                    **Centre 6**
Location: Cornwall
Duration: 7 days, July/August
Max. in group: 40
Levels: all
Min. age: 5
*Multiactivity, horse riding and watersports.*

**Ardmore Adventure Ltd**          **Centre 24**
Location: Buckinghamshire
Duration: 5 days-6 weeks, summer and Easter
Max. in group: varies
Levels: all
Min. age: 6
*Activity and English language programmes.*

**Avril Dankworth National Childrens Music Camps**          **Centre 30**
Location: Buckinghamshire
Duration: 7 days, July-August
Max. in group: 64
Levels: all
Min. age: 8
*Brings children with musical ability together for enjoyment.*

**Bearsports Outdoor Centres**          **Centre 38**
Location: Northumberland
Duration: varies, all year
Max. in group: 40
Levels: all
Min. age: 9

**Broadlands Riding Centre**          **Centre 63**
Location: Hampshire
Duration: 5 days, April-August
Max. in group: 7
Levels: all
Min. age: 10
*Instruction in all aspects of riding.*

**Byre Yard**          **Centre 72**
Location: Yorkshire
Duration: 3 days, August
Levels: all
Min. age: 8
*Children's creative holiday and a course on puppet making and performance.*

**Camp Aldenham**          **Centre 85**
Location: Hertfordshire
Duration: 5 days, Easter/Summer
Max. in group: 200
Levels: all
Min. age: 3
*Multiactivity holiday.*

**Eden Valley Woollen Mill**          **Centre 150**
Location: Cumbria
Duration: 2-5 days, half term and school holidays
Max. in group: 10
Levels: all
Min. age: 5
*Spinning, dyeing and weaving holidays.*

**English Country School**    **Centre 155**
Location: Hertfordshire
Duration: 7-28 days, July/August
Max. in group: 20
Levels: all
Min. age: 10
*Activities and English language programmes.*

**Genesis Leisure Ltd**    **Centre 184**
Location: Cambridgeshire
Duration: 5 days, school holidays
Max. in group: 120
Levels: all
Min. age: 4
*Multiactivity holidays.*

**International Warwick School
of Riding**    **Centre 232**
Location: Warwickshire
Duration: 5 days, April-August/October
Max. in group: 35
Levels: all
Min. age: 5
*Riding holidays.*

**ISCA Children's Holidays**    **Centre 236**
Location: Devon
Duration: 7 days, August
Levels: all
Min. age: 7
*Multiactivity, soccer and tennis coaching.*

**Kids Klub Activity Holidays**    **Centre 249**
Location: Suffolk
Duration: varies, all year
Max. in group: 64
Levels: all
Min. age: 7
*Multiactivity and language holidays.*

**Mill Farm Riding Centre**    **Centre 291**
Location: Shropshire
Duration: 5 days, July-August

Max. in group: 20
Levels: all
Min. age: 6
*Riding holiday for unaccompanied children 6-16 years. Instruction, competitions, stable management, gymkhana with evening entertainment.*

**Millfield School Village of
Education**    **Centre 293**
Location: Somerset
Duration: 5 days, July-August
Max. in group: 10
Levels: all
Min. age: 5
*Courses on drama, nature study, TV workshops, tennis, trampolining, cricket, communication and English language. Ring for brochure.*

**Mylor Sailing School**    **Centre 310**
Location: Cornwall
Duration: 1-7 days, April-November
Levels: all
Min. age: 8
*Dinghy sailing to Level 2 Junior.*

**PGL Adventure Holidays**    **Centre 345**
Location: Herefordshire
Duration: 3-7 days, July-August
Max. in group: varies
Levels: all
Min. age: 6
*Various courses on riding, cycling, rural activities, nature watch, sailing, windsurfing and drama.*

**Port Edgar Sailing School**    **Centre 353**
Location: West Lothian
Duration: 5 days, July-August
Max. in group: 6
Levels: beginners
Min. age: 8
*Canoeing courses.*

*Millfield School Village of Education*

**Pound Cottage Riding Centre  Centre 354**
Location: Dorset
Duration: 7 days, all year
Max. in group: 4
Levels: all
Min. age: 8
*A mixture of instruction, hacking, stable management and competition, often using BHS progressive tests.*

**Prime Leisure Activity
Holidays Ltd**  **Centre 358**
Location: Oxon
Duration: 5-6 days, July-August
Max. in group: varies
Levels: all
Min. age: 4
*Choices of many sports, arts and crafts.*

**Severn Valley Sports  Centre 392**
Location: Gloucestershire
Duration: 7 days, Easter/July-August
Max. in group: 65
Levels: all
Min. age: 6
*Choices of riding, languages, drama, sports and games.*

**Stonelands Activity Holidays  Centre 418**
Location: Devon
Duration: 6 days, July-August
Max. in group: 50
Levels: all
Min. age: 7
*Tuition for girls in all aspects of dance and drama.*

**Wasdale Mountain Walking
Holidays**  **Centre 467**
Location: Cumbria
Duration: 7 days, July-August
Max. in group: 4
Levels: all
Min. age: 10
*Guided walks to the tops of Englands highest mountains for ages 10-14.*

**Whizz-Kid Sailing**  **Centre 490**
Location: Cornwall
Duration: 7 days, April-October
Max. in group: 4
Levels: beginners/intermediate
Min. age: 8
*An introduction to boating, whilst living aboard a small yacht. Activities include*

# Special Interest and Study Holidays

If you are still looking for a subject to suit your needs the following pages offer a whole range of special interest and study holidays all over Britain, if you are looking to extend an existing knowledge or to start a subject completely from stratch.

The environment, for instance, is not only something which concerns most people - it is also there to be enjoyed. Whether you want to conserve it or learn more about its diversity, there are courses in the 'Natural History and Gardens' section on almost every aspect, ranging from birdwatching to the study of fungi. Many of these courses are run by the Field Studies Council with Centres located in National Parks and areas of outstanding natural beauty.

The unique diversity of the English garden and its associated arts of flower arranging and floristry provide an enormous variety of holiday courses. These courses incorporate visits to stately homes as well as tips for amateur gardeners on basic botany and soil structure. If however you are looking for a holiday where you will learn about other aspects of our culture try a weekend from the 'Heritage' section studying industrial architecture or Roman hillforts for instance.

For those who enjoy the pleasures of fine cuisine or just a good meal, the 'Food and Drink' section provides courses at all levels of ability, ranging from boiling an egg to making the perfect béarnaise sauce.

Do you already play an instrument or just need an extra push to start? Have you always wanted to dance Latin American style but never dared, or get up on stage and recite a soliloquy, which you perhaps have written yourself on a creative writing weekend? Look no further than the 'Dance, Drama and Music' section for some inspiring ideas.

Whatever your inclination there are courses in the following section catering for almost everyone's interest, however diverse or specific. They are offered by a vast number of organisations, often in quiet residential or outdoor centres which provide a relaxing environment as well as a chance to be inspired by expert tutors.

# Natural History and Gardens

## Birds of Prey Management

**British School of Falconry**     **Centre 60**
Location: Kent
Duration: 5 days, February-November
Max. in group: 8
Levels: all
Min. age:12
*Covers the handling, training and maintaining of birds of prey.*

**Falconry Otter & Wildlife
Sanctuary (The)**     **Centre 161**
Location: Staffordshire
Duration: 2 days, all year
Max. in group: 6
Levels: all
Min. age: 12
*Management and flying of birds of prey,
plus health, environment, equipment,
conservation and legal matters covered.*

**Traditional School of
Falconry**     **Centre 443**
Location: West Midlands
Duration: 5 days, all year
Max. in group: 4
Levels: all
Min. age: 14
*Introduction to the art of falconry, its
history, culture and modern day approach
to hunting and conservation.*

*Falconry Otter & Wildlife Sanctuary*

## Birdwatching

**Acorn Activities**     **Centre 3**
Location: Herefordshire
Duration: 2 days, all year
Levels: all
*Identification of birds in various habitats
according to season, with experienced
ornithologist.*

**Boswednack Manor**     **Centre 48**
Location: Cornwall
Duration: 7 days, September/October
Max. in group: 12
Levels: all
Min. age: 10
*A look at the Autumn migration.*

## Birdwatching continued

**Boultons Country House
Hotel**                          **Centre 49**
Location: Leicestershire
Max. in group: varies
Duration: 2 days, all year
Levels: all
*Guided tours of local nature reserve with
post field discussion and presentations.*

**Countrywide Holidays**        **Centre 114**
Location: nationwide
Duration: 7 days, May-June/September
Levels: all
*Ring for details.*

**Dale Fort Field Centre**      **Centre 121**
Location: Pembrokeshire
Duration: 5-7 days, April-June
Levels: all
Min. age: 16
*Particular emphasis on looking at seabirds
on the Pembrokeshire islands, Milford
Haven Waterway and River Cleddau.*

**Dorset Naturalist (The)**     **Centre 136**
Location: Dorset
Duration: 2 days, October-May
Max. in group: 12
Levels: all
Min. age: 14

**Drapers' Field Centre**       **Centre 137**
Location: Gwynedd
Duration: 3-7 days, March-May
Levels: all
Min. age: 16
*A look at estuary and woodland birdlife, as
well as the mountain birds and birds of prey
on the cliffs of Anglesey.*

**Earnley Concourse**           **Centre 141**
Location: Sussex
Duration: 2-3 days, all year
Max. in group: 15
Levels: all
Min. age: 16

**Flatford Mill Field Centre**  **Centre 169**
Location: Essex/Suffolk
Duration: 3-6 days, March-November
Levels: all
*Several courses during the different seasons
visiting local nature reserves and other
coastal and inland sites around Flatford.
Birdsong courses also offered.*

**Gibraltar Point Field Station  Centre 185**
Location: Lincolnshire
Duration: 2 days, May-November
Max. in group: 28
Levels: beginners/intermediate
Min. age: 18
*A detailed look at birds of the area -
emphasis on wildfowl, waders and Autumn
migrants.*

**Hilton Hotels**               **Centre 220**
Location: nationwide
Duration: 2-3 days, March-December
Max. in group: 35
Levels: all
Min. age: 12
*Weekends led by RSPB experts at peak bird
activity time to improve identification skills.*

**Juniper Hall Field Centre**   **Centre 243**
Location: Surrey
Duration: 3-7 days, May-November
Levels: all
*Heathland and woodland habitats are
explored during the different seasons in
lowland England.*

**Learn at Leisure**     Centre 260
Location: nationwide
Duration: 2-3 days, all year
Max. in group: 15-25
Levels: all
Min. age: 16

**Nettlecombe Court**     Centre 314
Location: Somerset
Duration: 3-7 days, all year
Levels: all
Min. age: 16
*Emphasis on reservoirs, coastal and woodland birds. Evening talks and slide shows.*

**Orielton Field Centre**     Centre 329
Location: Pembrokeshire
Duration: 7 days, May
Levels: all
Min. age: 16
*Birdwatching in the Pembrokeshire National Park including coastal islands.*

**Preston Montford Field Centre**     Centre 357
Location: Shropshire
Duration: 2-4 days, March-September
Levels: all
Min. age: 16
*A variety of courses looking at habitats in Wales and the Borderland to see resident and migratory birds. Also bird ringing courses.*

**Shorelands**     Centre 395
Location: Anglesey
Duration: 6 days, all year
Max. in group: 6
Levels: all
Min. age: 12
*Identification of bird species and other wildlife to understand their part in the ecosystem.*

**Slapton Ley Field Centre**     Centre 406
Location: Devon
Duration: 3 days, April
Levels: all
*Birds of wetland and woodland will be watched at Slapton Ley Nature Reserve and other localities of interest.*

**Snape Maltings**     Centre 411
Location: Suffolk
Duration: 2 days, May-September
Levels: all
*Ring for details.*

**Suffolk College Summer School**     Centre 422
Location: Norfolk/Suffolk
Duration: 5 days, July
Levels: all
Min. age: 16

**Trevone Hotel**     Centre 446
Location: Cornwall
Duration: 8 days, April-May/October
Max. in group: 48
Levels: all
Min. age: 12
*Birdwatching around estuaries, coastal paths and woodlands, and Cornwall's valleys.*

**University of Birmingham**     Centre 455
Location: Shropshire
Duration: 2 days, June
Max. in group: 25
Levels: all
Min. age: 18
*A look at breeding birds in the Long Mynd area.*

---

**Please refer to the Centres Index for details about accommodation**

---

## Birdwatching continued

**Wales Wildlife Holidays**     **Centre 464**
Location: Dyfed
Duration: 7 days, March-November
Max. in group: 6
Levels: all
Min. age: 12
*A study of birdsong, flight, feeding, perching and habitat. Birds of prey especially red kites included.*

**Wild Explorer Holidays**     **Centre 492**
Location: St. Kilda
Duration: 7 days, June
Max. in group: 10
Levels: all
Min. age: 15
*Cruise to St Kilda to see the highest density of seabirds in Europe.*

# Botany

**Dale Fort Field Centre**     **Centre 121**
Location: Pembrokeshire
Duration: 7 days, July
Levels: all
Min. age: 16
*Course to study the flora or both coastal and inland habitats.*

**Drapers' Field Centre**     **Centre 137**
Location: Gwynedd
Duration: 3-5 days, March-August
Levels: all
Min. age: 16
*Courses on mosses and liverworts, grasses, medicinal plants and ferns.*

**Flatford Mill Field Centre**     **Centre 169**
Location: Essex/Suffolk
Duration: 3-7 days, March-November
Levels: all
Min. age: 16
*A variety of courses on grasses, sedges and rushes, fruits of the forest, fungi, lichens, mosses and liverworts.*

**Gibraltar Point Field Station**   **Centre 185**
Location: Lincolnshire
Duration: 2 days, October-November
Max. in group: 28
Levels: beginners
Min. age: 18
*An introduction to fungi.*

**Juniper Hall Field Centre**     **Centre 243**
Location: Surrey
Duration: 3 days, March-October
Levels: all
Min. age: 16
*Courses on lichens, flowering grasses, fungi, mosses and liverworts.*

**Malham Tarn Field Centre**     **Centre 278**
Location: Yorkshire
Duration: 4-7 days, July-August
Levels: all
Min. age: 16
*Courses on grasses, lichens, mosses and liverworts.*

**Nairn Craft Holidays**     **Centre 311**
Location: Inverness-shire
Duration: 5 days, May
Max in group: 10
Levels: all
Min age: 16
*Introduction to bonsai. Demonstration of how to create a bonsai from nursery stock.*

**Nettlecombe Court**     **Centre 314**
Location: Somerset
Duration: 7 days, May-September
Levels: beginners
Min. age: 16
*Courses on mosses and fungi.*

**Orielton Field Centre**      Centre 329
Location: Pembrokeshire
Duration: 7 days, May-June
Levels: all
Min. age: 16
*Courses on coastal plants, lichens, mosses and liverworts, winkles and weeds.*

**Preston Montford
Field Centre**      Centre 357
Location: Shropshire
Duration: 2-7 days, June-October
Levels: all
Min age: 16
*Courses on waterside plants, grasses, mosses and liverworts, ferns, and fungi.*

**Slapton Ley Field Centre**      Centre 406
Location: Devon
Duration: 3 days, February-October
Levels: all
Min. age: 16
*Courses offered on mosses, lichens, fungi.*

# Conservation

**National Trust**      Centre 313
Location: nationwide
Duration: 2/7 days, all year
Max. in group: 12
Levels: all
Min. age: 17
*Outdoor conservation working weeks with the National Trust for enthusiastic and reasonably fit people.*

**Scotsell Ltd**      Centre 384
Location: Royal Deeside
Duration: 7 days, October-November
Max in group: 10
Levels: all
*Conservation work whilst visiting local National Nature Reserves.*

# Environment & Ecology

**Coleg Harlech**      Centre 100
Location: Gwynedd
Duration: 7 days, August
Max. in group: 12
Levels: all
Min. age: 14
*An introduction to the flora and fauna of Snowdonia.*

**Glenmore Lodge - Scottish National
Sports Centre**      Centre 189
Location: Inverness-shire
Duration: 6 days, May-September
Levels: beginners/intermediate
Min. age: 14
*Course deals with environmental issues of the area including endangered habitats, birdlife, erosion etc.*

**Mountain & Water**      Centre 302
Location: Powys
Duration: 2-7 days, April-October
Max. in group: 10
Levels: all
Min. age: 14
*Introduction to the principles of ecology, with advanced study available.*

**University of Birmingham**      Centre 455
Location: Derbyshire
Duration: 2 days, June
Max. in group: 25
Levels: all
Min. age: 18
*A field course to study the geology of the area.*

**Please refer to the Centres Index
for details about accommodation**

# Environment & Language

**English Country School**     **Centre 155**
Location: Hertfordshire
Duration: 7-28 days, July-August
Max. in group: 20
Levels: intermediate/advanced
Min. age: 10
*Environment study combined with English language tuition.*

# Environment & Wildlife

**Adventureline**     **Centre 11**
Location: Cornwall
Duration: 7 days, April-October
Max. in group: 10
Levels: all
Min. age: 8
*A look at Cornwall's unusual geography, geology, flora and fauna.*

**C-n-Do Scotland Ltd**     **Centre 74**
Location: Stirlingshire
Duration: 1-15 days, all year
Max. in group: 13
Levels: all
Min. age: 16
*Informal study of Scottish environment and wildlife within the context of a walking holiday.*

**High Force Training Centre**     **Centre 209**
Location: Co. Durham
Duration: varies, all year
Max. in group: 30
Levels: all
Min. age: 7
*Courses arranged to suit groups.*

**Summer Isles Marine**     **Centre 424**
Location: Ross-shire
Duration: 5 days, April-September
Max. in group: 6

Levels: all
Min. age: 5
*Study in the Ben Mhor estate and surrounding area.*

**Summer University**     **Centre 425**
Location: nationwide
Duration: 5 mornings, July-August
Max. in group: 12
Levels: all
Min. age: 18

# Floristry

**Valley School of Floristry**     **Centre 463**
Location: Shropshire
Duration: 4 days, except August
Max. in group: 6
Levels: beginners/intermediate
Min. age: 16
*Tuition in practical floristry, for bridal arrangements, funeral tributes etc.*

**Wansfell College**     **Centre 466**
Location: Essex
Duration: 2 days, July
Levels: all
Min. age: 18

# Gardening

**Juniper Hall Field Centre**     **Centre 243**
Location: Surrey
Duration: 3 days, April
Levels: all
Min. age: 16
*A course on biology for amateur gardeners who would like to know more about basic botany, zoology and soils structure.*

# Gardens

**Acorn Activities**     **Centre 3**
Location: Herefordshire

Duration: 4 days, all year
Levels: all
Visits to outstanding houses and gardens in the area.

**Action Extras**      **Centre 4**
Location: nationwide
Duration: 2 days, varies
Max. in group: 30
Levels: all
Min. age: 18
*Garden visits.*

**Carberry Tower**      **Centre 88**
Location: Midlothian
Duration: 3 days, May
Levels: all
Min. age: 21
*A holiday course at a stately home. Ring for details.*

**David Taylor's Interest Holidays**      **Centre 124**
Location: Midlands/Cotswolds
Duration: 2-7 days, April-September
Max. in group: 8
Levels: all
Min. age: 6
*Tours of gardens and national plant collections. Films and discussions included.*

**Headland Hotel**      **Centre 204**
Location: Cornwall
Duration: varies, April-May
Levels: all
Min. age: 7
*Opportunity to view some of Cornwalls's finest gardens, including some not normally open to the public.*

**HF Holidays Ltd**      **Centre 207**
Location: nationwide
Duration: 7 days, May-September
Max. in group: 30

Levels: all
*Guided tours of stately homes and gardens throughout Britain.*

**Hilton Hotels**      **Centre 220**
Location: nationwide
Duration: 2 days, May-September
Max. in group: 50
Levels: all
Min. age: 14
*Experts lead classes in horticulture with visits to public and private gardens.*

**How Hill Trust**      **Centre 222**
Location: Norfolk
Duration: 3 days, June
Min. age: 11
*Visits to Norfolk gardens. Resident gardener will be on hand to advise on cultivation and identification.*

**J.A.R. Services**      **Centre 238**
Location: Lincolnshire
Duration: 2-10 days, March-October
Max. in group: 45
Levels: all
Min. age: 15
*Visiting public and private gardens often in the company of well-known and professional hosts and guest speakers.*

**Learn at Leisure**      **Centre 260**
Location: nationwide
Duration: 3 days, June-September
Levels: all
*Various courses. Ring for details.*

**Maryland Residential College**      **Centre 281**
Location: Bedfordshire
Duration: 4 days, various months
Min. age: 18
*Ring for details.*

## Gardens continued

**Nettlecombe Court**          Centre 314
Location: Somerset
Duration: 7 days, August
Levels: all
Min age: 16
*A look at how Gertrude Jekyll, Vita Sackville West and Margery Fish have influenced gardens, with visits to various local gardens.*

**Northumbria Experience (The)**          Centre 323
Location: nationwide
Duration: 7 days, September
Max. in group: 50
Levels: all
Min. age: 16
*Exploration of country house estates and botanical gardens.*

**St. Michaels of Falmouth**          Centre 415
Location: Cornwall
Duration: 2-7 days, March-October
Levels: all
Min. age: 18
*Various options visiting national gardens with demonstrations and advice from resident gardeners.*

**Trevone Hotel**          Centre 446
Location: Cornwall
Duration: 7 days, May
Max. in group: 50
Levels: all
Min. age: 12
*Visits to the gardens and historic houses of Cornwall.*

# Gardens & Flowers

**Millfield School Village of Education**          Centre 293
Location: Somerset
Duration: 5 days, July-August
Max. in group: 10
Levels: all
Min. age: 13
*Dried flower workshop, 'The English Garden', and flower arranging courses offered.*

**Suffolk College Summer School**          Centre 422
Location: Suffolk
Duration: varies
Levels: all
*Courses in garden design, 'An English Tapestry of Gardens', and garden and patio brickcraft offered.*

# Geology

**Chichester Interest Holidays**          Centre 93
Location: Cornwall
Duration: 7 days, March-June/September-October
Max. in group: 7
Levels: all
Min. age: 18
*Collecting and identification of a wide variety of Cornish minerals. Excellent library on site.*

**Higham Hall Residential Study Centre**          Centre 214
Location: Cumbria
Duration: 2 days, June
Levels: all
*Geology of the Northern Lakes.*

**Juniper Hall Field Centre**        Centre 243
Location: Surrey
Duration: 2 days, February
Levels: beginners
Min. age: 16
*Course centred around the North Downs.*

**Mountain & Water**        Centre 302
Location: Powys
Duration: 2-7 days, all year
Max. in group: 10
Levels: all
Min. age: 14
*Introduction to the principles of geology, or more advanced study available.*

**Preston Montford
Field Centre**        Centre 357
Location: Shropshire
Duration: 7 days, July
Levels: all
Min. age: 16
*Emphasis on rocks, minerals and fossils.*

# Hedgelaying & Dry Stone Walling

**Flatford Mill Field Centre**        Centre 169
Location: Essex/Suffolk
Duration: 3 days, October-November
Max. in group: 8
Levels: beginners
Min. age: 16
*An introduction to the basic skills of laying hedges in the traditional way.*

**Ynys Hywel Countryside
Centre**        Centre 513
Location: Gwent
Duration: 2 days, November
Max. in group: 34
Levels: all
Min. age: 18

# Landscapes

**Juniper Hall Field Centre**        Centre 243
Location: Surrey
Duration: 3-7 days, July-October
Levels: all
*Natural history and geological study of the Surrey Downs and heathlands.*

**Preston Montford
Field Centre**        Centre 357
Location: Shropshire
Duration: 2-7 days, June-September
Levels: all
Min. age: 16
*A variety of courses on different aspects of the surrounding area.*

# Managing Nature Reserves

**Gibraltar Point Field Station**   Centre 185
Location: Lincolnshire
Duration: 2 days, August
Max. in group: 28
Min. age: 18
*A look at the conservation benefits of managing reserves.*

# Natural History

**Boswednack Manor**        Centre 48
Location: Cornwall
Duration: 7 days, May/July
Max. in group: 12
Levels: all
Min. age: 10
*Courses in Spring and Summer to look at habitat of West Penwith.*

**British Universities Accommodation
Consortium**        Centre 61
Location: various universities in Britain
Duration: varies, June-September
*Ring for programme.*

## Natural History continued

**Chichester Interest Holidays    Centre 93**
Location: Cornwall
Duration: 7 days, April-May/September
Max. in group: 7
Levels: all
Min. age: 18
*Introduction to different habitat, pond dipping, sea shores, moors, woodland and nature reserves. Some bird watching.*

**Cornwall Creative Activity Network (CCAN)                    Centre 111**
Location: Cornwall
Duration: varies, all year
Levels: all
*Various courses. Ring for details.*

**Countrywide Holidays    Centre 114**
Location: nationwide
Duration: 5-7 days, April-October
Levels: all
*Variety of flora and fauna in different habitats including Exmoor, Bodmin Moor, Peak District, Lake District and Norfolk.*

**Dale Fort Field Centre    Centre 121**
Location: Pembrokeshire
Duration: 4-7 days, April-August
Levels: all
Min. age: 16
*Botanical, geological and natural history exploration of the Pembrokeshire Coast National Park and Bristol Channel.*

**Dillington House    Centre 131**
Location: Somerset
Duration: 1-7 days, all year
Max. in group: 70
Levels: all
Min. age: 18
*Ring for details.*

**Dorset Naturalist (The)    Centre 136**
Location: Dorset
Duration: 3 days, May-August
Max. in group: 12
Levels: all
Min. age: 14
*Heathland, downland cliffs and marshes are visited to view wildlife.*

**Drapers' Field Centre    Centre 137**
Location: Gwynedd
Duration: 3-4 days, March-September
Levels: all
Min. age: 16
*A variety of courses to look at the geology and ecology of the Snowdonia National Park.*

**Fellowship Afloat Charitable Trust    Centre 164**
Location: Essex
Duration: 2 days, January-March/November-Devember
Max. in group: 36
Levels: all
Min. age: 11
*Study of estuary and saltmarsh environment combined with community living onboard light-vessel.*

**HF Holidays Ltd    Centre 207**
Location: nationwide
Duration: 7 days, May-October
Max. in group: 20
Levels: all
*Subjects of study include birdwatching, fossils, and wildflowers at a variety of locations.*

**Kindrogan Field Centre    Centre 250**
Location: Perthshire
Duration: 7 days, May-September
Levels: all
*Exploration and field trips to Highland forests, moors, lochs and mountains.*

**Learn at Leisure**  **Centre 260**
Location: nationwide
Duration: 3 days, May-October
Levels: all
*A variety of courses in different locations.*
*Ring for details.*

**Millfield School Village of**
**Education**  **Centre 293**
Location: Somerset
Duration: 5 days, July-August
Max. in group: 10
Levels: all
Min. age: 9

**Nettlecombe Court**  **Centre 314**
Location: Somerset
Duration: 3-7 days, February-October
Levels: all
*Exploration of the Bristol Channel, coastal*
*footpath and Exmoor National Park.*

**North-West Frontiers**  **Centre 318**
Location: Ross-shire
Duration: 7 days, May-October
Max. in group: 8
Levels: intermediate/advanced
Min. age: 15
*Walking up to 12 miles daily in wild country*
*to look at birds and plants.*

**Orielton Field Centre**  **Centre 329**
Location: Pembrokeshire
Duration: 7 days, May-September
Levels: all
Min age: 16
*A variety of courses centred around the cliffs*
*and beaches of Pembrokeshire, plus courses*
*on spiders, mammals and other vertebrates,*
*and bats.*

*Field Studies Council*

**Peak National Park**
**Study Centre**  **Centre 340**
Location: Derbyshire
Duration: 2-7 days, all year
Max. in group: 25
Levels: all
Min. age: 16

**Preston Montford Field Centre  Centre 357**
Location: Shropshire
Duration: 2-7 days, May-August
Levels: all
Min. age: 16
*Courses on badgers, otters, bats, butterflies*
*and moths. Also courses on wildlife sound*
*recording.*

**Scotsell Ltd**  **Centre 384**
Location: Isle of Bute/Skye/Shetland
Duration: 2-6 days, May-June
Max. in group: 8-18
Levels: all

## Natural History continued

**Slapton Ley Field Centre**     **Centre 406**
Location: Devon
Duration: 3 days, May-August
Levels: all
Min. age: 16
*Courses on wild mammals, bats, dragons and hoppers, butterflies and moths.*

**University of Birmingham**     **Centre 455**
Location: Perthshire
Duration: 5 days, July
Max. in group: 24
Levels: all
Min. age: 18
*Exploration of the semi-wilderness refuges for rare plants and animals.*

**University of Oxford
Summer School**     **Centre 458**
Location: Oxon
Duration: 7 days, July-August
Max. in group: 12
Levels: all
Min. age: 18
*Ring for details of topics covered.*

**Wales Wildlife Holidays**     **Centre 464**
Location: Dyfed
Duration: 7 days, March-November
Max. in group: 6
Levels: all
Min. age: 12
*A study of the natural history of different habitats.*

# Orchards

**Slapton Ley Field Centre**     **Centre 406**
Location: Devon
Duration: 3 days, February
Levels: all

Min. age: 16
*Orchard management is covered including planting, pruning and general care.*

# Organic Farming

**WWOOF**     **Centre 504**
Location: Sussex
Duration: 2+ days, all year
Max. in group: 6
Levels: all
Min. age: 16
*First hand experience of organic farming.*

**Ynys Hywell Countryside
Centre**     **Centre 513**
Location: Gwent
Duration: 2 days, November
Max. in group: 34
Levels: beginners/all
Min. age: 18

# People & Plants

**Gibraltar Point Field Station   Centre 185**
Location: Lincolnshire
Duration: 2 days, July
Max. in group: 28
Levels: all
Min. age: 18
*A study of the association between edible and medicinal plants and people.*

# Trees & Woodlands

**Flatford Mill Field Centre**     **Centre 169**
Location: Essex/Suffolk
Duration: 3-7 days, May-November
Levels: all
Min. age: 16
*A study of local woodlands, their management, woodland products, buildings, and wildlife. Tree planting also covered.*

**Juniper Hall Field Centre**    **Centre 243**
Location: Surrey
Duration: 7 days, August
Levels: all
Min. age: 16
*Identification and appreciation of the history of trees.*

**Orielton Field Centre**    **Centre 329**
Location: Pembrokeshire
Duration: 7 days, August
Levels: all
Min. age: 16
*Course proceeds from naturalised and introduced varieties to some of the more exotic.*

**Preston Montford
Field Centre**    **Centre 357**
Location: Shropshire
Duration: 2 days, September
Levels: all
Min. age: 16
*Tree identification in the Borderlands.*

## Weather Study

**Juniper Hall Field Centre**    **Centre 243**
Location: Surrey
Duration: 2 days, April
Levels: all
Min. age: 16
*An introduction through theory and practical field work.*

**Malham Tarn Field Centre**    **Centre 278**
Location: Yorkshire
Duration: 7 days, July
Levels: all
Min. age: 16
*Practical field work combined with discussion of modern meteorological techniques.*

**Nettlecombe Court**    **Centre 314**
Location: Somerset
Duration: 7 days, August
Levels: all
Min. age: 16
*Weather science and forecasting.*

## Wildflowers

**Earnley Concourse**    **Centre 141**
Location: Sussex
Duration: 3 days, June
Levels: all
Min. age: 16

**Flatford Mill Field Centre**    **Centre 169**
Location: Essex/Suffolk
Duration: 3-4 days, April/May
Levels: beginners/intermediate
*Courses in flower identification whilst visiting a variety of habitats.*

*National Trust*

## Wildflowers continued

**Juniper Hall Field Centre**     Centre 243
Location: Surrey
Duration: 3-7 days, June-September
Levels: all
Min. age: 16
*Courses on identification of wild flowers
and orchid flora around the Centre.*

**Nettlecombe Court**     Centre 314
Location: Somerset
Duration: 7 days, July
Levels: intermediate/advanced
Min. age: 16
*A chance to extend existing knowledge with
site visits.*

**Orielton Field Centre**     Centre 329
Location: Dyfed
Duration: 7 days, May
Levels: all
Min. age: 16
*Sea cliffs, sand dunes, woodland and
acquatic habitats are explored.*

**Preston Montford
Field Centre**     Centre 357
Location: Shropshire
Duration: 5 days, August
Levels: all
Min. age: 16
*Wildflower identification and trips to
interesting habitats.*

**Slapton Ley Field Centre**     Centre 406
Location: Devon
Duration: 3-7 days, May-July
Levels: all
Min. age: 16
*Dartmoor to the sea provides, the area of
study and identification.*

**Trevone Hotel**     Centre 446
Location: Cornwall
Duration: 7 days, May
Max. in group: 50
Levels: all
Min. age: 12
*An exploration of the gardens and
wildflowers of Cornwall.*

# Wildlife

**Acorn Activities**     Centre 3
Location: Herefordshire/Pembrokeshire
Duration: 2 days, all year
Levels: all
*A study of woodland, coastal and rural
habitats.*

**Bearsports Outdoor Centres**     Centre 38
Location: Northumberland
Duration: 2/5 days, all year
Max. in group: 40
Levels: all
Min. age: 12
*A look at renowned sites for birdlife, seals,
otters etc.*

**Falconry Otter and Wildlife
Sanctuary (The)**     Centre 161
Location: Staffordshire
Duration: 1 day, all year
Max. in group: 6
Min. age: 12
*Opportunity to see a Wildlife Rescue, and
involvement in the rehabilitation of wild
animals and birds brought into the sanctuary.*

**Flatford Mill Field Centre**     Centre 169
Location: Essex/Suffolk
Duration: 3 days, March-November
Levels: all
*Courses offered on flies, small mammals,
slugs and snails, bats, spiders, woodland and
hedgerow wildlife, butterflies and moths.*

**Focus Holidays**     Centre 171
Location: Gwynedd
Duration: 1-6 days, all year exc. February &
November
Max. in group: 10
Levels: all
Min. age: 12
*Walking and looking at a variety of
ecological habitats including birdlife.*

**How Hill Trust**     Centre 222
Location: Norfolk
Duration: varies, all year
Levels: all
Min. age: 11
*Various courses about nature in Broadland.*

**Juniper Hall Field Centre**     Centre 243
Location: Surrey
Duration: 3 days, April-October
Levels: all
Min. age: 16
*Courses covering pond and stream life,
insects and invertebrates, dragonflies,
spiders, badgers and small mammals, bats,
and mollusc.*

**Malham Tarn Field Centre**     Centre 278
Location: Yorkshire
Duration: 7 days, July-August
Levels: all
Min. age: 16
*Courses on fly-fishing and fly-tying,
butterflies and moths.*

**Nettlecombe Court**     Centre 314
Location: Somerset
Duration: 7 days, August
Levels: all
*A family course on wildlife watching.*

**Scottish Youth Hostels**     Centre 388
Location: Isle of Skye/Raasay
Duration: 7 days, May-June/September

Max. in group: 15
Levels: all
Min. age: 12
*Exploration of the flora and fauna of the
islands, golden eagles, otters, seals and
visits to classic geological and archaeological sites.*

**Uist Outdoor Centre**     Centre 454
Location: Isle of North Uist
Duration: 7 days, all year
Max. in group: 50
Levels: all

**West Cornwall Learning
Holidays**     Centre 479
Location: Cornwall
Duration: 2 days, July-August
Max. in group: 10
Levels: all
Min. age: 16
*Badger watching. Field visits and evening
films.*

**West Country Wildlife**     Centre 480
Location: Devon
Duration: 7 days, April-July
Max. in group: 4
Levels: all
Min. age: 13
*A general study tour of Dartmoor, Exmoor,
River Exe and its estuary, plus badger
watching.*

**Wild Explorer Holidays**     Centre 492
Location: Isle of Skye/Raasay
Duration: 5-7 days, June/September
Max. in group: 11
Levels: all
Min. age: 10
*Introduction to the wildlife of these islands
with emphasis on Eurasian otters, eagles,
seals, dolphins, whales and red deer.*

# Heritage

## Archaeology & Industrial Archaeology

**Acorn Activities**                    **Centre 3**
Location: South Wales
Duration: 3 days, June/August/October
Levels: all
*Course looks at the workplace of mines, ironworks and mills alongside canals and railways.*

**Bearsports Outdoor Centres**    **Centre 38**
Location: Northumberland
Duration: 2-5 days, all year
Max. in group: 40
Levels: all
Min. age: 18
*Archaeological and architectural scenery of Northumberland.*

**Boswednack Manor**              **Centre 48**
Location: Cornwall
Duration: 7 days, August/September
Max. in group: 12
Levels: all
Min. age: 10
*Course visits archaeological sites in Cornwall with illustrated talks on specific subjects.*

**Chichester Interest Holidays**    **Centre 93**
Location: Cornwall
Duration: 7 days, May/October
Max. in group: 10
Levels: all
Min. age: 18
*Introduction to the archaeology of Cornwall. Flint collecting included.*

**Headland Hotel**                **Centre 204**
Location: Cornwall
Duration: 2 days, Spring/Autumn
Max. in group: 25
Levels: all
Min. age: 10
*A guided tour of Cornwall's mining industry*

**Cornwall of Mine Ltd**          **Centre 112**
Location: Cornwall
Duration: 3 days, all year
Levels: all
Min. age: 8
*Course provides an insight through field trips into the Cornish tin, copper and china clay mining industries.*

**Talland Bay Hotel**             **Centre 433**
Location: Cornwall
Duration: 6 days, April/October
Max. in group: 12
Levels: all
Min. age: 16
*A study of Cornish archaeological sites.*

# Architecture

**Dillington House**    **Centre 131**
Location: Somerset
Duration: 2 days, February
Levels: all
*A study of 17th and 20th century British architects.*

**Flatford Mill Field Centre**    **Centre 169**
Location: Essex/Suffolk
Duration: 2-5 days, February-November
Levels: all
Min age: 16
*Various courses exploring Suffolk villages, churches, and medieval buildings.*

**Gateway Education & Arts
Centre**    **Centre 183**
Location: Shropshire
Duration: 2 days, March
Levels: all
*A study of the architecture and history of London.*

**Grantley Hall**    **Centre 194**
Location: Yorkshire
Duration: 3 days, March
Levels: all
*An exploration of the architecture, technology and art of medieval ecclesiastical buildings.*

# Cathedral Restoration

**Cathedral Camps**    **Centre 90**
Location: nationwide
Duration: 8 days, July-September
Levels: all
Min. age: 16
*Preservation of cathedrals. Volunteers given the opportunity to undertake the conservation and restoration of cathedrals and their environments.*

# Genealogy

**Institute of Heraldic &
Genealogical Studies**    **Centre 229**
Location: Kent
Duration: 1-5 days, January-October
Max. in group: 25
Levels: beginners/advanced
Min. age: 18
*Various courses including tracing family history, art and language of heraldry, use of legal records and genealogy for librarians.*

**University of Stirling**    **Centre 459**
Location: Stirlingshire
Duration: 5 days, August
Max. in group: 15
Levels: all
Min. age: 16
*Practical assistance given to trace family history. Visits to archives included.*

# Heraldry

**Dale Fort Field Centre**    **Centre 121**
Location: Dyfed
Duration: 3 days, March
Levels: all
Min age: 16
*An introduction to heraldry with trips to local cathedrals.*

# Historic Buildings & Sites

**Acorn Activities**    **Centre 3**
Location: Pembrokeshire
Duration: 3 days
Max. in group: varies
Levels: all
*A study of Pembrokeshire's early history, Celtic Christianity, and 11th and 12th century castles.*

# Special Interest and Study Holidays

## Heritage continued

**Ammerdown Study Centre**　　　Centre 17
Location: Avon
Duration: 4 days, April
Max. in group: 40
Levels: all
*Study course on monasteries, churches and cathedrals in the West Country.*

**Britannia Study Tours**　　　Centre 58
Location: various
Duration: 3 days, April-September
Max. in group: 50
Levels: all
Min. age: 7
*Various courses covering the archaeology of East Anglia, castles of Yorkshire, North Wales and Northumberland, prehistoric Wiltshire, Hadrian's Wall, and ancient monuments in Wessex.*

**British Universities Accommodation Consortium**　　　Centre 61
Location: various universities in Britain
Duration: varies, June-September
*Ring for details.*

**Chichester Interest Holidays**　　　Centre 93
Location: Cornwall
Duration: 7 days, April-October
Max. in group: 10
Levels: all
Min. age: 18
*A study of the archaeology, natural history, geology and history of Cornwall, with some walking.*

**Countrywide Holidays**　　　Centre 114
Location: nationwide
Duration: 4-7 days, all year
Levels: all
*Visits to National Trust Properties,*

*treasures of Northumbria, castles of North Wales, maritime heritage, castles and stately homes of the Isle of Wight and Cornwall, canal heritage, railways and bridges.*

**Countrywide Holidays**　　　Centre 114
Location: nationwide
Duration: 7 days, all year
Levels: all
*Holidays include 'Scottish Heritage', '4 Scottish cities', 'Scottish Safari', visits to a variety of castles, stately homes and gardens, and an introduction to canals in Scotland.*

**Dale Fort Field Centre**　　　Centre 121
Location: Dyfed
Duration: 8 days, June
Levels: all
Min. age: 16
*An exploration of Pembrokeshire castles and ancient monuments.*

**David Taylor's Interest Holidays**　　　Centre 124
Location: Worcestershire
Duration: 2-7 days, Easter-end September
Max. in group: 8
Levels: all
Min. age: 8
*Interest holidays arranged on a variety of themes: castles, cathedrals, churches, the Romans, and factory tours to various industries.*

**Drapers' Field Centre**　　　Centre 137
Location: Gwynedd
Duration: 3-7 days, May/September
Levels: all
Min. age: 16
*Historic houses and gardens, Welsh farmhouses and Edwardian castles covered.*

**Focus Holidays**                     **Centre 171**
Location: Gwynedd
Duration: 1-6 days, January/March-October/
December
Max. in group: 10
Levels: beginners/intermediate
Min. age: 12
*Exploration of areas of historical interest in
or near Snowdonia National Park.*

**Higham Hall Residential
Study Centre**                        **Centre 214**
Location: Cumbria
Duration: 3-4 days, April-June
Levels: all
Min. age: mostly 16
*Courses on British castles and Romans in
the North.*

**Instep Linear Walking
Holidays**                            **Centre 228**
Location: Henney/Avon
Duration: 5 days, September
Max. in group: 16
Min. age: 16
*A study of the Henney to Avon and Brecon
to Abergavenny canal.*

**Juniper Hall Field Centre**         **Centre 243**
Location: Surrey
Duration: 2 days, April/September
Levels: all
Min. age: 16
*Surrey churches.*

**Learn at Leisure**                  **Centre 260**
Location: nationwide
Duration: 2 days, February-November
Levels: all
*Many courses on industrial landscapes,
religious buildings, historic houses and
gardens, castles and medieval towns. Ring
for programme.*

**Malham Tarn Field Centre**          **Centre 278**
Location: Yorkshire
Duration: 7 days, July
Levels: all
Min. age: 16
*Courses on the 'Settle to Carlisle Railway'
and 'Old Roads of the Yorkshire Dales'.*

**Millfield School Village
of Education**                        **Centre 293**
Location: Somerset
Duration: 5 days, July-August
Max in group: 10
Levels: all
Min age: 13
*Courses include 'Cathedrals of England',
'Church & Chapel', 'Exploring Local
History', 'Farm & Cottage', 'Somerset
Churches', 'Stately Houses in Somerset',
and 'Arthur & Avalon'.*

**Northumbria Experience (The) Centre 323**
Location: Northumberland
Duration: 6-7 days, July-September
Max. in group: 50
Levels: all
Min. age: 16
*Various courses on Northumbria heritage
from the Romans to the Edwardians,
Christian and maritime heritage.*

**Preston Montford Field
Centre**                              **Centre 357**
Location: Shropshire
Duration: 2-7 days, February-October
Levels: all
Min. age: 16
*Various courses on industrial buildings,
medieval buildings, heraldry, local battle-
fields and historical landscapes.*

## Heritage continued

**Slapton Ley Field Centre          Centre 406**
Location: Devon
Duration: 2-7 days, May-July
Levels: all
Min. age: 16
*Courses on evolving landscapes, smuggling, and industrial archaeology.*

**Suffolk College Summer School          Centre 422**
Location: Suffolk
Duration: varies
*Various courses on antique English furniture, the history of Ipswich, castles of Norfolk, maritime Suffolk, Suffolk's churches and architecture and women in late Stuart and Georgian England.*

**Summer Academy          Centre 423**
Location: Kent
Duration: 7 days, June-September
Max. in group: 40
Levels: all
Min. age: 16
*Many courses offered on castles, medieval towns, Hadrian's Wall and the Roman army, British history, historic houses and gardens, European history and religious buildings. Ring for programme.*

**Summer University          Centre 425**
Location: Leicestershire/nationwide
Duration: 5 days, July-August
Max. in group: 24
Levels: all
Min. age: 18
*Study of the historic buildings from various centuries, with lectures and off-campus visits.*

*Summer Academy*

**University of Birmingham**  **Centre 455**
Location: nationwide
Duration: 2-7 days, March-October
Max. in group: 25
Levels: all
Min. age: 18
*Various courses on English country houses, hillforts of Dorset, stone circles of Wessex, archaeology of Yorkshire, historic towns of the Welsh borders and Victorian Liverpool.*

**University of Cambridge**  **Centre 456**
Location: Cambridgeshire
Duration: 2 days, all year
Levels: all
Min. age: 18
*Many courses offered on British and world history, local history, architecture and archaeology. Ring for programme.*

# Historic Houses & Gardens

**Acorn Activities**  **Centre 3**
Location: Herefordshire
Duration: 4 days, June-July/September
Levels: all
*Course on antiques, churches and historic houses and gardens.*

**Alston Hall Residential College**  **Centre 16**
Location: Lancashire
Duration: 2 days, July
Levels: all
Min. age: 16
*Courses on historic houses.*

**Boultons Country House Hotel**  **Centre 49**
Location: Leicestershire
Duration: 4-7 days, April-September
Max. in group: varies
Levels: all

*Tours of castles, museums, and historic houses in the area.*

**Burton Manor College**  **Centre 70**
Location: Cheshire
Duration: 2 days, May
Max. in group: 16
Levels: all
Min. age: 14
*Historic houses and medieval towns.*

**Chichester Interest Holidays**  **Centre 93**
Location: Cornwall
Duration: 7 days, June
Max. in group: 7
Levels: all
Min. age: 50
*Cornwall historic houses and gardens, with boat trips to Tresco on the Scillies.*

**Dillington House**  **Centre 131**
Location: Somerset
Duration: 2 days, March/April
Levels: all
*Somerset gentry estates, houses and gardens.*

**Earnley Concourse**  **Centre 141**
Location: Sussex
Duration: 2/7 days, all year
Max. in group: 25-30
Levels: all
Min. age: 16
*A variety of courses on historic houses and gardens. Ring for details.*

**Hawkwood College**  **Centre 200**
Location: Gloucestershire
Duration: 6 days, June
Max. in group: 40
*Guided visits to country houses and gardens in the Cotswolds.*

## Historic Houses & Gardens continued

**HF Holidays Ltd**                      **Centre 207**
Location: nationwide
Duration: 7 days, April-September
Max. in group: 30
Levels: all
*Visits to stately homes and gardens with an expert leader. Holidays at a variety of locations in Britain.*

**Hilton Hotels**                        **Centre 220**
Location: nationwide
Duration: 2 days, April-November
Max. in group: 50
Levels: all
Min. age: 16
*Participants learn about history, heritage and antiques through talks and visits to houses, museums and galleries.*

**Peak National Park Study Centre**                      **Centre 340**
Location: Derbyshire
Duration: 7 days, July-August
Max. in group: 25
Levels: all
Min. age: 50
*Coach based guided tour of the villages and communities of Derbyshire villages.*

**Trevone Hotel**                        **Centre 446**
Location: Cornwall
Duration: 8 days, May
Max. in group: 48
Levels: all
Min. age: 12
*Cornish heritage.*

# Dance, Drama and Music

## Dance

**Acorn Activities**                     **Centre 3**
Location: Herefordshire
Duration: 2 days, varies
Levels: all
*Modern sequence and ballroom dancing.*

**Alston Hall Residential College**                          **Centre 16**
Location: Lancashire
Duration: 2 days, May
Levels: all
*Folk dancing.*

**Brighton Natural Health Centre**                         **Centre 56**
Location: Sussex
Duration: 2-5 days, Easter and summer
Max. in group: varies
Levels: all
*Contemporary, Afro-Caribbean, African, and circle dancing.*

**Burton Manor College**                 **Centre 70**
Location: Cheshire
Duration: 1-5 days, all year
Max. in group: 16
Levels: all
Min. age: 14
*Folk, circle, and ballroom dancing.*

**Carberry Tower**          Centre 88
Location: Midlothian
Duration: 2 days, March
Max. in group: 90
Levels: all
Min. age: 18
*Dance in worship.*

**Countrywide Holidays**     Centre 114
Location: nationwide
Duration: 7 days, May-September
Levels: all
*Scottish, country, old time and modern
sequence and international folk dancing.*

**Dolmetsch Historical Dance
Society**                   Centre 135
Location: Hertfordshire
Duration: 7 days, July
Max. in group: 48
Levels: all
Min. age: 16
*A practical study of theatre, court and
country dances of the 18th century.*

> **Please refer to the Centres Index
> for details about accommodation**

**HF Holidays Ltd**          Centre 207
Location: nationwide
Duration: 4-7 days, all year
Levels: all
*Scottish country, folk, English country,
ballroom, Latin American, sequence,
International folk dancing.*

**Millfield School Village of
Education**                 Centre 293
Location: Somerset
Duration: 5 days, July-August
Max. in group: 10
Levels: all
Min. age: 9
*Tap, English country, Latin American, and
ballroom dancing.*

*Dolmetsch Historical Dance Society*

# Drama

**East 15 Acting School**          **Centre 142**
Location: Yorkshire
Duration: 7 days, July-August
Levels: all
Min. age: 15

**Harrogate Theatre Courses**    **Centre 199**
Location: Yorkshire
Duration: 2-7 days, August
Max. in group: 40
Levels: all
Min. age: 12-18
*Design, playwriting, acting and general theatre skills covered.*

**National Operatic & Dramatic Association**          **Centre 312**
Location: Avon
Duration: 8 days, July
Max. in group: 60
Levels: all
Min. age: 18
*Basic techniques, stagecraft, voice production, movement and directing.*

**National Operatic & Dramatic Association**          **Centre 312**
Location: London
Duration: 8 days, August
Max. in group: 60
Levels: all
Min. age: 18
*Technical theatre skills, stage management, lighting, wardrobe and costumes.*

**Suffolk College Summer School**          **Centre 422**
Location: Suffolk
Duration: July/August
Levels: all
*Actors' workshops.*

**Wetherby**          **Centre 482**
Location: Berkshire
Duration: varies, all year
Max. in group: 6
Levels: all
Min. age: 6

# Music

**Alston Hall Residential College**          **Centre 16**
Location: Lancashire
Duration: 2 days, April-September
Levels: all
*Courses on string quartets, viol consort playing, Monteverdi's music, British musicals, recorder playing, lieder performing, Mahler's music and choral singing.*

**Avril Dankworth National Children's Music Camps**          **Centre 30**
Location: Buckinghamshire
Duration: 7 days, July-August
Max. in group: 64
Levels: all
Min. age: 8
*Music camps for children.*

**Belstead House**          **Centre 39**
Location: Suffolk
Duration: 2 days, all year
Levels: all
Min. age: 16
*Various courses. Ring for details.*

**Little Benslow Hills**          **Centre 266**
Location: Hertfordshire
Duration: 2-7 days, all year
Levels: all
*Many courses including individual instrument workshops, chamber music, quartets, opera, singing, orchestra and brass ensembles. Extensive summer school programme.*

**Burton Manor College**  **Centre 70**
Location: Cheshire
Duration: 1-5 days, all year
Max. in group: 16
Levels: all
Min. age: 14
*Courses on music in facsimile,*
*Rachmaninov, understanding opera,*
*songwriting, recorder and guitar playing.*

**Countrywide Holidays**  **Centre 114**
Location: nationwide
Duration: 7 days, all year
Levels: all
*Classical guitar, opera appreciation,*
*recorder playing and singing.*

**Dillington House**  **Centre 131**
Location: Somerset
Duration: 1-7 days, all year
Max. in group: 70
Levels: all
Min. age: 18
*Courses on Puccini, Bach and Mozart.*

**Earnley Concourse**  **Centre 141**
Location: Sussex
Duration: 2-7 days, May-September
Levels: all
Min. age: 16
*Courses on jazz, opera and piano.*

**Grantley Hall**  **Centre 194**
Location: Yorkshire
Duration: 2 days, all year
Levels: all
*Courses on Rachmaninov, Tchaikovsky and*
*choral singing.*

**Hawkwood College**  **Centre 200**
Location: Gloucestershire
Duration: 7 days, August
Max. in group: 45
Levels: intermediate/advanced

Min. age: 12
*Orchestral summer school.*

**HF Holidays Ltd**  **Centre 207**
Location: nationwide
Duration: 4-7 days, all year
Levels: all
*Playing in an orchestra or folk dance band,*
*or singing from madrigals to Music Hall.*

**Higham Hall Residential**
**Study Centre**  **Centre 214**
Location: Cumbria
Duration: 2-7 days, March/May/August
Levels: all
*Jazz, early music and Rachmaninov.*

**Learn at Leisure**  **Centre 260**
Location: nationwide
Duration: 2-7 days, all year
Levels: all
*Many courses. Ring for details.*

**Millfield School Village of**
**Education**  **Centre 293**
Location: Somerset
Duration: 5 days, July-August
Max. in group: 10
Levels: all
Min. age: 9
*Electronic keyboard, multi-activity music,*
*and singing.*

**Missenden Abbey**  **Centre 296**
Location: Buckinghamshire
Duration: 2 days, all year
Levels: all
Min. age: 16
*Courses include singing, composing and*
*early music.*

## Music continued

**National Operatic & Dramatic
Association**      **Centre 312**
Location: Yorkshire
Duration: 8 days, August
Max. in group: 150
Levels: intermediate/advanced
Min. age: 18
*Opera, operetta and musicals.*

**Northumbrian Recorder &
Violin School**      **Centre 325**
Location: Co Durham
Duration: 7 days, July-August
Max. in group: 100+
Levels: all
Min. age: 13
*All aspects of early music.*

**Sceptre Promotions**      **Centre 380**
Location: nationwide
Duration: 7 days, April/May/October
Max. in group: 1000
Levels: all
*Tutorials and talent contests.*

**Suffolk College Summer
School**      **Centre 422**
Location: Suffolk
Duration: July/August
Levels: all
*Opera.*

**Summer Academy**      **Centre 423**
Location: nationwide
Duration: 7 days, July
Max. in group: 40
Levels: all
Min. age: 16
*Music at the Gower Festival.*

**Summer University**      **Centre 425**
Location: Leicestershire
Duration: 5 days, July-August
Max. in group: 20
Levels: all
Min. age: 18
*Opera, European music.*

**University of Cambridge**      **Centre 456**
Location: Cambridgeshire
Duration: 2-7 days, all year
Levels: all
Min. age: 16
*Courses on jazz, Strauss, Tannhauser,
Bach, string quartet playing and history of
the harpsichord.*

**University of Manchester**      **Centre 457**
Location: Manchester
Duration: 2 days, all year
Levels: all
Min. age: 16
*Various courses. Ring for details.*

**University of Stirling**      **Centre 459**
Location: Stirlingshire
Duration: 5 days, July
Max. in group: 15+
Levels: intermediate/advanced
Min. age: 16
*Shetland fiddle techniques.*

**West Dean College**      **Centre 481**
Location: Sussex
Duration: 2-4 days, all year
Levels: all
*Courses on opera, guitar playing and
singing. Also courses on making musical
instruments.*

**Please mention this guide when
booking courses**

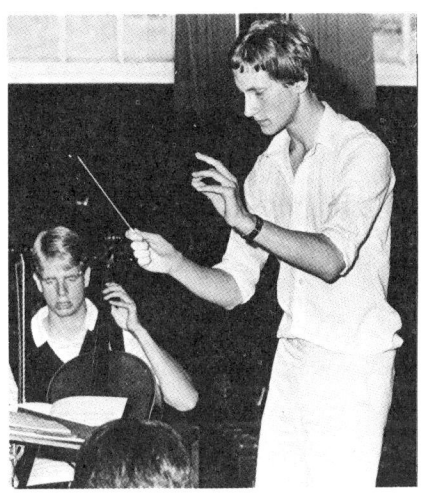

*Wycombe Music Summer School*

**Wycombe Music Summer School**     **Centre 506**
Location: Buckinghamshire
Duration: 7 days, August
Max in group: 150
Levels: all
Min age: 8
*Courses on symphony orchestra playing, choral, conducting, string and woodwind music.*

# Music Appreciation

**Acorn Activities**     **Centre 3**
Location: Worcestershire/Herefordshire
Duration: 2 days, varies
Levels: all
*A listening tour of locations where Elgar drew inspiration.*

**Braziers Adult College**     **Centre 53**
Location: Oxon
Duration: 2 days, June-July
Levels: all
*Courses on Berlioz and Liszt and general music appreciation.*

**Philharmonic Study Tour Club**     **Centre 347**
Location: nationwide
Duration: 2-7 days, March-October
Max in group: 15
Levels: all
Min age: 20
*Talks at UK music festivals.*

# Languages and Literature

## Creative Writing

**Arvon Foundation**     Centre 27
Location: Yorkshire
Duration: 4 days, April-December
Max. in group: 16
Levels: all
Min. age: 16
*Course to work alongside professional writers to improve and practise writing skills.*

**Braziers Adult College**     Centre 53
Location: Oxon
Duration: 2 days, all year
Max. in group: 10
Levels: all
Min. age: 18
*Courses on autobiographical writing, turning novels into film and general creative writing.*

**British Universities Accommodation Consortium**     Centre 61
Location: nationwide
Duration: varies, June-September
Levels: all
*Many courses. Ring for details.*

**Burton Manor College**     Centre 70
Location: Cheshire
Duration: 1-5 days, all year
Max. in group: 16
Levels: all
Min. age: 14
*Creative writing and poetry courses.*

**Coleg Harlech**     Centre 100
Location: Gwynedd
Duration: 7 days, August
Max. in group: 14
Levels: all
Min. age: 18
*Writers' workshop.*

**Dillington House**     Centre 131
Location: Somerset
Duration: 1-2 days, all year
Max. in group: varies
Levels: all
Min. age: 18
*Creative writing and short story workshops.*

**Eden Centre (The)**     Centre 148
Location: Devon
Duration: 7 days, May-July
Max. in group: 12
Levels: all
Min. age: 18
*Writing retreat on the mainland and islands.*

**Fen Farm Arts**     Centre 166
Location: Suffolk
Duration: 5 days, March-December
Max. in group: 10
Levels: all

Min age: 16
*Courses to develop writing techniques.*
*Discussion with specialist tutor.*

**Grantley Hall**                    **Centre 194**
Location: Yorkshire
Duration: 2 days, all year
Levels: all

**Hawkwood College**              **Centre 200**
Location: Gloucestershire
Duration: 2 days, March
Max. in group: 25
Levels: all
Min. age: 18
*Poetry writing.*

**Millfield School Village of
Education**                          **Centre 293**
Location: Somerset
Duration: 5 days, July-August
Max. in group: 10
Levels: all
Min. age: 8
*Creative writing, poetry, and writing for TV
and radio.*

**Nettlecombe Court**            **Centre 314**
Location: Somerset
Duration: 7 days, July
Levels: all

**Summer Academy**               **Centre 423**
Location: Chester/Sheffield
Duration: 7 days, June/July
Max. in group: 40
Levels: all
Min. age: 16

**Summer University**            **Centre 425**
Location: Leicestershire
Duration: 5 days, July-August
Max. in group: 12

Levels: all
Min. age: 18
*Short stories, plays and poetry.*

**Taliesin Trust**                   **Centre 432**
Location: Gwynedd
Duration: 5 days, June/August
Max. in group: 16
Levels: all
Min. age: 16

**University of Birmingham**     **Centre 455**
Location: Shropshire
Duration: 2 days, March
Max. in group: 23
Levels: all
Min. age: 18
*Individual writing workshops, group work
and tutorials.*

**University of Cambridge**      **Centre 456**
Location: Cambridgeshire
Duration: 2 days, May
Levels: all
Min. age: 18
*All aspects plus an overview of the publish-
ing industry.*

# English Language

**British Universities Accommodation
Consortium**                         **Centre 61**
Location: nationwide
Duration: varies, June-September
Levels: all
*Many courses. Ring for details.*

**Please mention this guide when
booking a course**

## English Language continued

**Cornish Study Holidays          Centre 110**
Location: Cornwall
Duration: 5/10/15 days, April-September
Max. in group: 10
Levels: intermediate/advanced
Min. age: 20
*English as a foreign language.*

**English Country School          Centre 155**
Location: Hertfordshire
Duration: 7-28 days, July-August
Max. in group: 20
Levels: all
Min. age: 10
*English language learning combined with activities.*

**English Language &
Equestrian Centre (The)          Centre 157**
Location: Sussex
Duration: 19 days, April/June-August
Max. in group: 24
Levels: all
Min. age: 12
*English language tuition with horse-riding plus other activities.*

**Jordanhill College          Centre 242**
Location: Glasgow
Duration: 7-28 days, July-August
Max. in group: 100
Levels: intermediate/advanced
Min. age: 12
*English as a foreign language plus British culture.*

**Lydbury English Centre          Centre 274**
Location: Shropshire
Duration: 5 days, all year
Max. in group: 10

Min. age: 19
*To improve language appreciation and ability.*

**Millfield School Village of
Education          Centre 293**
Location: Somerset
Duration: 5 days, July-August
Max. in group: 10
Levels: all
Min. age: 8

**Scot-ed Courses          Centre 383**
Location: Edinburgh
Duration: 21 days, all year
Max. in group: 25
Levels: intermediate/advanced
Min. age: 14
*General English for foreign students.*

# Languages

**Acorn Activities          Centre 3**
Location: Herefordshire
Duration: varies, all year
Levels: all
*Courses in French, German, Italian, Spanish, Russian and Swedish.*

**British Universities Accommodation
Consortium          Centre 61**
Location: nationwide
Duration: varies, June-September
Levels: all
*Many courses. Ring for details.*

**Burton Manor College          Centre 70**
Location: Cheshire
Duration: 1-5 days, all year
Max. in group: 16
Levels: all
Min. age: 14
*Courses on Italian, French and German.*

**Coleg Harlech**      **Centre 100**
Location: Gwynedd
Duration: 2-7 days, April-August
Max. in group: 12-100
Levels: all
Min. age: 14
*Welsh and French courses.*

**Dillington House**      **Centre 131**
Location: Somerset
Duration: 1-2 days, all year
Max. in group: varies
Levels: all
Min. age: 18
*Courses on Italian, Greek, Turkish and French.*

**Earnley Concourse**      **Centre 141**
Location: Sussex
Duration: 2 days, all year
Max. in group: 16
Levels: all
Min. age: 16
*French and Italian.*

**Grantley Hall**      **Centre 194**
Location: Yorkshire
Duration: 2 days, all year
Levels: all
*French, German and Spanish.*

**Hill Residential College**      **Centre 218**
Location: Gwent
Duration: 2-7 days, all year
Max. in group: 12
Levels: all
Min. age: 16
*French, German, Spanish and Italian.*

**Millfield School Village
of Education**      **Centre 293**
Location: Somerset
Duration: 5 days, July-August

Max. in group: 10
Levels: all
Min. age: 8
*Conversational French.*

**Suffolk College Summer
School**      **Centre 422**
Location: Suffolk
Duration: 5 days, July
Levels: all
Min. age: 16
*French, Italian and Spanish.*

**University of Cambridge**      **Centre 456**
Location: Cambridgeshire
Duration: 2 days, all year
Levels: all
Min. age: 18
*French, German, Spanish, Italian, Russian, Latin, classical Greek and Slavonic languages.*

**University of Stirling**      **Centre 459**
Location: Stirlingshire
Duration: 5 days, July
Max. in group: 20
Min. age: 16
*Gaelic language.*

**Wansfell College**      **Centre 466**
Location: Essex
Duration: 2 days, January-March/June
Levels: all
Min. age: 18
*Scottish Gaelic, Italian, modern Greek, Spanish and German.*

**Wetherby**      **Centre 482**
Location: Berkshire
Duration: all year
Max. in group: 6
Levels: all
Min. age: 6
*Spanish and French.*

# Literature

**Alston Hall**                    Centre 16
Location: Lancashire
Duration: 2 days, June-August
Levels: all
*East European literature and 'Writers and Places'.*

**Ammerdown Study Centre**    Centre 17
Location: Avon
Duration: 2-7 days, May/August
Max. in group: 40
Levels: all
*A study of Shakespeare, Thomas Hardy, and the poems of Donne and Eliot.*

**Braziers Adult College**       Centre 53
Location: Oxon
Duration: 2-7 days, all year
Max. in group: 10
Levels: all
Min. age: 14
*Various courses on writers and poets. Ring for details.*

**British Universities Accommodation Consortium**           Centre 61
Location: nationwide
Duration: varies, June-September
Levels: all
*Many courses. Ring for details.*

**Coleg Harlech**                Centre 100
Location: Gwynedd
Duration: 7 days, August
Max. in group: 12
Levels: all
Min. age: 18
*Courses on Victorian literature, and Wales in fiction.*

**Cornish Study Holidays**       Centre 110
Location: Cornwall
Duration: 5 days, August
Max. in group: 10
Levels: all
Min. age: 20
*Romantic poets.*

**Eden Centre (The)**            Centre 148
Location: Devon
Duration: 7 days, May-July
Max. in group: 12
Levels: all
Min. age: 18

**Goldnib Leisure**              Centre 192
Location: Yorkshire
Duration: 2 days, June-August
Max. in group: 30
Levels: all
Min. age: 18
*Agatha Christie workshop in Harrogate.*

**Higham Hall Residential Study Centre**              Centre 214
Location: Cumbria
Duration: 2-7 days, May-July
Levels: all
*Courses on George Eliot, Wordsworth and poetry.*

**Suffolk College Summer School**                     Centre 422
Location: Suffolk
Duration: 5 days, July
Levels: all
Min. age: 16
*19th century novels.*

**Summer Academy**               Centre 423
Location: nationwide
Duration: 7 days, June-September
Max. in group: 40
Levels: all

Min. age: 16
*Various courses on British and European literature. Ring for details.*

**Summer University**          **Centre 425**
Location: Leicestershire
Duration: 5 days, July-August
Max. in group: 12
Levels: all
Min. age: 18
*A study of selected playwrights.*

**University of Birmingham**   **Centre 455**
Location: Shropshire
Duration: 2 days, April-September
Max. in group: 23
Levels: all
Min. age: 18
*Courses include a study of the Brontës and the Country House in literature.*

**University of Cambridge**    **Centre 456**
Location: Cambridgeshire
Duration: 2 days, all year
Levels: all
Min. age: 18
*Over 20 courses on British and world literature from all centuries.*

**University of Oxford
Summer School**                **Centre 458**
Location: Oxford
Duration: 7 days, July-August
Max. in group: 12
Levels: all
Min. age: 18
*Seminars on all aspects of literature and creative writing.*

**University of Stirling**     **Centre 459**
Location: Stirlingshire
Duration: 5 days, August
Max. in group: 15

Min. age: 16
*20th century Scottish literature.*

## Literature & Theatre

**HF Holidays Ltd**            **Centre 207**
Location: nationwide
Duration: 2-7 days, all year
Max. in group: 20-30
Levels: all

## Sign Language

**Butterfields**               **Centre 71**
Location: Clwyd
Duration: 5 days, all year
Max. in group: 12
Levels: beginners/intermediate
Min. age: 12
*To achieve stages I or II level of assessment, laid down by the Council for the Advancement of Communication with deaf people.*

**Millfield School Village of
Education**                    **Centre 293**
Location: Somerset
Duration: 5 days, July-August
Max. in group: 10
Levels: all
Min. age: 8

**Please refer to the Centres Index for details about accommodation**

# Food and Drink

## Cookery Courses

**Bath School of Cookery**    Centre 36
Location: Avon
Duration: 4 days-4 weeks, all year
Max. in group: 10
Levels: all
Min. age: 17
*Learn to cook or expand your repertoire in small classes in a house party atmosphere.*

**Bonne Bouche School of Cookery**    Centre 45
Location: Devon
Duration: 1-25 days, all year
Max. in group: 6
Levels: beginners/all
Min. age: 20
*Variety of courses including 'French, International Cuisine', 'Healthy Eating', 'Cooking with Sauces', 'Fish Cookery', 'English Cuisine', special weekend, day classes and foundation courses.*

**Cookery At The Grange**    Centre 107
Location: Somerset
Duration: 2 days - 4 weeks, varies
Max. in group: 14-16
Levels: beginners/all
Min. age: 18
*Variety of courses including 'Basics to Bearnaise', 'Food with Flair', and 'Weekend Cooking'.*

**Dillington House**    Centre 131
Location: Somerset
Duration: 1-2 days, all year
Max. in group: varies
Levels: all
Min. age: 18
*Various courses demonstrating versatile uses of vegetables, herbs and fish.*

**Manor School of Fine Cuisine**    Centre 279
Location: Nottinghamshire
Duration: 2 days - 1 month, varies
Max. in group: 8-10
Levels: beginners/all
Min. age: 12-16
*A variety of courses including 'Chocolate, Gourmet Weekends', 'Game Fare', 'Vegetarian Entertaining', Foundation Courses and Certificate Courses.*

**Millfield School Village of Education**    Centre 293
Location: Somerset
Duration: 5 days, July-August
Max. in group: 10
Levels: all
Min. age: 9
*Course including cake decorating, basic cookery, and Eastern cookery.*

**Suffolk College Summer School**    Centre 422
Location: Suffolk
Duration: 5 days, July

*The Lutterworth Guide to* Activity and Study Holidays

Max. in group: varies
Levels: all
Min. age:16
*Various courses in breadmaking, French cuisine, and finishing touches.*

**Young Cooks of Britain**     **Centre 516**
Location: Sussex
Duration: 5 days, August (2 courses)
Max. in group: 20
Levels: all
Min. age: 11
*Familiarises young people with cookery techniques, whilst having fun with quizzes, competitions, sports, picnics and barbeques.*

# Food & Drink

**Earnley Concourse**     **Centre 141**
Location: Sussex
Duration: 2 days, all year
Max. in group: 12
Levels: all
Min. age: 16
*A variety of courses.*

# Food & Walking

**HF Holidays Ltd**     **Centre 207**
Location: nationwide
Duration: 2-3 days, February-March
Levels: all
*Walks include a gourmet picnic and a six-course evening dinner menu with wine to round off a day of walking.*

# Specialty Foods

**Countrywide Holidays**     **Centre 114**
Location: North Yorkshire
Duration: 7 days, September
Levels: all
*An opportunity to look at Yorkshire through*

*the heart of its villages - the Pub. Walks of about 10 miles daily across moors, valleys and along the coast. History and legends told.*

**Countrywide Holidays**     **Centre 114**
Location: nationwide
Duration: 7 days, October
Levels: all
*Indulge in old fashioned delicacies such as spotted dick, treacle pudding, boiled beef and carrots. Not a stodge week but not for weightwatchers either!*

**Countrywide Holidays**     **Centre 114**
Location: Scotland
Duration: 7 days, July
Levels: all
*A taste of real Scotland. Try rumbledethumps, tipsy laird, mussels macduff as well as fresh salmon, venison and highland beef. Visits to distilleries.*

# Gardens & Gourmet

**Wharton Lodge Gourmet**     **Centre 484**
Location: Herefordshire
Duration: 1 day, July-September
Max. in group: 20
*Our Chef de Cuisine demonstrates on 3 occassions Wharton Lodge favourites that can be prepared simple at home. Includes luncheon and tour of extensive gardens.*

# Gourmet Cooking

**Acorn Activities**     **Centre 3**
Location: Herefordshire
Duration: 2 days, all year
Levels: all
*Indian, Italian, French and English cooking taught.*

# Wine Tasting

**Acorn Activities**      **Centre 3**
Location: Herefordshire
Duration: 2 days
Max. in group: varies
*Visits to vineyards and cider producers with tasting and tours.*

**Headland Hotel**      **Centre 204**
Location: Cornwall
Duration: 2 days, Spring/Autumn
Max. in group: 50
Levels: all
Min. age: 18
*Tasting of wines from all over the world arranged informally, aiming to dispel some of the mystery of the subject.*

**Upper House Farm**      **Centre 460**
Location: Herefordshire
Duration: 2 days, all year
Max. in group: 12
Levels: all
Min. age: 17
*To educate and humour guests while enjoying wine tasting.*

**Wineweekends**      **Centre 500**
Location: Herefordshire
Duration: 2 days, all year
Max. in group: 12
Levels: all
Min. age: 17

# Games

## Bridge

**Acorn Activities**      **Centre 3**
Location: Herefordshire
Duration: 2 days
Max. in group: varies

**Alston Hall Residential College**      **Centre 16**
Location: Preston
Duration: 2 days, July

**Boultons Country House Hotel**      **Centre 49**
Location: Leicestershire
Duration: 2 days, all year
Levels: all

**Bradford & Ilkley College**      **Centre 51**
Location: Yorkshire
Duration: 7 days, July
Max. in group: 60
Levels: all
Min. age: 20

**HF Holidays Ltd**      **Centre 207**
Location: nationwide
Duration: 4-7 days, all year
Levels: all

**Higham Hall Residential Study Centre**      **Centre 214**
Location: Cumbria
Duration: 4-7 days, May-August
Max. in group: varies
Levels: all
Min. age: 18
*Bridge playing combined with walking.*

**Hill Residential College**     **Centre 218**
Location: Gwent
Duration: 2-4 days, all year
Max. in group: 32
Levels: all
Min. age: 16

**Millfield School Village of
Education**     **Centre 293**
Location: Somerset
Duration: 5 days, July-August
Max. in group: 10
Levels: all
Min. age: 15
*Part of a multiactivity week.*

# Chess

**Millfield School Village of
Education**     **Centre 293**
Location: Somerset
Duration: 5 days, July-August
Max. in group: 10
Levels: all
Min. age: 8
*Part of multiactivity week.*

# Scrabble

**HF Holidays Ltd**     **Centre 207**
Location: nationwide
Duration: 2-7 days, all year
Levels: all
*A chance to learn the in's and out's of the game with an expert leader.*

# Technical Courses

## Computing

**Earnley Concourse**     **Centre 141**
Location: Sussex
Duration: 2 days, May-September
Max. in group: varies
Levels: all
Min. age: 16
*Various courses including desktop publishing.*

**Learn at Leisure**     **Centre 260**
Location: Nottinghamshire
Duration: 2 days, July
Levels: all
*Desktop publishing.*

**Millfield School Village of
Education**     **Centre 293**
Location: Somerset
Duration: 5 days, July-August
Max. in group: 10
Levels: beginners
Min. age: 18
*Various courses.*

**Premier**     **Centre 355**
Location: Cambridgeshire
Duration: 1-2 days, March-October
Max. in group: 1
Levels: beginners
Min. age: 16
*Introduction to various desktop publishing systems.*

## Computing continued

**Suffolk College Summer School**                    **Centre 422**
Location: Suffolk
Duration: 5 days, July
Max. in group: varies
Levels: all
Min. age: 16
*Various courses.*

# D.I.Y.

**Juvan Courses**                    **Centre 245**
Location: Gloucestershire
Duration: 2 days, April-November
Max. in group: 6
Levels: all
Min. age: 16
*Courses in plastering, bricklaying, electrical, plumbing and basic home maintenance.*

**Suffolk College Summer School**                    **Centre 422**
Location: Suffolk
Duration: 5 days, July
Max. in group: varies
Levels: all
Min. age: 16
*Courses in bricklaying, brickcraft and welding.*

# Driving

**Acorn Activities**                    **Centre 3**
Location: Herefordshire
Duration: 2-5 days
Levels: beginners
Min. age: 17
*Learn to drive with test on the fifth day.*

**Ballater Driving School**                    **Centre 32**
Location: Aberdeenshire
Duration: 5 days, all year
Max. in group: 2
Levels: all
Min. age: 17
*Teaches people to drive and pass their test in 5 days.*

**EP Training Services Ltd**                    **Centre 159**
Location: Surrey
Duration: 5 days, all year
Max. in group: 6
Levels: all
Min. age: 17
*Learn to drive and pass car test.*

**Fallowfield School of Motoring**                    **Centre 162**
Location: Gwynedd
Duration: 5+ days, all year
Max. in group: 6
Levels: all
Min. age: 17
*Learn to drive and pass car test.*

**Highland Drovers**                    **Centre 215**
Location: Inverness-shire
Duration: 2 days, all year exc. November
Max. in group: 1-2
Levels: all
Min. age: 16
*Off-road driving instruction in 4 x 4 vehicles.*

**Highland Drovers**                    **Centre 215**
Location: Inverness-shire
Duration: 5 days, July-September
Max. in group: 8
Levels: all
Min. age: 17
*4 x 4 or 8-wheel driving tuition.*

**Intensive Driving Course**     Centre 231
Location: Essex
Duration: varies, all year
Max. in group: 3
Levels: all
Min. age: 17
*Beginner, refresher, or advanced tuition.*

**Motor Safari**     Centre 301
Location: Clwyd
Duration: 1-7 days, all year
Max. in group: 32
Levels: all
Min. age: 17
*Off-road and 4-wheel adventure driving.*

## First Aid

**Kevin Walker Mountain
Activities**     Centre 248
Location: Powys
Duration: 2 days, all year
Max. in group: 16
Levels: all
Min. age: 18
*Training to MLTB/NCA requirements.*

# Model Engineering

**Summer University**     Centre 425
Location: Leicestershire
Duration: 5 days, July-August
Max. in group: 20-24
Levels: intermediate/advanced
Min. age: 18
*Individual tuition on participant's chosen
project.*

# Motor Cycle Driving

**Acorn Activities**     Centre 3
Location: Herefordshire
Duration: 2 days
Max. in group: varies
Levels: beginners
Min. age: 17
*Basic training course for those wishing to
take their test.*

# Personal Development

**Acorn Activities**     Centre 3
Location: Herefordshire
Duration: 5 days, all year
Max. in group: 10
Levels: all
*Personal Development and Management
training courses covering leadership,
personal effectiveness, resource manage-
ment and self awareness.*

**Allenheads Lodge Outdoor
Centre**     Centre 15
Location: Northumberland
Duration: 2/5/7 days, all year
Max. in group: 20
Levels: all
Min. age: 14
*Courses in team work, team building and
personal development using outdoor
pursuits.*

## Personal Development continued

**Alston Hall Residential
College**                       Centre 16
Location: Lancashire
Duration: 2 days, May/July/September
Levels: all
Min. age: 16
*Course develops talking with confidence.*

**Bearsports Outdoor Centres**   Centre 38
Location: Northumberland
Duration: any, all year
Max. in group: 40
Levels: all
Min. age: 16
*Through a structured programme of
challenging activities participants are given
feedback from their tutors and peers.*

**Braziers Adult College**       Centre 53
Location: Oxon
Duration: 2 days, all year
Levels: all
*Courses on yoga, massage, problem
solving, learning from dreams, living with
more meaning.*

**Brighton Natural Health
Centre**                        Centre 56
Location: Sussex
Duration: 2-5 days, Easter/Summer
Max. in group: varies
Levels: all
*A range of courses including dance, yoga,
Tai Chi, Shiatsu, and assertiveness training.
Contact organisation for more details.*

**Burton Manor College**        Centre 70
Location: Cheshire
Duration: 1-5 days, all year
Max. in group: 16
Levels: all

Min. age: 14
*Courses on Tai Chi, dance, stress manage-
ment, aromatherapy and Alexander
technique.*

**CAER**                        Centre 78
Location: Cornwall
Duration: 3-5 days, March-August
Max. in group: 16-18
Levels: all
*Courses on enlightenment training,
humanistic psychology, the art of loving,
tantra enhancing and choices in work.*

**Compass Christian Centre**    Centre 103
Location: Perthshire
Duration: 2-6 days, all year
Max. in group: 20
Min. age: 18
*Tailor made courses looking at personal
development through team building and
leadership issues. Suitable for companies,
voluntary organisations, church groups etc.*

**Cornish Study Holidays**      Centre 110
Location: Cornwall
Duration: 5 days, April-September
Max. in group: 10
Levels: beginners/intermediate
Min. age: 20
*Increase self-confidence in all areas of
personal communication including public
speaking, group participation and interview
technique.*

**Country Venture Activities**   Centre 113
Location: Cumbria
Duration: 2-7 days, February-December
Max. in group: 20
Min. age: 16
*Courses in leadership, team work, working
with people, management development, and
communication skills.*

160                  *The Lutterworth Guide to* Activity and Study Holidays

**Countrywide Holidays**          Centre 114
Location: nationwide
Duration: 4-7 days, April/July/October
Levels: all
*Yoga classes for families.*

**Dartmoor Expedition Centre**     Centre 123
Location: Devon
Duration: 6 days, March/November-
December
Max. in group: 32
Levels: all
Min. age: 18
*Introductory course for people wishing to
lead groups on hills and mountains. Also
courses for personal development through
outdoor activities.*

**David Taylor's Interest
Holidays**          Centre 124
Location: Worcestershire
Duration: 2-7 days, October-March
Max. in group: 8
Levels: all
Min. age: 18
*This course aims to bring about better
parenthood through discussions and talks
on various aspects of parenthood.*

**Dillington House**          Centre 131
Location: Somerset
Duration: 2 days, all year
Levels: all
*Courses in complementary therapies, yoga,
life planning, Alexander technique,
massage, self hypnosis, Chinese exercise,
and the creative self.*

**Earnley Concourse**          Centre 141
Location: Sussex
Duration: 2 days, all year
Max. in group: 16
Levels: all
Min. age: 16

*Courses on yoga, massage, assertiveness,
and speaking confidently.*

**East Down Centre**          Centre 144
Location: Devon
Duration: 2 days, all year
Max. in group: 12
Levels: all
Min. age: 18
*For existing groups only. Using the
experiential learning cycle with outdoor
and indoor exercises to develop individual
interaction and team work.*

**Grantley Hall**          Centre 194
Location: Yorkshire
Duration: 3 days, March
*A programme of yoga disciplines of posture,
breathing exercises, and meditation.*

**HF Holidays Ltd**          Centre 207
Location: London
Duration: 2-7 days, all year
Max. in group: 20
Levels: all
*Courses in assertiveness, positive thinking,
public speaking, alexander technique and yoga.*

**High Force Training Centre**     Centre 209
Location: Co. Durham
Duration: any, all year
Max. in group: 30
Levels: all
Min. age: 7

**High Loaning Head
Adventure Centre**          Centre 210
Location: Cumbria
Duration: varies. Ring for details
Levels: all
*Mountain leaders' training.*

## Personal Development continued

**Howtown Outdoor**                 **Centre 223**
Location: Cumbria
Duration: 5-7 days, all year
Max. in group: 60
Levels: all
Min. age: 12
*A variety of outdoor activities as a catalyst for personal development.*

**Ladytrek-Ladytour**               **Centre 253**
Location: Wester Ross
Duration: 4-7 days, February-November
Max. in group: 8
Levels: beginners/intermediate
Min. age: 17
*Confidence building through group experience - walking camping for women only.*

**Metamorphic Association**         **Centre 287**
Location: London
Duration: 2 days, all year
Max. in group: 15
Levels: beginners
Min. age: 18
*Introduction to the practice and theory of the Metamorphic Technique for self-growth and transformation.*

**Mill on the Brue Activity Centre**                         **Centre 292**
Location: Somerset
Duration: 2-4 days, February-March/ September-November
Max. in group: 18
Levels: beginners/intermediate
Min. age: 18
*For women only, a course to develop self awareness and self confidence.*

**Millfield School Village of Education**                       **Centre 293**
Location: Somerset
Duration: 5 days, July-August
Max. in group: 10
Levels: all
Min. age: 16
*Courses in family therapy, personal development and self-confidence.*

**Millnain**                        **Centre 294**
Location: Ross-shire
Duration: varies, all year
Max. in group: 6
Levels: all
Min. age: 18
*One-to-one guidance on stress management, time management, creativity and positive thinking combined with various activities.*

**Minerva Training**                **Centre 295**
Location: Dyfed
Duration: 2-5 days, all year
Max. in group: 30-40
Levels: all
Min. age: 10
*Courses for all age groups to enable greater self awareness.*

**Mountain Stream Activities**      **Centre 305**
Location: Devon
Duration: 3 days
Max. in group: 34
Levels: all
*Management training, staff development, and communication skills.*

**Mountain Ventures Ltd**           **Centre 306**
Location: Liverpool
Duration: 2/3/5-7 days, all year
Levels: all
Min. age: 14
*Develop self confidence through challeng-*

*ing training experiences, in a fun low key environment.*

**North York Moors Adventure
Centre**      **Centre 320**
Location: Yorkshire
Duration: 5 days, April-October
Max. in group: 20
Levels: all
Min. age: 16
*Management training courses, group work, problem solving and character building.*

**Scottish Centres**      **Centre 385**
Location: Lanarkshire
Duration: March-October
Max. in group: 10-250
Min. age: 8
*Group bookings for 10 minimum in personal development.*

**Summer University**      **Centre 425**
Location: Leicestershire
Duration: 5 days, July-August
Max. in group: 20
Levels: all
Min. age: 18
*A course to help students become more confident in their relationships with others.*

**Uist Outdoor Centre**      **Centre 454**
Location: Isle of North Ulst
Duration: 7 days, all year
Max. in group: 20
Levels: all
Min. age: 12
*Courses to develop motivation skills, communication, leadership and teamwork using a stimulating natural environment.*

**University of Stirling**      **Centre 459**
Location: Stirlingshire
Duration: 1-2 days, June-August
Max. in group: 20

Min. age: 16
*Courses include Alexander technique, aromatherapy, and reflexology.*

**Wansfell College**      **Centre 466**
Location: Essex
Duration: 2 days, July
*Course to develop a positive attitude to retirement.*

**West Cornwall Learning
Holidays**      **Centre 479**
Location: Cornwall
Duration: 7 days, April/June-August
Max. in group: 10
Levels: all
Min. age: 20
*Course to explore new career possibilities, learn job search skills and improve confidence. Includes psychometric assessment and career counselling.*

**YMCA National Centre**      **Centre 512**
Location: Cumbria
Duration: 7 days, July-September
Max. in group: varies
Levels: advanced
Min. age: 18
*Mountain Walking Leader's training course.*

**Ynys Hywel Countryside
Centre**      **Centre 513**
Location: Gwent
Duration: 2 days, September-November
Max. in group: 34
Levels: beginners/all
Min. age: 18
*Reflexology courses.*

**Yoga For Health Foundation**      **Centre 514**
Location: Bedfordshire
Duration: 1-7 days, May-October
Levels: all
*Variety of yoga courses available.*

# Health and Fitness

**Acorn Activities**      **Centre 3**
Location: varies, all year
Max. in group: varies
*Assessment including measurement of lung volume, percentage of body fat, endurance, flexibility, cardiovascular ability, etc. followed by an individually tailored weight training programme.*

**Action Extras**      **Centre 4**
Location: nationwide
Duration: 2 days, varies
Max. in group: 30
Levels: all
Min. age: 18
*Ring for details.*

**Brighton Natural Health Centre**      **Centre 56**
Location: Sussex
Duration: 2-5 days, Easter/Summer
Max. in group: varies
Levels: all
*A range of courses are offered. Ring for details.*

**Burton Manor College**      **Centre 70**
Location: Cheshire
Duration: 1-5 days, all year
Max. in group: 16
Levels: all
Min. age: 14

*Tai chi, dance, stress management, aromotherapy.*

**Earnley Concourse**      **Centre 141**
Location: Sussex
Duration: 2/4 days, all year
Levels: all
Min. age: 16

**Hilton Hotels**      **Centre 220**
Location: nationwide
Duration: 2 days, March/October/November
Max. in group: 60
Levels: all
Min. age: 16
*Structured fitness sessions with demonstrations.*

**Millfield School Village of Education**      **Centre 293**
Location: Somerset
Duration: 5 days, July-August
Max. in group: 10
Levels: all
Min. age: varies
*Aerobics, Alexander technique, yoga and massage.*

**St. Michaels of Falmouth**      **Centre 415**
Location: Cornwall
Duration: 2 days, all year

Levels: all
Min. age: 18
*With the help of resident professional expert, you will have a comprehensive physical assessment and a tailor-made exercise plan. Massage available.'*

**Suffolk College Summer School**     Centre 422
Location: Suffolk
Duration: 5 days, July
Levels: all
Min. age: 16
*Introductory aromatherapy workshop for women and face and body workshop.*

**Summer University**     Centre 425
Location: Leicestershire
Duration: 5 days, July-August
Max. in group: 15
Min. age: 18
*Courses in yoga and complementary therapies.*

# Miscellaneous Subjects

## Art Therapy

**Carberry Tower**     Centre 88
Location: Midlothian
Duration: 2 days, various months
Max. in group: 24
Levels: all
Min. age: 21

**Summer University**     Centre 425
Location: Leicestershire
Duration: 5 days, July/August
Max. in group: 15
Levels: all
Min. age: 18
*Exploration of the unconcious mind through spontaneous drawing.*

## Astronomy

**Wansfell College**     Centre 466
Location: Essex
Duration: 2 days, March
Levels: all
Min. age: 18

## Christian Festivals

**Hawkwood College**     Centre 200
Location: Gloucestershire
Duration: 2 days, April
Max. in group: 35
Levels: all
Min. age: 21
*A look at celebrating Christian festivals within the family settting with discussion and practical craftmaking.*

---

**Please refer to the Centres Index for details about accommodation**

---

## Miscellaneous Subjects continued

## Counselling

**Alston Hall Residential
College**                    **Centre 16**
Location: Lancashire
Duration: 2 days, May
*An introductory course.*

## Crossword Puzzles

**Cartoon School (The)**          **Centre 89**
Location: Yorkshire
Duration: 2 days, May
Max. in group: 30
Levels: all
Min. age: 18
*Learn to write crossword puzzles for profit.
This course will take participants through
the various stages of crossword compilation
and clue writing to produce publishable,
saleable puzzles.*

## Green Business

**Flatford Mill Field Centre**    **Centre 169**
Location: Essex/Suffolk
Duration: 3 days, February
Levels: all

## Growing Together

**Acorn Activities**              **Centre 3**
Location: Welsh Border
Duration: 2 days, various months
*This weekend course is designed to deepen
and enrich the relationship of couples who
are committed to make their marriage work.*

# Hygiene

**Yeoldon Country House Hotel Centre 511**
Location: Devon
Duration: 5 days, October-May
Max. in group: 20
Levels: all
Min. age: 18
*Course covers the 1990 Hygiene Act.*

# Managing a B&B

**Premier**                       **Centre 355**
Location: Cambridgeshire
Duration: 2 days, February-October
Max. in group: 4
Levels: beginners
Min. age: 18
*How to run a Bed & Breakfast establishment,
understanding all regulations, certificates
needed, food hygiene, marketing, etc.*

# Murder Mystery

**Acorn Activities**              **Centre 3**
Location: Herefordshire
Duration: 2 day, various months
*Detective playing and brain teasing weekend.*

**Boultons Country House
Hotel**                           **Centre 49**
Location: Leicestershire
Duration: 2 days, all year
*A weekend revolving around the solving of
a murder committed on Friday evening,
including a mystery tour of Rutland.*

**Headland Hotel**                **Centre 204**
Location: Cornwall
Duration: 2 days, September
Max. in group: 60
Levels: all
Min. age: 7

**HF Holidays Ltd**          **Centre 207**
Location: nationwide
Duration: 2-3 days, all year
Levels: all
*A weekend of detective playing, mystery and suspense.*

# Personal Finance

**Gateway Education &**
**Arts Centre**          **Centre 183**
Location: Shropshire
Duration: 2 days, February
Levels: all

**Hill Residential College**          **Centre 218**
Location: Gwent
Duration: 2 days, February/November
Max. in group: 25
Levels: beginners
Min. age: 16
*This course will help you sort out your own investments and plan your long term income strategies.*

**Hill Residential College**          **Centre 218**
Location: Gwent
Duration: 2 days, February-November
Max. in group: 25
Levels: beginners
Min. age: 16

# Writers' Workshop

**Coleg Harlech**          **Centre 100**
Location: Gwynedd
Duration: 7 days, August
Max. in group: 14
Levels: all
Min. age: 18
*A course designed to help writers get published.*

# Britain's most dynamic holiday magazine!

## On sale in your newsagents from January

A MUST FOR ANYONE WHO LIKES TO GET UP AND GO ON HOLIDAY

BRITAIN'S MOST DYNAMIC HOLIDAY MAGAZINE

**ACTION HOLIDAYS**

JANUARY-FEBRUARY

MICROLIGHTING
SURFING
TREKKING
SHARK SHOOTING
BIKING

Plus features on Outward Bound, Outback Adventures, Sail Training, Panning for Gold, Activity Holidays in Bermuda, Spain and Ireland.

WIN a Headwater Holiday in France
WIN a holiday on Lake Lugano
WIN a Learn to Dive weekend

Austria

MARCH-APRIL 1992 £1.75

**ACTION HOLIDAYS**

Activity holidays in Italy, Zambia, France, Austria, Wales
Scuba Diving
Flotilla Sailing
Angling
Summer Skiing
Cycling

WIN a diving holiday with Travellers Interests
A holiday in St. Cyprien
Stylish luggage from Equator

**Cover price: £1.75**

**Packed with ideas destinations and information on activity holidays**

## The magazine for getting bums out of beds, off beaches and out of

This section lists the organisations from whom you can obtain more information about the courses listed.

**Key to symbols used:**

| | |
|---|---|
| 🏃 | children can be accommodated |
| ♿ | disabled facilities on site |
| 🐕 | pets are welcome |
| est. | date organisation was established |
| all types | full or half board, B&B or self-catering available |

Facilities vary from Centre to Centre, therefore readers are advised to always check before making a booking.

# Centres Index

## Centre 1
**Abernethy Outdoor Centre**   est. 1971
Nethy Bridge
Inverness-shire
PH25 3ED
Tel: 0479 821279
Contact: Pamela Boyd
Accommodation: for 76, full board at the Centre or self-catering in chalets.
🏃

## Centre 2
**Achanalt House Guided Mountain Bike Holidays**   est. 1990
Achanalt House
Achanalt by Garve
Ross-shire
IV23 2QD
Tel: 0997 414283
Contact: Peter Davison
Accommodation: for 6, all types, in private house.
🏃♿🐕

*'Based at our 18th century coaching house we travel to different tracks daily, exploring the northern high-lands. Excellent biking, quality accommodation and wonderful meals.'*

## Centre 3
**Acorn Activities**   est. 1989
7 East Street
Hereford
Herefordshire
HR1 4RY
Tel: 0432 357335
Contact: Charles Cordle
Accommodation: all types in hotel, guest house or farmhouse.
🏃♿🐕

*'Acorn activities, Britain's leading activity holiday company offers a choice of over 100 activities for all interests and ages. With group, farmhouse or hotel accommodation.'*

## Centre 4
**Action Extras**   est. 1981
Hilton National Hotels
P.O. Box 137
Watford
Hertfordshire
WD1 1DN
Tel: 0923 246464
Contact: Jean Butler
Accommodation: full board in hotels throughout Britain.
🏃♿🐕

## Centre 5
**Active Edge Paragliding**    est. 1991
Watershed Mill
Langcliffe Road
Settle
Yorkshire
BD24 9LY
Tel: 0729 822311/0423 712539
Contact: Tony Johnston/Dean Crosby
Accommodation: all types in hotels,
guest houses, hostels or camping.

*'Active Edge is based in the Yorkshire
Dales, offering excellent training
throughout the year in this area of
outstanding beauty. The school is fully
registered and acknowledged by the
BADC.'*

## Centre 6
**Adventure & Computer
Holidays**    est. 1983
28 Gowrie Road
London
SW11 5NR
Tel: 071 350 1896
Contact: Sarah Bradley
Accommodation: for 52, all types in
private house or camping if preferred.

## Centre 7
**Adventure Cycles**    est. 1985
2 Snows Cottages
Mamhead
Kenton
Devon
EX6 8HW
Tel: 0626 864786
Contact: Ian Shields
Accommodation: for 10, half board or
B&B in guest house.

## Centre 8
**Adventure International**    est. 1980
Belle Vue
Bude
Cornwall
EX23 8JP
Tel: 0288 355551
Contact: Keith Marshall
Accommodation: for 360, full board or
B&B in a former hotel, now a residen-
tial centre.

## Centre 9
**Adventure Sky Sports U.K.**   est. 1991
15 St Mary's Green
Biggin Hill
Kent
TN16 3R
Tel: 0959 573996
Contact: Derek Bond
Accommodation: all types, in various
locations, according to clients require-
ments.

*'ASS U.K. is an independent booking
agency. When enquiries are received
we are able to discuss the relative
costs, physical demands, courses,
duration and costs. And offer choices
e.g. Sussex, Devon, Wales etc.'*

## Centre 10
**Adventure Sports**    est. 1982
Carnkie Farm House
Carnkie
Redruth
Cornwall
TR16 6RZ
Tel: 0209 218962
Contact: Lester Cruse
Accommodation: for 20, self-catering
in farmhouse, chalet or camping.

## Centre 11

**Adventureline**                    est. 1988
North Trefula Farm
Redruth
Cornwall
TR16 5ET
Tel: 0209 820847
Contact: Martin or Elizabeth Hunt
Accommodation: for 10, all types in
farmhouse, cottage or hotel.

*'Cornwall's spectacular diversity of
landscapes and her stunning coastline
make a perfect opportunity for a
walking holiday which explores the
natural history, archaeology, geography and geology of this beautiful
county.'*

## Centre 12

**Airborne Hang Gliding &
Paragliding Centre**              est. 1976
Hey End Farm
Luddendfoot
Halifax
Yorkshire
HX2 6NJ
Tel: 0422 834989
Contact: Tony Delaney/Sue White
Accommodation: B&B in local
farmhouse.

## Centre 13

**Alan Baxter Pottery**          est. 1979
The White House Studio
Lower Somersham
Ipswich
Suffolk
IP8 4QA
Tel: 0473 831256
Contact: Alan or Pat Baxter
Accommodation: for 8, full board in
private house or camping.

## Centre 14

**Albion Rides** est. 1987
Duck Row
Cawston
Norwich
Norfolk
NR10 4EZ
Tel: 0603 871725
Contact: Clementina Sutton
Accommodation: for 6, all types in
hotel, cottage or camping.

## Centre 15

**Allenheads Lodge Outdoor
Centre**                           est. 1988
Allenheads Lodge
Allenheads
Northumberland
NE47 9HW
Tel: 0434 685374
Contact: Roger Ward
Accommodation: for 20, full board or
self-catering at residential centre.

*'The lodge is situated in the old lead
mining village of Allenheads, 1300' up
in the rugged North Pennines.'*

## Centre 16

**Alston Hall Residential
College**                           est. 1956
Longridge
Preston
Lancashire
PR3 3BP
Tel: 0772 784661
Contact: The Administrator
Accommodation: for 42, full board in
residential adult education college.

# Centres Index

**Centre 17**
**Ammerdown Study Centre** est. 1973
Radstock
Bath
Avon BA3 5SW
Tel: 0761 433709
Contact: The Course Secretary
Accommodation: for 40, full/half board
and B&B in study centre.

&#9855;

*'Ammerdown is set in Ammerdown
Park near to Lord Hylton's private
residence where some of the parkland
and gardens are open to guests.'*

**Centre 18**
**Anglia Cycling Holidays** est. 1978
Ballintuim
Blairgowrie
Perthshire PH10 7NJ
Tel: 0250 886 201
Contact: Kenneth Todd
Accommodation: in B&B's, farm-
houses and pubs.

**Centre 19**
**Anne Justina Carhart** est. 1987
70 Harcourt Drive
Harrogate
Yorkshire HG1 5AB
Tel: 0423 506630
Contact: Anne J. Carhart
Accommodation: for 2-4, half board or
B&B on premises or in guest houses.

**Centre 20**
**Anvil Yacht Charters** est. 1968
13 Harbour View Road
Parkstone
Poole
Dorset BH14 0PD
Tel: 0202 741637
Contact: Ray Saunders

Accommodation: for 12, self-catering,
on board yacht.

**Centre 21**
**Apollo Water-Ski School** est. 1989
Apollo Tavern
96 Northgate Street
Great Yarmouth
Norfolk
NR30 1BP
Tel: 0493 856052
Contact: Don Bryan
Accommodation: in B&B's, pubs or
hotel.

**Centre 22**
**Ardeonaig Outdoor Centre** est. 1984
Killin
Perthshire
FK21 8SY
Tel: 0567 820523
Contact: Rachel Macdonald
Accommodation: for 40, full board at
residential centre.

**Centre 23**
**Ardmiddle Enterprises** est. 1992
Ardmiddle Mains
Turriff
Aberdeenshire
AB53 8AL
Tel: 0888 62443
Contact: Kate Ferguson
Accommodation: all types in cottages
or farmhouse.

*'The courses are held in a spacious,
newly renovated farmhouse studio set
in quiet, picturesque countryside.
Excellent farmhouse cooking. Ideal
location for golf and fishing.'*

*The Lutterworth Guide to* Activity and Study Holidays

**Centre 24**
**Ardmore Adventures Ltd**   est. 1983
11-15 High Street
Marlow
Buckinghamshire
SL7 1AU
Tel: 0628 890060
Contact: Richard Tobias
Accommodation: for 60-300, full board
in residential centres.

**Centre 25**
**Argyll & Isles Cruising
Tuition**   est. 1982
8 Kilmory Road
Lochgilphead
Argyll
PA31 8SZ
Tel: 0546 60 2670
Contact: Liz Carver
Accommodation: for 5, full board on
board sailing cruiser.

**Centre 26**
**Artscape Painting
Holidays Ltd**   est. 1952
Suite 4
18 Hamlet Court Road
Westcliff-on-Sea
Essex
SS0 7LX
Tel: 0702 435990
Contact: Sally-Anne Howard
Accommodation: for 15, full/half board
in colleges and hotel.

*'Over forty years of experience of
tutored painting courses, to suit first-
time, improvers and experienced artists
in all media. Modern, impressionist
and traditional courses. Brochure
available.'*

**Centre 27**
**Arvon Foundation**   est. 1975
Lumb Bank
Heptonstall
Hebden Bridge
Yorkshire HX7 6DF
Tel: 0422 843714
Contact: Ann Anderton
Accommodation: for 16, full board in
former mill owner's house.

**Centre 28**
**Avalon Trekking Scotland**   est. 1988
Bowerswell Lane
Kinnoull
Perthshire PH2 7DL
Tel: 0738 24194
Contact: Tom Sandiford
Accommodation: for 10, half board in
hotels or guest houses.

**Centre 29**
**Aviemore Ski School**   est. 1963
Aviemore Mountain Resort
Aviemore
Inverness-shire
PH22 1PL
Tel: 0479 810310
Contact: A.W. Caird
Accommodation: for up to 1000, all
types.

**Centre 30**
**Avril Dankworth National Children's
Music Camps**   est. 1971
Ye Barn - Spinney Lane
Aspley Guise
Milton Keynes
Buckinghamshire
MK17 8JT
Tel: 0908 58325
Contact: Yvonne Speller

Accommodation: for 64, full board camping.

*'Musically these holidays are unique. Children come because they love music and the timetable is tailored according to their instruments, ability and interests.'*

## Centre 31
**Ayrshire Equitation Centre**                            est. 1950
Castlehill Stables
Hillfoot Road
Ayr
Ayrshire
KA7 3LF
Tel: 0292 266267
Contact: Kevin Galbraith
Accommodation: for 15, full/half board or B&B in residential centre.

## Centre 32
**Ballater Driving School**        est. 1987
Creag Meggan
Bridge of Gairn
Ballater
Aberdeenshire
AB35 5UD
Tel: 03397 55767
Contact: Graham or Margaret Johnson
Accommodation: for 6, half board or B&B in guest houses.

*'Intensive 5 day learn-to-drive courses with test. Suitable for the beginner and those with driving experience. Available all year in Aberdeen or Ballater, from £275.'*

## Centre 33
**Balloon Base**                         est. 1988
Vauxhall House - Coronation Road
Southville

Bristol
Avon
BS3 1RN
Tel: 0272 633333
Contact: Jo Phillip
Accommodation: various options. Ring for details.

## Centre 34
**Barend Properties Ltd**        est. 1977
Barend
Sandyhills
Dalbeattie
Kirkcudbrightshire
DG5 4NU
Tel: 038 778 663
Contact: The Central Office.
Accommodation: for 8-10, self-catering in chalets.

*'Situated on the coast in South West Scotland the centre provides treks through Dalbeattie forest or lessons, courses using our excellent facilities from outdoor manège to cross-country jumps.'*

## Centre 35
**Barry Skinner**                        est. 1986
Turnpike Cottage
Traeth
Beddgelert
Gwynedd LL55 4YF
Tel: 076 686 283
Contact: Barry Skinner
Accommodation: all types. Ring for details.

*'Walking, scrambling, navigation, cross-country skiing available through-out year for all ages and experience. School parties. Accommodation can be arranged day, weekend or week.'*

## Centre 36

**Bath School of Cookery**  est. 1988
Bassett House
Claverton
Bath
Avon BA2 7BL
Tel: 0225 722498
Contact: Sallie Caldwell
Accommodation: for 10, full board
residential at centre.

## Centre 37

**Beaconhill - East Kent**
**Field Centre**  est. 1985
Beaconhill Cottage
Great Mongeham
Deal
Kent CT14 OHW
Tel: 0304 372809
Contact: Tony Wiggins
Accommodation: for 14, full board,
residential at centre.
🚶‍♂️ ♿ (limited)

## Centre 38

**Bearsports Outdoor**
**Centres**  est. 1973
Windy Gyle
West Street
Belford
Northumberland
NE70 7QE
Tel: 0668 213289
Contact: Peter or Phillipa Clark
Accommodation: for 80, all types in
outdoor centres, hotels or camping.
🚶‍♂️

*'We provide extensively equipped and*
*'outdoor proof' accommodation in*
*Northumberland close to heritage*
*coast. Excellent equipment, staff,*
*locations and approved by RYA, BCU,*
*BAHA, CARP, and MLTB.*

## Centre 39

**Belstead House**
Residential Centre  est. 1947
Belstead
Suffolk IP8 3NA
Tel: 0473 686321
Contact: The Manager
Accommodation: for 43, full board
residential at centre.

## Centre 40

**Bicycle Beano**  est. 1983
59 Birch Hill Road
Clehonger
Hereford
Herefordshire HR2 9RF
Tel: 0981 251087
Contact: Jane Barnes
Accommodation: for 30, half board in
guest houses or camping.
🚶‍♂️

## Centre 41

**Blidworth Pottery**  est. 1990
Woodstock, Ricket Lane
Blidworth
Nottinghamshire NG21 0QW
Tel: 0623 795704
Contact: Janet or David Charlton
Accommodation: for 6, full board with
family.
🚶‍♂️

## Centre 42

**Blisland Porcelain**  est. 1988
Tregreenwell Farm Craft Centre
St Teath
Bodmin
Cornwall PL30 3JJ
Tel: 0208 851171
Contact: Mary-Jane Hill
Accommodation: half board, self-
catering and B&B in guest house.
🚶‍♂️

## Centre 43
**Blue Skies Parachute Training
School** est. 1972
4 Shalford Terrace
Whitford
Axminster
Devon EX13 7PL
Tel: 0297 553300
Contact: The Manager
Accommodation: ring for details.

## Centre 44
**Bobsport (Scotland) Ltd** est. 1982
32 Pentland Gardens
Edinburgh
EH10 6NW
Tel: 031 447 3500
Contact: Bob Brownless/Atholl Pirie
Accommodation: for 50, half board,
self-catering and B&B in hotels or
guest houses.

⚄⚄

## Centre 45
**Bonne Bouche School of
Cookery** est. 1986
Lower Beers
Brithem Bottom
Cullompton
Devon EX15 1NB
Tel: 0884 32257
Contact: Gerald Nicholls
Accommodation: for 10, full board in
private house.

*'Small groups, around 6 people. Practical
hands-on classes. Personal tuition,
informal, fun. Professional teachers. All
levels. Own bedrooms with private
facilities. Many leisure attractions nearby.'*

## Centre 46
**Booker Gliding Club** est. 1982
Wycombe Air Park

Marlow
Buckinghamshire
SL7 3DR
Tel: 0494 442501/529263
Contact: The Administrator
Accommodation: half board at Bisham
Abbey National Sports Centre or B&B.

⚄

## Centre 47
**Border Parachute Centre** est. 1983
Eastwell House
Embleton
Northumberland
NE66 3UX
Tel: 0661 844444
Contact: Dave Porter
Accommodation: for 40, full board,
residential at centre.

⚄⚄

## Centre 48
**Boswednack Manor** est. 1986
Zennor
St Ives
Cornwall
TR26 3DD
Tel: 0736 794183
Contact: Dr Gynn
Accommodation: for 12-15, full/half
board and B&B in guest houses.

⚄

## Centre 49
**Boultons Country House
Hotel** est. 1985
Catmose Street
Oakham
Leicestershire
Tel: 0572 722844
Contact: The Manager
Accommodation: for 12-45, half board
in hotel.

⚄⚄

## Centre 50
**Bowles Outdoor Centre**    est. 1964
Eridge Green
Tunbridge Wells
Sussex TN3 9LW
Tel: 0892 665665
Contact: B. Rudkin
Accommodation: for 60, full board,
residential at centre.

## Centre 51
**Bradford & Ilkley College**    est. 1984
Easby Road
Bradford
Yorkshire BD7 1QZ
Tel: 0274 733291
Contact: Jane Wilson
Accommodation: for 200, all types
residential at College.

## Centre 52
**Brasshouse Centre**    est. 1975
50 Sheepcote Street
Birmingham
West Midlands B16 8AJ
Tel: 021 643 0114
Contact: Deborah Cobbett
Accommodation: half board staying
with families.

## Centre 53
**Braziers Adult College**    est. 1950
Ipsden
Oxford
Oxon OX9 6AN
Tel: 0491 680221
Contact: Dr Faithfull
Accommodation: for 24, full board,
residential at College.

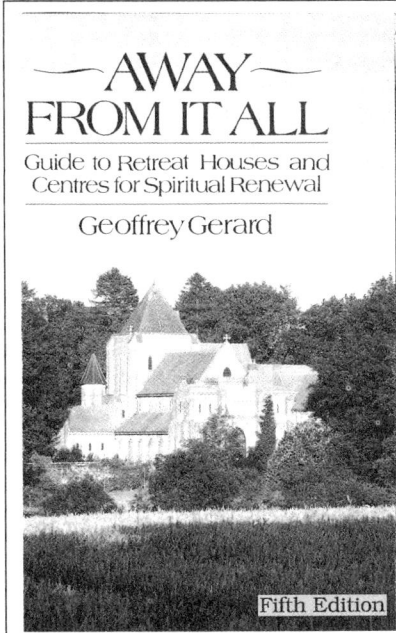

*Breakaway Survival School*

## Centre 54

**Breakaway Survival School** est. 1983
17 Hugh Thomas Avenue
Holmer
Hereford
Herefordshire
HR4 9RB
Tel: 0432 267097
Contact: Mick Taylor
Accommodation: for 30, self-catering in countryclub, barns, shelters or camping.

*'Management initiative, motivation and team building courses. Come and enjoy the unspoilt beauty of the very scenic area, head of the Neath Valley, south of Brecon Beacons.*

## Centre 55

**Breaside Sports**                    est. 1988
26 Western Hill
Sunderland
Tyne & Wear
SR2 7PH
Tel: 091 565 4801
Contact: George Walton
Accommodation: for 25, B&B in guest houses.

*'Puma Centre is set in large green sports complex on outskirts of Sunderland a seaside holiday resort which boasts good restaurants, nightclubs at northern England down-to-earth budget prices.'*

## Centre 56
**Brighton Natural Health Centre** est. 1981
27 Regent Street
Brighton
Sussex
BN1 1UL
Tel: 0273 6000010
Contact: Jeddi Bassan
Accommodation: ring for details.

## Centre 57
**Bristol & Gloucestershire Gliding Club** est. 1956
Nympsfield
Stonehouse
Gloucestershire GL10 3TX
Tel: 0453 860342
Contact: G. Dale
Accommodation: for 10, all types in clubhouse.

🏃🐑

## Centre 58
**Britannia Study Tours** est. 1990
20 Henry Road
West Bridgford
Nottingham
Nottinghamshire
NG2 7NA
Tel: 0602 815963
Contact: Colin Groves
Accommodation: for 50, full board residential in adult educational colleges and country houses.

🏃

## Centre 59
**British Offshire Sailing School** est.1991
Hamble Point Marina
Southampton
Hampshire SO2 0SF
Tel: 0703 227724
Contact: P. Ellis/L. Peacock
Accommodation: full board on board yacht or B&B in guest house.

## Centre 60
**British School of Falconry** est. 1982
Stelling Minnis
Canterbury
Kent CT4 6AQ
Tel: 0227 87575
Contact: Stephen or Emma Ford
Accommodation: full board at local hotels, or self-catering in off-site cottages.

## Centre 61
**British Universities Accommodation Consortium** est. 1971
University Park
Nottingham
Nottinghamshire
NG7 2RD
Tel: 0602 504571
Contact: Carole Formon
Accommodation: all types in residential colleges.

🏃

## Centre 62
**Broadland Arts Centre** est. 1989
43 The Crossways
Westcliffe on Sea
Essex SS0 8PU
Tel: 0692 536320
Contact: Angela Dammery
Accommodation: B&B at Centre, or local B&B's and hotels.

*'Set in beautiful Broadland National Park. 2-8 day courses in all forms of painting, drawing, printmaking, crafts. Summer school afloat - art study, painting tours abroad.'*

**Centre 63**

**Broadlands Riding Centre**   est. 1946
Lower Paice Lane
Mestead
Alton
Hampshire
GU34 5PX
Tel: 0420 63382
Contact: S.M. Stratford
Accommodation: for 7, full board in
private house.

🚶

**Centre 64**

**Brookhouse Pottery
Workshop**   est. 1963
The Malt House
Brookhouse Lane
Denbigh
Clwyd
LL16 4RE
Tel: 0745 812805
Contact: David Frith
Accommodation: for 8, in local hotels,
guest houses or camping.

♿

**Centre 65**

**Brunel University Arts Centre** est. 1967
Brunel University
Uxbridge
Middlesex
UB8 3PH
Tel: 0895 273482
Contact: Christine Garner
Accommodation: B&B, in university
halls of residence.

**Centre 66**

**Bryn Ffynnon Farm Riding
Centre**   est. 1960
Cefneurgain Lane
Rhosesmor
Mold
Clwyd
CH7 6PG
Tel: 0352 86664
Contact: Netta Rowlands
Accommodation: for 10, all types in
farmhouse, guest house or camping.

🚶 ♿ 🐑

*'Bryn Ffynnon is 12 miles from the
historic town of Chester. All ages
catered for in this informal farmhouse.
5 leisure centres near, always plenty to
do.'*

**Centre 67**

**Budleigh Farm Target Shooting
Centre**   est. 1983
Moretonhampstead
Newton Abbot
Devon
TQ13 8SB
Tel: 0647 40835
Contact: J. Harvey
Accommodation: for up to 20, all types
in guest houses or camping.

🚶 ♿

**Centre 68**

**Bulldog Sailing Centre**   est. 1987
Ocean Village Marina
Canute Road
Southampton
Hampshire
SO1 1JJ
Tel: 0703 230260
Contact: Eddie Edrich
Accommodation: full board on board
yacht.

🚶

**Centre 69**

**Burton Hotel**   est. 1988
Mill Street
Kington

Herefordshire
HR5 3BQ
Tel: 0544 230323
Contact: Lisa Richardson
Accommodation: for 30, full/half board
or B&B at hotel.

🏃🐕

## Centre 70
**Burton Manor College**     est. 1948
Burton
South Wirral
Cheshire
L64 5SJ
Tel: 051 336 5172
Contact: Janet Hooper
Accommodation: for 72, full/half
board, residential at College.

♿

## Centre 71
**Butterfields**     est. 1985
Pen y Nant Cottage
Minera
Wrexham
Clwyd
LL11 3DA
Tel: 0978 750547
Contact: Ken or Janet Butterfield
Accommodation: for 12, all types at
hostel.

🏃🐕

## Centre 72
**Byre Yard**     est. 1989
Tanton Hall Farm
Stokesley
Yorkshire TS9 5JT
Tel: 0642 711371
Contact: Barbara Agar
Accommodation: for 19, full board or
B&B.

🏃♿

*'Year-round art and craft courses in
attractive rural setting including
sketching, painting, printing, textiles,
basketry, papermaking, paper sculpture, carnival structures, children's
creative activities.'*

## Centre 73
**C-Charters Sea School**     est. 1987
Deacon's Boatyard
Bursledon
Southampton
Hampshire SO3 8AZ
Tel: 0703 406420
Contact: S. Godwin/M. Clark
Accommodation: for 5, full board on
board yacht.

🏃

*'Learn to sail in sail training certifi-
cated yachts in the Solent Area gaining
RYA certificates if required.'*

## Centre 74
**C-n-Do Scotland Ltd**     est. 1983
77/78 John Player Building
Springbank Road
Stirling
Stirlingshire FK7 7RP
Tel: 0786 445703/812355
Contact: Margaret Porter
Accommodation: for 13, all types in
guest houses, hotel, hostel or camping.

🏃♿

## Centre 75
**C.A.C. Watersports**     est. 1985
Mylor Yacht Harbour - Mylor
Falmouth
Cornwall
TR11 5UF
Tel: 0326 376191
Contact: Brian Phipps
Accommodation: for 30, all types.

**Centre 76**

**Cabair Group Ltd**  est. 1969
Elstree Aerodrome
Borehamwood
Hertfordshire WD6 3AW
Tel: 081 953 4411
Contact: Julia Hines
Accommodation: all types, various
options. Ring for details.

**Centre 77**

**Cader Ventures**  est. 1992
2 Llanegryn Street
Abergynolwyn
Tywyn
Gwynedd LL36 9YE
Tel: 0654 782699
Contact: Hugo Iffla
Accommodation: all types, various
options. Ring for details.

**Centre 78**

**CAER**  est. 1978
Rosemerryn
Lamorna
Penzance
Cornwall TR19 6BN
Tel: 0736 810530
Contact: Jo May
Accommodation: for 22, full board or
B&B at centre.

**Centre 79**

**Cairnwell Hang Gliding
School**  est. 1975
Cairnwall
Braemar
Aberdeenshire AB3 5XS
Tel: 03397 41331
Contact: Gustav Fischnaller
Accommodation: B&B in hotel or
guest house.

*'Learn to fly in the scenic Grampion
Range of the Scottish Highlands. Safety
and fun is our motto in Scotland's
longest established hang gliding
school.'*

**Centre 80**

**Cairnwell Ski School**  est. 1971
Braemar
Aberdeenshire
AB3 5XS
Tel: 03397 41331
Contact: Gustav Fischnaller
Accommodation: ring for details.

*'Cairnwell Ski School conveniently
situated at the Ski Centre under the
direction of Austrian Gustav
Fischnaller. Our qualified instructor
ensures your safety and enjoyment.'*

**Centre 81**

**Calder Valley Cruising**  est. 1986
The Marina
New Road
Hebden Bridge
Hebden
Yorkshire HX7 8AD
Tel: 0422 844833
Contact: Phil Kennedy
Accommodation: for 20, full/half
board, in hotels and guest houses.

**Centre 82**

**Calluna Workshops**  est. 1990
Hill House
Creech St Michael
Taunton
Somerset TA3 5DP
Tel: 0823 443335
Contact: Heather Luke
Accommodation: various B&B's.

## Centre 83
**Calshot Activities Centre**  est. 1965
Calshot Road
Calshot
Southampton
Hampshire SO4 1BR
Tel: 0703 892077
Contact: D. Evans
Accommodation: for 150, all types,
residential at Centre.

## Centre 84
**Calvert Trust Kielder**  est. 1984
Kielder Water
Hexham
Northumberland NE48 1BS
Tel: 0434 250232
Contact: The Director
Accommodation: for 50, full/half board
in hotel.

## Centre 85
**Camp Aldenham**  est. 1982
Aldenham School
Elstree
Hertfordshire WD6 3AJ
Tel: 0923 857553
Contact: David Mead
Accommodation: ring for details.

## Centre 86
**Campions Crafts**  est. 1988
Campions
Buzzacott Lane
Combe Martin
Devon EX34 0NL
Tel: 0271 882626
Contact: F. Ward
Accommodation: all types at centre,
hotel, guest house, pubs or camping.

*'Craft centre is located on edge of*

*beautiful Exmoor National Park, with
easy access to North Devon beaches
and other holiday facilities.'*

## Centre 87
**Canopy Training**  est. 1989
146 Oakland Road
Sheffield
Yorkshire S6 4QQ
Tel: 0742 326055
Contact: Louise Johnson
Accommodation: for 6-14, full board at
outdoor centre or guest house.

## Centre 88
**Carberry Tower**  est. 1961
Musselburgh
Midlothian
EH21 8PY
Tel: 031 665 3135
Contact: The Warden
Accommodation: for 92, full/half board
or B&B at residential centre.

## Centre 89
**Cartoon School (The)**  est. 1989
33 Saint Catherine's Road
Harrogate
Yorkshire HG2 8JZ
Tel: 0423 887880
Contact: P. Coupe/D. Robinson
Accommodation: for 30, full board in
hotel.

## Centre 90
**Cathedral Camps**  est. 1981
Manor House
High Birstwith
Harrogate
Yorkshire HG3 2LG
Tel: 0423 771179
Contact: Robert Aagaard
Accommodation: camping on church
premises. Ring for details.

**Centre 91**

**Cefn-y-Dre**                          est. 1989
Fishguard
Dyfed SA65 9QS
Tel: 0348 874499
Contact: Roy or Elaine Ayres
Accommodation: for 6, full board and
B&B.

𝕏

**Centre 92**

**Chatsworth & Purbeck Activity
Centres**                          est. 1924
Ulwell Road
Swanage
Dorset BH19 1LG
Tel: 0929 422123
Contact: Karen Hamilton
Accommodation: up to 400, full board,
residential at Centres.

𝕏

*'The Chatsworth & Purbeck Centres
specialize in a multi-activity holidays
and courses for groups of young
people, led by qualified instructors who
provide a safe and fun approach.
Within walking distance is the beach
and town.'*

**Centre 93**

**Chichester Interest Holidays** est.1982
14 Bay View Terrace
Newquay
Cornwall TR7 2LR
Tel: 0637 874216
Contact: Sheila Harper
Accommodation: for 10, full board in
guest house.

**Centre 94**

**Chichester Sailing Centre**   est. 1954
Chichester Marina
Chichester

Sussex PO20 7EL
Tel: 0243 512557
Contact: The Manager
Accommodation: for 50 in various
locations. Ring for details.

𝕏 ♿

**Centre 95**

**Cinderhill House**                est. 1989
St Briavels
Gloucestershire
GL15 6RH
Tel: 0594 530393
Contact: G. Peacock
Accommodation: full board, ring for
details.

♿

**Centre 96**

**Clay Farm - Sporting Heights** est. 1980
Clows Top
Kidderminster
Worcestershire
DY14 9NN
Tel: 0299 832421
Contact: Ella Grinnall
Accommodation: for 6, B&B at
farmhouse.

𝕏

**Centre 97**

**Clive Powell Mountain Bikes**  est. 1985
The Mount
East Street
Rhayader
Powys
KD6 5DN
Tel: 0597 810585
Contact: Clive Powell
Accommodation: for 16, full board in
guest house or camping.

𝕏

## Centre 98
**Clyde Offshire Sailing Centre**  est. 1985
Kip Marina
Inverkip
Renfrewshire
PA16 0AS
Tel: 0475 521210
Contact: D. Miles
Accommodation: for 6-10, full board
on board yachts.

🏃

*'Clyde Offshore is the premier sailing
school and yacht charter company in
Scotland. Courses at all levels including novice, family and yacht master.'*

## Centre 99
**Cold Keld Guided Walking
Holidays**  est. 1989
Fell End
Ravenstonedale
Cumbria CA17 4LN
Tel: 05396 23273
Contact: K. Trimmer
Accommodation: for 10, full board at
the farmhouse, active blind people
welcome.

🐑

*'We are happy to take active blind
people with or without chaperon.'*

## Centre 100
**Coleg Harlech**  est. 1927
Harlech
Gwynedd
LL46 2PU
Tel: 0766 780363
Contact: Mena Ifans
Accommodation: for 100, full board at
residential centre.

🐑

*'In Snowdonia National Park, adjacent
to golf course and miles of sandy
beach. Social activities; own theatre
and bar, lounge.'*

## Centre 101
**Colwall Park Hotel**  est. 1981
Colwall
Malvern
Worcestershire
WR13 6QG
Tel: 0684 40206
Contact: Simon Lowe
Accommodation: for 20, full board at
hotel.

🏃🐑

## Centre 102
**Combe Lodge Hotel**  est. 1986
Chambercourse Park Road
Ilfracombe
Devon EX34 9QW
Tel: 0271 864518
Contact: Bryan or Janet Lath
Accommodation: for 20, half board or
B&B in hotel.

🏃🐑

## Centre 103
**Compass Christian Centre**  est. 1968
Glenshee Lodge
Blairgowrie
Perthshire PH10 7QD
Tel: 0250 885209
Contact: Roger Clare
Accommodation: for 42, all types at
centre.

🏃

## Centre 104
**Compass Ventures**  est. 1990
Tarbet House
Loch Lomond
Arrochar

Dunbartonshire G83 7DE
Tel: 03012 349
Contact: John Harvey
Accommodation: up to 8, full board or
B&B in guest house.

*'Compass Ventures holidays are
designed for adults and based at Tarbet
House. 2-Crown commended. With
tennis court. Magnificently situated in
7 acres overlooking Loch Lomond.'*

## Centre 105
**Compass West - International School
of Rock Climbing**     est. 1978
Compass West
Sennen
Nr. Lands End
Cornwall TR19 7AR
Tel: 0736 871447
Contact: Rowland Edwards
Accommodation: for 24, residential at
centre, or hotel.

## Centre 106
**Contessa Riding Centre**     est. 1976
Willow Tree Farm
Colliers End
Ware
Hertfordshire
SG11 1EN
Tel: 0920 821792
Contact: S. Layton
Accommodation: for 10, half board on-
site or in caravans.

## Centre 107
**Cookery At The Grange**     est. 1981
Whatley Vineyard
Frome
Somerset
BA11 3LA
Tel: 0373 836579
Contact: Jane Croswell-Jones

Accommodation: for 16, full board in
private house.

## Centre 108
**Coombe Farm Studios**     est. 1983
Dittisham
Dartmouth
Devon TQ6 0JA
Tel: 080422 352
Contact: Tina Riley
Accommodation: for 14, full/half board
or B&B, residential at centre or in
hotel.

*'Situated in rural valley, 1 mile from
Dart estuary. Relaxed atmosphere,
good food. Local facilities include
sailing, hiking, beaches, tennis etc.
Expert tuition in all areas.'*

## Centre 109
**Copley Stables**     est. 1978
Newpark Cottages
Copley
Bishopston
West Glamorgan
Tel: 0792 234428
Contact: W.P. Hemms-Tucker
Accommodation: half board or B&B in
hotel.

## Centre 110
**Cornish Study Holidays**     est. 1992
Roskennals Mill
Newbridge
Penzance
Cornwall TR20 8RW
Tel: 0736 62459
Contact: R. Trewellard
Accommodation: for 10, half board or
B&B at guest house.

*'The study centre forms part of a property which dates back at least 300 years. An idyllic location for a study course.'*

## Centre 111
**Cornwall Creative Activity Network (CCAN)**   est. 1990
Cornwall CAN
Fairhope, 5 Rose Terrace
Mitchell
Nr. Newquay
Cornwall
TR8 5AU
Tel: 0872 510551
Contact: Jackie Usher
Accommodation: for 4-50, arrangements vary, contact organisation.

*'Cornwall Creative Activity Network CAN offer in one brochure, holidays with tuition by individual expert operators; choose from arts, crafts, study, nature, archaeology, land/water sports.'*

## Centre 112
**Cornwall of Mine Ltd**   est. 198
24 Pembridge Crescent
London
W11 3DS
Tel: 071 229 2616
Contact: Paul Saulter
Accommodation: varies according to requirements. Ring for details.

## Centre 113
**Country Venture Activities**   est. 1982
Country Venture
The Old School
Tebay
Cumbria
CA10 3TP
Tel: 05874 286
Contact: D. Weatherley

Accommodation: for 46, all types residential at centre.

## Centre 114
**Countrywide Holidays**   est. 1893
Birch Heys
Cromwell Range
Manchester
M14 6HU
Tel: 061 225 1000
Contact: The Reservations Office
Accommodation: for up to 70, full board in guest house.

## Centre 115
**Craft Supplies Ltd**   est. 1978
The Mill
Millers Dale
Buxton
Derbyshire
SK17 8SN
Tel: 0298 871636
Contact: Eve Middleton
Accommodation: for 4, full board in adjacent farmhouse.

## Centre 116
**Craigower Lodge Outdoor Centre**   est. 1980
Golf Course Road
Newtonmore
Inverness-shire
PH20 1AT
Tel: 0540 673319
Contact: Bob Telfer
Accommodation: for 50, full board in outdoor centre.

# Centres Index

## Centre 117

**Cumbrae - The Scottish National Sports Centre** est. 1974
Burnside Road
Largs
Ayrshire
KA30 8RW
Tel: 0475 674666
Contact: Anne Dippie
Accommodation: for 36, full/half board, self-catering or on-site chalet.

&

## Centre 118

**Cwm Uchaf** est. 1987
Outdoor Activity Centre
Crai
Nr Sennybridge
Brecon
Powys LD3 8YN
Tel: 0874 636 703
Contact: Lionel Charlwood
Accommodation: for 18, all types in private house or camping.

*'The centre is in the heart of Brecon Beacons National Park with facilities for all outdoor activities including guided walks nearby Dan-y-orgof Caves. Big pit mining museum, many other attractions.'*

## Centre 119

**Cycle Tracks** est. 1991
Inverearn
St Fillians
Perthshire
PH6 2NF
Tel: 0764 85 322
Contact: John Chadwick/April D'Arcy
Accommodation: for 6, all types, in guest houses or hotels.

## Centre 120

**Cyclists' Touring Club** est. 1878
Cotterell House
69 Meadrow
Godalming
Surrey
GU7 3HS
Tel: 0483 417217
Contact: The Administrator
Accommodation: varies according to tour in hotels, hostels or camping.

## Centre 121

**Dale Fort Field Centre** est. 1947
(Field Studies Council)
Haverfordwest
Dyfed
SA62 3RD
Tel: 0646 636205
Contact: The Warden
Accommodation: for 36, full board, residential at the Centre.

## Centre 122

**Dane Lodge Hotel** est. 1992
92 Northenden Road
Sale
Cheshire
M33 3HB
Tel: 061 969 4440
Contact: Charles C. Hickson
Accommodation: for 50, half board or B&B at hotel.

*'2-6 nights course on landscape painting. Studio activities combined with outdoor projects. From beginners to advanced. Demonstrations, lectures, project development, individual tuition.'*

*The Lutterworth Guide to* Activity and Study Holidays

## Centre 123
**Dartmoor Expedition**
**Centre**                          est. 1971
Rowden Farm
Widecombe in the Moor
Newton Abbot
Devon TQ13 7TX
Tel: 03642 249
Contact: John Earle
Accommodation: for 32, full board or
self-catering in bunk house.

## Centre 124
**David Taylor's Interest**
**Holidays**                        est. 1989
Victoria Guest House
31 Victoria Road
Bromsgrove
Worcestershire
B61 0DW
Tel: 0527 75777
Contact: David L. Taylor
Accommodation: for 8, full/half board
or B&B in guest house or hotel.

## Centre 125
**Derbyshire & Lancashire Gliding**
**Club**                            est. 1958
Great Hucklow
Tideswell
Derbyshire SK17 8RQ
Tel: 0298 871270
Contact: John McKenzie
Accommodation: for 12, full board in
farmhouse.

*'Situated within the heart of the
beautiful Peak District National Park
the club offers superb soaring opportunities matched by the comfortable and
attractive facilities.'*

## Centre 126
**Derbyshire Action Holidays** est. 1982
Kirby House
Main Street
Winster
Derbyshire
DE4 2DH
Tel: 0629 650716
Contact: Geoff William
Accommodation: for 20, all types, in
guest house, hostel or camping.

*'We arrange tailor made, individually
instructed holidays in the White Peak
of Derbyshire throughout the year. We
offer a choice of activities and
accomodation and you are free to
choose your dates. Mid-week and off-
season rates are economical.'*

## Centre 127
**Derbyshire Ski Action**           est. 1982
Kirby House
Main Street
Winster
Derbyshire
DE4 2DH
Tel: 0629 650716
Contact: Geoff William
Accommodation: all types in guest
house or hostel.

*'Cross country ski instruction with
equipment. Daily in season in the
White Peak of Derbyshire on a daily or
period basis. Especially suitable for
novices and as a pre-introduction to ski
holidays.'*

Hartford Barton, Gittisham

*Devon Woodcrafts*
*'Fully qualified woodworking instruction in a purpose built workshop with six of the top English lathes. Ten hours per day creative learning with your own lathe.'*

## Centre 128
**Devon & Dorset Activities**   est. 1968
6 Kew Green
Kew
Richmond
Surrey TW9 3BH
Tel: 081 940 7782
Contact: Chris McCarthy
Accommodation: for 200+, full board in residential centres.

*'3 multi-activity centres, 2 in Devon, 1 in Dorset. 35+ activities inc waterskiing, windsurfing, speed sailing, surfing, canoeing, river crossing and many more.'*

## Centre 129
**Devon Woodcrafts**   est. 1977
Hartford Barton
Gittisham

Honiton
Devon
EX14 0AW
Tel: 0404 44155
Contact: Oliver Plant
Accommodation: for 6, full/half board or B&B in 17th century coaching inn.

## Centre 130
**Diane Hoare**   est. 1988
Upper House Farm
Dilwyn
Hereford
Herefordshire HR4 8JJ
Tel: 05447 245
Contact: Diane Hoare
Accommodation: for 6, in farmhouse or B&B's.

## Centre 131
**Dillington House** est. 1950
Ilminster
Somerset TA19 9DT
Tel: 0460 52427
Contact: The Booking Secretary
Accommodation: for 60, full board in
16th century manor house.

&

*'Dillington House is a beautiful manor
house set in superb grounds. It offers a
very wide range of adult education
courses. Free prospectus.'*

## Centre 132
**Discover** est. 1991
Brown Hill House
Annat
Torridon
Ross-shire
IV22 2EZ
Tel: 044 587 218
Contact: C. Macleay
Accommodation: half board or self-
catering in guest house or hotel.

*'Loch Torridon is surrounded by
magnificent scenery, some of Britain's
most spectacular mountains, with an
excellent chance to see wild life in its
natural habitat.'*

## Centre 133
**Diver Training School** est. 1972
The Quayside
Exmouth Harbour
Exmouth
Devon
EX8 1ER
Tel: 0395 266300
Contact: Tim Stevens
Accommodtion: for 36, half board or
B&B in guest house.

## Centre 134
**Diving Leisure Ltd** est.
Rockley Park
Hamworthy
Poole
Dorset
BH15 4LZ
Tel: 0202 680898
Contact: Cindy Wood
Accommodation: half board or B&B
guest house.

&

## Centre 135
**Dolmetsch Historical Dance
Society** est. 1976
Redmire
Ardley End
Hatfield Heath
Hertfordshire CM22 7AL
Tel: 0279 730530
Contact: E. Wright
Accommodation: for 60, full board,
residential at Centre.

&

## Centre 136
**Dorset Naturalist (The)** est. 1984
9 Little Britain
Dorchester
Dorset DT1 1NN
Tel: 0305 267994
Contact: Jamie McMillan
Accommodation: for 12, full board in
hotel or guest house.

## Centre 137
**Drapers' Field Centre** est. 1968
Rhyd-y-creuau
Betws-y-coed
Gwynedd
LL24 0HB
Tel: 0690 710494
Contact: The Warden

Accommodation: for 66, full board, residential at Centre.

🧍🧍

## Centre 138
**Drywell Farm Riding Centre**   est. 1972
Widecome-in-the-Moor
Newton Abbot
Devon
TQ13 7PN
Tel: 03643 349
Contact: Ruth Parnell
Accommodation: for 10, half board in farmhouse.

🧍🧍

## Centre 139
**Dunolly House Activity Centre**   est. 1988
Dunolly House
Taybridge Drive
Aberfeldy
Perthshire
PH15 2BP
Tel: 0887 820298
Contact: H. Telford/A. Bowen
Accommodation: for 60, full board, self-catering or B&B, residential at Centre.

🧍🧍

## Centre 140
**Eaglescott Parachute Centre**   est. 1988
Eaglescott Airfield
Ashreigney
Chulmleigh
Devon
EX1 7PH
Tel: 0769 60726/0769 3552
Contact: Dave Tylcoat
Accommodation: all types in pubs, farmhouses or guest houses.

## Centre 141
**Earnley Concourse**   est. 1975
Earnley
Chichester
Sussex PO20 7JL
Tel: 0243 670392
Contact: The Booking Secretary
Accommodation: for 90, full board, at residential centre.

🧍🧍♿

*'Comfortable and very well equipped centre in attractive rural setting close to the sea. Leisure facilities include indoor heated swimming pool, squash and snooker.'*

## Centre 142
**East 15 Acting School**   est. 1961
Sheriff Hutton Park
Sheriff Hutton
York
Yorkshire
Y02 1RH
Tel: 03477 442
Contact: C. Feakins
Accommodation for 16, self-catering in grade I, listed historic house.

## Centre 143
**East Anglian School of Sailing** est. 1973
Studio One
Fox's Marina
Ipswich
Suffolk IP2 8NJ
Tel: 0473 684884/780246
Contact: Peggy Fuller
Accommodation: for 26, full board on board yacht or in guest houses.

🧍🧍♿

# Special Interest Courses and Summer Activity Weeks

Our wide range of weekend courses and summer activity weeks includes Drawing and Painting, Wildlife and Walking, Musical History, Antiques and Country Houses, Fitness and Health, Swimming, Creative Writing, Cookery and Wine Tasting, Computer Studies, Bridge for All, Golf Coaching.

Comfortable accommodation, good food and excellent leisure facilities for tuition and leisure. Places for residents and non-residents. Minimum age 16.

Our free brochure is available on request.

### *The Earnley Concourse*
Earnley, Chichester, Sussex PO20 7JL
Tel: (0243) 670392 — Fax: (0243) 670832

## Centre 144

**East Down Centre**          est. 1983
Dunsford
Exeter
Devon EX6 7AL
Tel: 0647 24546
Contact: R.P. Jones
Accommodation: for 16, all types, residential at centre.

*'A 16th century thatched barn and roundhouse sympathetically converted to provide comfortable accommodation. Set in beautiful countryside on the edge of the Dartmoor National Park.'*

## Centre 145

**Eastbourne Marine**          est. 1981
1 Church Street
Eastbourne
Sussex BN21 1HN
Tel: 0323 32171
Contact: Peter Towner
Accommodation: self-catering.

## Centre 146

**Eclipse Outdoor Discovery**  est. 1989
Cragwood House
Windermere
Cumbria LA23 1LQ
Tel: 05394 44033
Contact: Philip Poole
Accommodation: for 40, full/half board or B&B in hotel or guest house.

## Centre 147

**Edale YHA Activity Centre** est. 1930
Rowland Cote
Edale
Sheffield
Yorkshire
S30 2ZH
Tel: 0433 670302
Contact: The Manager
Accommodation: for 139, full/half
board or self-catering in youth hostel.

*'YHA activity centre in open moorland
on side of Kinder Scout in Peak
National Park. Full range of outdoor
courses and leisure breaks year round.'*

## Centre 148

**Eden Centre (The)** est. 1987
Eden House
38 Lee Road
Lynton
Devon
EX35 6BS
Tel: 0598 53440
Contact: Jenny Davis
Accommodation: for 15, all types at
centre or various locations. Ring for
details.

## Centre 149

**Eden Valley Centre** est. 1978
Ainstable
Carlisle
Cumbria
CA4 9QA
Tel: 076 886 202
Contact: Matthew Ellis
Accommodation: for 37, all types
residential in 18th century building.

## Centre 150

**Eden Valley Woollen Mill** est. 1988
Front Street
Armathwaite
Carlisle
Cumbria
CA4 9PB
Tel: 06992 457
Contact: Steve or Belinda Wilson
Accommodation: for 10, all types in
local guest houses.

## Centre 151

**Edinburgh College of Art Festival
Summer School** est. 1991
Lauriston Place
Edinburgh
EH3 9DF
Tel: 031 229 9311 x249
Contact: Sheena Milligan
Accommodation: self-catering or B&B
in hotels and hostels.

## Centre 152

**Elvaston Castle Riding
Centre** est. 1982
Thulston
Derby
Derbyshire
DE7 3EP
Tel: 0332 751927
Contact: Peter Coe
Accommodation: for 6, full board or
self-catering in guest houses, pubs,
hotels.

## Centre 153

**EME Yacht Charter** est. 1967
Falmouth Yacht Marina
North Parade
Falmouth
Cornwall

TR11 2TD
Tel: 0326 211121
Contact: David Eastburn
Accommodation: for 60+, full/half
board or self-catering on board yachts.

*'Coastal and cross channel cruises for
all ages including youth flotillas (under
25) to Brittany. Good food and wine.
Excellent sailing in modern yachts.'*

## Centre 154
**Emsworth Sailing School**    est. 1957
The Port House
Port Solent
Portsmouth
Hampshire
PO6 4TH
Tel: 0705 210510
Contact: Jacqui McKendry
Accommodation: for 75-100, full/half
board or B&B in hotels, guest houses,
family homes and campsite.

## Centre 155
**English Country School**    est. 1987
Lockleys
Welwyn
Hertfordshire
AL6 0BL
Tel: 061 486 1824
Contact: Sarah Etchells
Accommodation: for 70, full board in
residential private school.

## Centre 156
**English County Cruises**    est. 1975
Wrenbury Mill
Wrenbury
Nantwich
Cheshire
CW5 8HG

Tel: 0270 780544
Contact: Jenny Monk
Accommodation: for 8 per narrowboat,
self-catering.

*'Our superb fleet of luxury
narrowboats are based on the
Llangollen Canal. Chirk & Beeston
Castle, Wigan Pier, are all in our
beautiful countryside.'*

## Centre 157
**English Language & Equestrian
Centre (The)**    est. 1967
Friars Gate Farm
Marden Hill
Crowborough
Sussex
TN6 1XH
Tel: 0892 661195
Contact: D.R.C. Forsyth
Accommodation: for 24, full board,
residential at Centre.

## Centre 158
**English Wanderer**    est. 1979
6 George Street
Ferryhill
Co Durham
DL7 0DT
Tel: 0740 653169
Contact: Philip Scriver
Accommodation: for 15, full board in
hotel or guest house.

## Centre 159
**EP Training Services Ltd**    est. 1980
6A High Street
Esher
Surrey
KT10 9RT

Tel: 0372 466183
Contact: R. Taylor
Accommodation: for 6, full/half board
in hotel or guest house.

&

*'5 and 10 day intensive car driving
courses. Manual and automatic cars,
off road training area. Established
1974, over 3000 students. Accommodation available.'*

## Centre 160
**Fairhope Fine Furniture
Restoration**                   est. 1989
5 Rose Terrace
Mitchell
Newquay
Cornwall TR8 5AU
Tel: 0872 510551
Contact: Jackie Usher
Accommodation: for 7, in farmhouses
and various guest houses.

*'Fairhope Fine Furniture Restoration
Course - 3, 5, 6 day courses in all
aspects of furniture restoration, french
polishing, marquetry, veneering,
upholstery. Max 4 students hands-on
accommodation.'*

## Centre 161
**Falconry Otter & Wildlife Sanctuary
(The)**                         est. 1987
Sprinks Lane
Kingsley
Nr Cheadle
Staffordshire
ST10 2BX
Tel: 0538 754784
Contact: V Hodges
Accommodation: for 6, B&B in guest
house.

*'Situated in the beautiful Churnet
Valley, the sanctuary also provides
educational and guided tours for day
visitors (by appointment).'*

## Centre 162
**Fallowfield School of
Motoring**                      est. 1972
The Cherries
Benllech
Anglesey
Gwynedd
LL74 85R
Tel: 0248 852029
Contact: Mr & Mrs Botham
Accommodation: for 6, half board,
self-catering or B&B in private house.

## Centre 163
**Farsyde Stud & Riding
Centre**                        est. 1957
Robin Hood's Bay
Whitby
Yorks
YO22 4UG
Tel: 0947 880249
Contact: Angela Green
Accommodation: full board or self-
catering in private cottages.

*'Yorkshire stone cottages in secluded
position amid spectacular coastal,
country and moors scenery. Close to old-
world village of Robin Hood's Bay and 6
miles from the ancient port of Whitby.'*

## Centre 164
**Fellowship Afloat Charitable
Trust**                         est. 1969
The Sail Lofts
Woodrolfe Road
Tollesbury
Essex CM9 8SE

Tel: 0621 868113
Contact: David Hillyer
Accommodation: for 36, full board on
floating residential centre.

𝄢

## Centre 165
**Felpham Sailing & Sports
School**          est. 1958
Sea Road
Felpham
Bognor Regis
Sussex PO22 7AN
Tel: 0243 826125
Contact: Bob Bonner:G7 871302
Contact: Chris South
Accommodation: for 50, half board,
self-catering or B&B in guest house,
caravan or camping.

## Centre 166
**Fen Farm Arts**          est. 1991
Fen Road
Blo Norton
Diss
Norfolk IP22 2JH
Tel: 0284 753110
Contact: Sally Worboyes
Accommodation: for 8, full board in resi-
dential converted 17th century barn.

*'17th century farmhouse and converted barn
in quiet country location. Walks, pub, windmill entirely suitable writing environment.
Comfortable accommodation. Excellent facilities and food (including vegetarian).'*

## Centre 167
**Fibrecrafts at Barnhowe**    est. 1985
Barnhowe
Elterwater
Cumbria
LA22 9HW
Tel: 096 67 346

Contact: M. Riley
Accommodation: for 5, B&B in guest
house.

## Centre 168
**First Ascent**          est. 1986
Far Cottage
Church Street
Longnor
Derbyshire
SK17 0PE
Tel: 0298 83545
Contact: Lizzie Hamer
Accommodation: for 8, full board in large
cottage.

## Centre 169
**Flatford Mill Field Centre**   est.1943
East Bergholt
Colchester
Essex
CO7 6UL
Tel: 0206 298283
Contact: The Warden
Accommodation: for 62, full board
residential at Centre.

## Centre 170
**Fly High Parascending/
Paragliding**          est. 1972
101 Heath Road
Barming
Maidstone
Kent
ME16 9JT
Tel: 0622 728230/0860 351130
Contact: Barry Clark
Accommodation: for 12, all types in
bunkhouse or camping

# Centres Index

**Centre 171**
**Focus Holidays**          est. 1987
Argoed Guest House
Trefriw
Llanrwst
Gwynedd LL27 0TX
Tel: 0492 640091
Contact: P. or K. Booth
Accommodation: for 10, full/half board
or B&B in guest house.
kids 🐐

**Centre 172**
**Forest of Arden Hotel**       est. 1989
Maxstoke Lane
Meriden
Warwickshire
CV7 7HR
Tel: 0676 22335
Contact: Louise Pritchard
Accommodation: half board at hotel.

**Centre 173**
**Fort Bovisand Underwater
Centre**                 est. 1970
Plymouth Ocean Projects Ltd
Plymouth
Devon PL9 0AB
Tel: 0752 408021
Contact: Jill Williams
Accommodation: for 120, all types in
dormitories, twin rooms or self-
catering units.

*'19th Century Fort on edge of Plymouth
Sand. Own harbour Bar with wonderful
views, cafe. Diving activities, marine
biology, underwater archaeology.'*

**Centre 174**
**Fortify the Spirit**          est. 1989
Wellrash Barn
Boltongate
Carlisle

Cumbria
CA5 1DH
Tel: 09657 522
Contact: Clive or Gaynor Wragg
Accommodation: for 12, full/half board
in hotels or self- catering.

**Centre 175**
**Fowey Cruising School**       est. 1972
32 Fore Street
Fowey
Cornwall
PL23 1AQ
Tel: 0726 832129
Contact: John Myatt
Accommodation: for 15, on board yacht
or in hotel.

**Centre 176**
**Freetime Activities**         est. 1988
Sun Lea
Joss Lane
Sedbergh
Cumbria
LA10 5AS
Tel: 05396 20828
Contact: Paul Ramsden
Accommodation: for 6, B&B in private
house.

**Centre 177**
**Freetime Holidays**          est. 1989
Runnelstone Cottage
St. Levan
Penzance
Cornwall
TR19 6LU
Tel: 0736 871302
Contact: Chris South
Accommodation: for 50, half board, self-
catering or B&B in guest house, caravan
or camping.

## Centre 178
**Freewheeling Trekking**
**Expeditions** est. 1992
Northcommon Farm
Golf Links Lane
Selsey
Sussex PO20 9DP
Tel: 0243 602725
Contact: Andrew Bunn
Accommodation: in hotel or guest
house or self-catering if client wishes.

## Centre 179
**Further Afield** est. 1989
Warcarr
Greenhead
Northumberland CA6 7HY
Tel: 06977 47358
Contact: D. Rozario
Accommodation: B&B in hotel, guest
house or farmhouse.

## Centre 180
**G & C Holidays Ltd** est. 1974
98 Coniston Road
Basingstoke
Hampshire RG22 5HZ
Tel: 0256 22303
Contact: C. Stefanopoulos
Accommodation: for 30, half board,
residential in school.

*'Located in picturesque Devon near
Exeter equipped with heated swimming
pool, sauna, solarium, gymnasium,
massage. Friendly bar and attractive
sun lounge.'*

## Centre 181
**Galloway Sailing Centre** est. 1989
Shirmers Bridge
Loch Ken

Castle Douglas
Kirkcudbrightshire
DG7 3NQ
Tel: 06442 626
Contact: Roddy Hermon
Accommodation: for 25+, camping on-
site or various local guest houses.

*'A friendly family run centre set in
beautiful Galloway. Excellent clubhouse facilities with kitchen and hot
showers. Private owners launching and
large selection of boats for hire.'*

## Centre 182
**Garden of England Cycling**
**Holidays** est. 1986
Barn Cottage
Boxley
Maidstone
Kent ME14 3DN
Tel: 0622 675891
Contact: J. Munson
Accommodation: in private houses,
farms or guest houses.

## Centre 183
**Gateway Education & Arts**
**Centre** est. 1984
Chester Street
Shrewsbury
Shropshire
SY1 1NB
Tel: 0743 367682
Contact: The Manager
Accommodation: lists of farm or
country accommodation available.
Ring for details.

*'This purpose built luxury centre on the
River Severn and 5 minutes walk from
medieval town centre offers a wide
variety of holidays breaks.'*

## Centre 184

**Genesis Leisure Ltd**        est. 1989
213 Belsize Avenue
Woodston
Peterborough
Cambridgeshire
PE2 9HY
Tel: 0733 555152
Contact: Martyn Price

## Centre 185

**Gibraltar Point Field Station**  est. 1972
Gibraltar Road
Skegness
Lincolnshire
PE24 4SU
Tel: 754 762677
Contact: Carl Hawke
Accommodation: for 28, full board at field station.

## Centre 186

**Gidleigh Park**        est. 1978
Chagford
Devon
TQ13 8HH
Tel: 0647 432367
Contact: Paul Henderson
Accommodation: for 32, half board in hotel.

## Centre 187

**Glanhelyg Painting Courses** est. 1984
Llechryd
Cardigan
Dyfed SA43 2NJ
Tel: 0239 87 482
Contact: Robin Holtom
Accommodation: for 8, full board in private country house.

## Centre 188

**Glencoe Outdoor Centre**     est. 1988
Glencoe
Argyllshire PA39 4HS
Tel: 08552 350
Contact: Chris Williams
Accommodation: for 36, full/half board or B&B in guest house or hotel.

## Centre 189

**Glenmore Lodge - Scottish National Sports Centre**        est. 1948
Aviemore
Inverness-shire
PH22 1QU
Tel: 0479 861276
Contact: Martin Burrows-Smith
Accommodation: for 60, full/half board residential or self-catering in chalets.

## Centre 190

**Glenmulliach Nordic Ski Centre**        est. 1987
Stronauaich
Tomintoul
Ballindalloch
Banffshire AB3 9ES
Tel: 08074 356
Contact: Jane Lannagan
Accommodation: all types in hotel, guest house or self-catering.

## Centre 191

**Gloucestershire Mountain Bike Tours**        est. 1992
4 Cheviot Close
Quedgeley
Gloucester
Gloucestershire
GL2 6TR
Tel: 0452 883936

Contact: Neil Webb
Accommodation: for 4-8, self-catering or B&B in farmhouse or hotel.

## Centre 192
**Goldnib Leisure**  est. 1991
33 St Catherine's Road
Harrogate
Yorkshire
HG2 8JZ
Tel: 0423 887880
Contact: P./D. Coupe-Robinson
Accommodation: for 30, full board in hotel.

*'Harrogate - historical spa town renowned for its elegant buildings and floral displays; offering speciality shops, Betty's tearooms, restaurants, concerts, theatre and the beautiful Yorkshire Dales.'*

## Centre 193
**Grafham Water Centre**  est. 1968
Perry
Huntingdon
Cambridgeshire PE18 0BX
Tel: 0480 810521
Contact: Mrs Illston/Mrs Dawson
Accommodation: for 56, full/half board or B&B at residential centre.

*'Grafham Water Centre is situated on the south shore of beautiful Grafham Water in the Huntingdonshire wolds sixty miles from London. Major credit cards accepted.'*

## Centre 194
**Grantley Hall**  est. 1949
Ripon
Yorkshire HG4 3ET
Tel: 0765 620259

Contact: Louise Dart
Accommodation: for 65, full board at residential college.

## Centre 195
**Great Glen School of
Adventure**  est. 1989
Great Glen Water Park
South Laggan
Spean Bridge
Inverness-shire
PH34 4EA
Tel: 08093 381
Contact: Ian Macleod
Accommodation: for 150 self-catering at centre or B&B and camping nearby.

## Centre 196
**Greenholme Holidays**  est. 1989
Greenholme Farm
Bewcastle
Carlisle
Cumbria
CA6 6PW
Tel: 06978 630
Contact: Geoff Price
Accommodation: for 16, full/half board in hotels and guest houses.

## Centre 197
**Hamble Dinghy Sailing
School**  est. 1985
Mercury Marina
Satchell Lane
Southampton
Hampshire SO3 5HQ
Tel: 0400 73003
Contact: C.P. Overton
Accommodation: for 50, all types in hotel or camping.

## Centre 198
**Harbour Sports Windsurfing**
**Centre** est. 1978
The Harbour
Paignton
Devon
TQ4 6DT
Tel: 0803 550180
Contact: F. Sobey/J. Smith
Accommodation: various off-site. Ring for details.

## Centre 199
**Harrogate Theatre Courses** est. 1988
Oxford Street
Harrogate
Yorkshire
HG2 8TH
Tel: 0423 502710
Contact: Jennifer Granville
Accommodation: for 40, full board in private house, guest house or hotel.
👟♿🐑

## Centre 200
**Hawkwood College** est. 1970
Painswick Old Road
Stroud
Gloucestershire
GL6 7QW
Tel: 0453 764607/759034
Contact: Stephanie Cooper
Accommodation: for 52, full/half board or B&B at residential college.

*'On the edge of the Cotswolds, Hawkwood in its peaceful 45 acres of gardens, fields and woods, commands a panoramic view of the Severn Vale.'*

## Centre 201
**Hazel Tree Farm** est. 1983
Hassell Street
Hastingleigh

Ashford
Kent TN25 5JE
Tel: 0233 750324
Contact: C. Gorell Barnes
Accommodation: for 12, full board in private house or guest house.

## Centre 202
**Head for the Hills** est. 1976
The Recreation Hall
Garth
Builth Wells
Powys LD4 4AT
Tel: 059712 388
Contact: Laurence Golding
Accommodation: for 12, full board in mobile camping unit.

*'Join guided group walkers gently penetrating Britains wild magical areas for few days. Vehicle-borne hotel-under-canvas enables us to travel light with rare freedom.'*

## Centre 203
**Headcorn Parachute Club**
Headcorn Aerodrome
Headcorn
Kent TN27 9HX
Tel: 0622 890862
Contact: Allison Drew
Accommodation: for 24, self-catering, residential on-site or camping.

## Centre 204
**Headland Hotel** est. 1987
Fistral Bay
Newquay
Cornwall TR7 1EW
Tel: 0637 872211
Contact: Mrs Armstrong/Miss Pearson
Accommodation: for 250, half board or B&B at hotel.
👟♿🐑

## Centre 205
**Heathfield House**          est. 1988
Okehampton
Devon
EX20 1EW
Tel: 0837 54211
Contact: Jane Seigal
Accommodation: for 10, half board or
B&B in guest house.

## Centre 206
**Helvellyn Youth Hostel**     est. 1984
Greenside
Glenridding
Penrith
Cumbria CA11 0QR
Tel: 07684 82269
Contact: The Warden
Accommodation: for 64, all types in
youth hostel.

## Centre 207
**HF Holidays Ltd**          est. 1913
Imperial House
Edgware Road
London NW9 5AL
Tel: 081 905 9556
Contact: The Reservations Dept
Accommodation: for 80, full board at
19 hotels nationwide.

*'HF country houses are located
throughout Britain, ususally in areas of
outstanding beauty, all with a traditional warm welcome and a unique
friendly atmosphere.'*

## Centre 208
**High Adventure**          est. 1981
Coastguard Lane
Freshwater Bay
Isle of Wight
PO40 9QX
Tel: 0983 752322
Contact: Mike McMillan
Accommodation: for 20, full/half board
or B&B at hotel.

## Centre 209
**High Force Training Centre** est. 1990
Forest in Teesdale
Barnard Castle
Co Durham
DL12 0HA
Tel: 0833 22302
Contact: Anthony Kelton
Accommodation: for 40, full board/
self-catering or B&B in dormitory at
residental centre.

## Centre 210
**High Loaning Head Adventure
Centre**                 est. 1982
Carrigill
Alston
Cumbria CA9 3EY
Tel: 0434 381929
Contact: The Administrator
Accomodation: for 20, all types in
outdoor education hostel.

## Centre 211
**High Plains Adventure Centre** est. 1988
High Plains Lodge
Alston
Cumbria
CA9 3DD
Tel: 0434 381886
Contact: D. Simpson
Accommodation: for 46, full board or
self-catering at Centre. Camping on
request.

## Centre 212
**High Trek Snowdonia**      est. 1986
Tal y Waen
Deiniolen
Gwynedd LL55 3NA
Tel: 0286 871232
Contact: Mandy Whitehead
Accommodation: for 7, full board, in various locations.

## Centre 213
**Higher Humber Farm**      est. 1992
Bishopsteignton
Teignmouth
Devon TQ14 9TD
Tel: 0626 775385
Contact: Sally Lang
Accommodation: 6, B&B in private house.
人

## Centre 214
**Highham Hall Residential Study Centre**      est. 1974
Bassenthwaite Lake
Cockermouth
Cumbria
CA13 9SH
Tel: 07687 76276
Contact: Freda Shaw
Accommodation: for 42, full board at Centre.
&

*'The Lake District's Residential Conference & Study Centre. Small and intimate. Well appointed. Wide range of courses. Good food. Spectacular situation with views over Skiddow.'*

## Centre 215
**Highland Drovers**      est. 1988
Kincardine Croft
Boat of Garten

Inverness-shire
PH24 3BY
Tel: 0479 83 329
Contact: Ailsa Clark
Accommodation: all types in hotels and guest houses.
人

## Centre 216
**Highland Riding Centre**      est. 1963
Borlum Farm
Drumnadrochit
Inverness-shire
IV3 6XN
Tel: 045 62 358
Contact: Ad MacDonald-Haig
Accommodation: B&B in farmhouse, self-catering in cottages and camping.
人

## Centre 217
**Highlander Mountaineering** est. 1989
Highlea
Auchnarrow
Glenlivet
Banffshire
AB37 9JN
Tel: 08073 250
Contact: Ravelle Hill
Accommodation: varying types in hotel, guest house, bunkroom or camping.

## Centre 218
**Hill Residential College**      est. 1967
Pen-y-Pound
Abergavenyy
Gwent
NP7 7RP
Tel: 0873 855221
Contact: L.J. Newcombe
Accommodation: for 82, full board on-site.

## Centre 219

**Hillscape Walking Holidays** est. 1984
Blaen-y-Dol
Pontrhydygroes
Ystrad Meurig
Dyfed
SY25 6DS
Tel: 097422 640
Contact: Richard or Anne Wilson
Accommodation: for 8, full board in guest house.

## Centre 220

**Hilton Hotels** est. 1986
PO Box 137
Watford
Hertfordshire
WD1 1DN
Tel: 0923 246464
Contact: Jean Butler
Accommodation: full board in hotel.

## Centre 221

**Holmhead Guest House** est. 1983
Greenhead-in-Northumberland
Carlisle
Cumbria
CA6 7HY
Tel: 06977 47402
Contact: P. Staff
Accommodation: for 12, half board, self-catering, and B&B in guest house.

*'Farmhouse situated in quiet valley on foundations of Hadrians Wall near river and 500 yards from golf course. 4 en-suite bedrooms and self-catering flat. Candlelit evening meals, dinner party style, using fresh produce.'*

## Centre 222

**How Hill Trust** est. 1984
How Hill Trust
Ludham
Great Yarmouth
Norfolk NR29 5PG
Tel: 0692 62 555
Contact: Sue Holmes
Accommodation: for 46, full/half board in guest house.

## Centre 223

**Howtown Outdoor** est. 1966
Ullswater
Penrith
Cumbria
CA10 2ND
Tel: 0768 486 508
Contact: Steve Mitchell
Accommodation: for 60, full board in dormitories.

*'The centre is owned by Durham Educational Authority. The centre head is a member of the Association of Heads of Outdoor Education Centres.'*

## Centre 224

**Icelandic Tapestry School** est. 1988
The Little Lynch
6 Behind Berry
Somerton
Somerset
TA11 7PD
Tel: 0458 73111
Contact: Jona Sparey
Accommodation: for 20, half board, self-catering and B&B in hotel and guest house.

# Centres Index

## Centre 225
**Images on Silk** est. 1989
Tregreenwell Farm Craft Centre
St Teath
Bodmin
Cornwall PL30 3JJ
Tel: 0208 851171
Contact: Jenni Milne
Accommodation: for 6, half board in
guest house within 1 mile of centre.

🏃🏃

## Centre 226
**Inniemore School of
Painting** est. 1967
Inniemore Lodge
Carsaig
Isle of Mull PA70 6HD
Tel: 06814 201
Contact: Julia Wroughton
Accommodation: for 20, full board/
self-catering in private house.

*'Painting courses run continuously
from May - mid-Sept. Full board in
lovely highland home overlooking the
Firth of Lorn. Professional tuition in a
relaxed and peaceful setting.'*

## Centre 227
**Inscape Fine Art Tours** est. 1986
Austins Farm
High Street
Stonesfield
Oxon OX7 8PU
Tel: 0993 891726
Contact: Carole Friend
Accommodation: half board in hotel.

*'An expert but companionable lecturer
and efficient courier accompany each
small group ensuring you maximum
involvement and minimum fuss.
Comfort at all times is top priority.'*

## Centre 228
**Instep Linear Walking
Holidays** est. 1987
35 Cokeham Road
Lancing
Sussex BN15 0AE
Tel: 0903 766475
Contact: Ann or Mick Hartley
Accommodation: for 16, in farm-
houses, guest houses and family run
hotels.

## Centre 229
**Institute of Heraldic & Genealogical
Studies** est. 1962
79-82 Northgate
Canterbury
Kent CT1 1BA
Tel: 0227 768664
Contact: Janet Carter
Accommodation: for 20-25, full board
in guest house.

*'Close to the city centre and archives.
Students can use the institute's
extensive genealogical facilities and
enjoy the tradition hospitality and
enthusiasm.'*

## Centre 230
**Instow Sailing Tuition
Centre** est. 1974
Cross Trees
Tavern Gardens
Weare Giffard
Devon EX39 4QR
Tel: 0237 421684
Contact: J.L. Bowers
Accommodation: various types
available locally.

*'RYA certificate courses all grades
over 6 days. Many sailing and shorter
courses available.'*

**Centre 231**
**Intensive Driving Course**    est. 1988
480 Sutton Road
Southend-on-Sea
Essex
SS2 5PN
Tel: 0702 600789
Contact: The Administrator
Accommodation: for 3, half board in
private guest house.
&

**Centre 232**
**International Warwick School**
**of Riding**    est. 1974
Guys Cliffe
Coventry Road
Warwick
Warwickshire
CV34 5YD
Tel: 0926 494313
Contact: Jan Martinez
Accommodation: for 35, full board in
residential dormitories.

**Centre 233**
**Inverclyde - Scottish National Sports**
**Centre**    est. 1980
Burnside Road
Largs
Ayrshire KA30 8RW
Tel: 0475 674666
Contact: Maureen Chantry
Accommodation: for 24, full board at
residential centre.

**Centre 234**
**Inversnaid Photography**
**Centre**    est. 1987
Inversnaid Lodge
Aberfoyle
Stirlingshire FK8 3TU
Tel: 087 786 254

Contact: Linda Middleton
Accommodation: for 12, full board in
restored hunting lodge.

*'Basic to advanced levels. Professional
tuition, studio,darkroom. Excellent
food and accommodation in restored
hunting lodge overlooking Loch
Lomond and spectacular mountain
scenery.'*

**Centre 235**
**Iris-Activity Breaks**    est. 1990
29 Alandale Drive
Pinner
Middlesex HA5 3UP
Tel: 081 866 3002
Contact: Iris Henry
Accommodation: B&B in hotel.

**Centre 236**
**ISCA Children's Holidays**    est. 1982
Bonnaford
Brentor
Tavistock
Devon PL19 0LX
Tel: 0822 810514
Contact: Paddy or Margaret Shephard
Accommodation: full board in boarding
school.

**Centre 237**
**Island Cruising Club**    est. 1951
10 Island Street
Salcombe
Devon TQ8 8DR
Tel: 0548 843481
Contact: Jools Bennett
Accommodation: for 60, full board/
B&B in cabins on a ferry.

**Centre 238**
**J.A.R. Services**            est. 1985
Garden House
45 Church Road
Saxilby
Lincolnshire LN1 2HH
Tel: 0522 703773
Contact: John Ramsbottom
Accommodation: for 45, full board in a
hotel.
&

**Centre 239**
**Jeremy Williams**
**Woodcarving**            est. 1982
Sycamore Cottage
Traboe
Helston
Cornwall TR12 6EA
Tel: 0326 23609
Contact: Jeremy Williams
Accommodation: half board in hotel or
guest house.

**Centre 240**
**John Bull School of**
**Adventure**            est. 1984
12 Littlethorpe Park
Ripon
Yorkshire
HG4 1UQ
Tel: 0765 604071
Contact: John Bull
Accommodation: for 20, all types in a
farmhouse, log cabins or converted
watermill.

**Centre 241**
**John Sharp Sailing (Fowey)** est. 1971
Brockles Quay
St Veep
Lostwithiel

Cornwall
PL22 0NT
Tel: 0208 872470
Contact: J. Sharp
Accommodation: for 10/20, cottages
are available and others types can be
arranged.

**Centre 242**
**Jordanhill College**            est. 1975
76 Southbrae Drive
Glasgow
G13 1PP
Tel: 041 950 3320
Contact: David Wilkie
Accommodation: for 230, all types in
hostel.

**Centre 243**
**Juniper Hall Field Centre**   est. 1943
(Field Studies Council)
Dorking
Surrey RH5 6DA
Tel: 0306 883849
Contact: Diane Seabright
Accommodation: for 14, full board in
residential Centre.

**Centre 244**
**Just Pedalling**            est. 1979
9 Church Street
Coltishall
Norfolk
NR12 7DW
Tel: 0603 737201
Contact: Alan Groves
Accommodation: B&B in guest house
and farmhouse.

## Centre 245
**Juvan Courses**                    est. 1987
Lower House
Mill Lane
Longhope
Gloucestershire
GL17 0AA
Tel: 0452 831348
Contact: Carol or Tony Lush
Accommodation: for 6, B&B in
residential and off-site guest house.

*'Juvan courses are run at Lower House
the home of Carol and Tony Lush.
Situated on the edge of the Forest of
Dean, Gloucestershire.'*

## Centre 246
**Kelly's Antiques**                    est. 1989
23/7 Stevenston Industrial Estate
Stevenston
Ayrshire
KA20 3LR
Tel: 0294 602920
Contact: Kris Edwin
Accommodation: for 5-6, all types in
hotel, guest house or camping.
泰 占 ㅠ

## Centre 247
**Keswick Mountaineering
School**                    est. 1988
24 Skiddaw Street
Keswick
Cumbria
CA12 4BY
Tel: 07687 73809
Contact: Paul Ross
Accommodation: B&B in guest house.

## Centre 248
**Kevin Walker Mountain
Activities**                    est. 1978
74 Beacons Park

Brecon
Powys
LD3 9BQ
Tel: 0874 625111
Contact: Kevin Walker
Accommodation: for 20, all types in
guest house and in chalet/bunkhouse.

*'Recognised by the mountainwalking
leader training board and the national
caving association training committee
as providers of official outdoor activity
training courses.'*

## Centre 249
**Kids Klub Activity Holidays**   est. 1987
The Hall
Great Finborough
Stowmarket
Suffolk
IP14 3EF
Tel: 0449 675907
Contact: Mike or Maggie Garling
Accommodation: for 300, full/half
board in dormitories.
泰 占

*'Independent school set in magnificent
grounds, with woodlands and river.
Individuals and groups catered for.
Please call Maggie or Mike for further
information and prices.'*

## Centre 250
**Kindrogan Field Centre**           est. 1965
Enochdu
Blairgowrie
Perthshire PH10 7PG
Tel: 0250 881286
Contact: Alastair Lavery
Accommodation: for 66, full board at
Centre.
泰 占

## Centre 251

**Kirkbeag Craft**                est. 1987
Kincraig
Kingussie
Inverness-shire PH21 1ND
Tel: 0540 651298
Contact: John Paisley
Accommodation: for 5, full board at
establishment.

＊＊

*'Pleasant homely workshop in con-
verted church. Workshop days can be
supplemented by exploring our
beautiful countryside by foot, car,
bicycle or canoe. Non-participating
partners welcome.'*

## Centre 252

**KLC Interior Design
Training**                est. 1982
KLC House
Sprinvale Terrace
London W14 0AE
Tel: 071 602 8592
Contact: Julia Bottwood
Accommodation: varies, contact
registrar for list of local families, etc.

*'KLC is based in West London in easy
reach of a wide range of galleries,
museums and theatres.'*

## Centre 253

**Ladytrek-Ladytour**                est. 1988
'Junipers'
Leacanashie
Lochcarron
Wester Ross IV54 8YD
Tel: 05202 238
Contact: Jean Stewart
Accommodation: for 6-8, full board in
on-site cottage.

&

## Centre 254

**Lakeland Photographic
Holidays**                est. 1986
Fern Howe
Braithwaite
Keswick
Cumbria
CA12 5SZ
Tel: 07687 78459
Contact: Lesley Dent
Accommodation: for 12, full board in
guest house.

＊＊

## Centre 255

**Lancaster University Summer
Programme**                est. 1980
Cartmel College
Lancaster
Lancashire
LA1 4YL
Tel: 0524 382118
Contact: Ralph Maddams
Accommodation: for 1000, full board
in campus student residence.

＊＊ &

*'Free evening entertainment including
barn dance, quizzes, competitions,
debates, music. Close to lakes and
Dales. Friendly atmosphere. Use of
University Sports Centre.'*

## Centre 256

**Land Ends**                est. 1991
Watermillock
Ullswater
Cumbria
CA11 0NB
Tel: 07684 86438
Contact: Roy Murphy
Accommodation: for 39, all types, on-
site rooms and log cabins.

＊＊ &

*'3 miles from Ullswater. Converted farmhouse in 7 acres ground with 2 small lakes. All ensuite facilites. Bar. Spectacular scenery. Peaceful location. 2 studios.'*

**Centre 257**
**Laneside Weavers**          est. 1984
Bonnngate
Crook
Kendal
Cumbria LA8 8JX
Tel: 0539 821269
Contact: Joanna Somervell
Accommodation: for 5, full board/B&B in private house.
♁ 14+

*'Weekly holiday courses weaving, spinning, dyeing. Full board or tuition only. Beginners welcome. Small groups. April-October. Lake district in beautiful, peaceful surroundings.'*

**Centre 258**
**Laser School & Cat. Clinic** est. 1984
Grafham Water
Perry
Cambridgeshire PE18 0BU
Tel: 0480 812288
Contact: Pat Oxley
Accommodation: for 20, B&B in hotel, guest house or self-catering camping or in cottages.
♁

**Centre 259**
**Lasham Gliding Society**     est. 1956
Lasham Aerodrome
Alton
Hampshire GU34 5SS
Tel: 0256 381322/381270
Contact: The Manager
Accommodation: for 17, full board, single bed rooms on-site.

**Centre 260**
**Learn at Leisure**          est. 1985
Dept of Adult Education
University of Nottingham
Nottingham
Nottinghamshire
NG1 4FJ
Tel: 0602 516526
Contact: Sylvia Stephens
Accommodation: for groups of 15-25 at hotels, field stations or university campus.

**Centre 261**
**Lejair Ltd**                est. 1985
Shetland
Chapel Lane
Beeston
Norfolk PE32 2NG
Tel: 0328 701602
Contact: Tony or Rona Webb
Accommodation: for 15, B&B/half board at guest house/private house/ hotel, or camping.
♁

*'Wide open spaces purpose made field for flying microlight flights, paragliding possibilities coastal activities sailing, walking, wild life in North Norfolk windsurfing.'*

**Centre 262**
**Lightfoot**                 est. 1990
Nanquitho
Leedstown
Hayle
Cornwall TR14 8QQ
Tel: 0736 850715
Contact: Stuart MacKenzie
Accommodation: for 30, full board at hotels/B&B/guest houses/farmhouses or inns.

**Centre 263**
**Limes Farm Holiday Centre** est. 1983
Hawkinge
Folkestone
Kent CT18 7DZ
Tel: 0303 892335
Contact: Ann Berry
Accommodation: for 12, full board at
hostel.

**Centre 264**
**Linguisport Sailing School** est. 1991
8 Gunton Cliff
Lowestoft
Suffolk NR32 4PE
Tel: 0502 564442
Contact: Alison Knights
Accommodation: for 15, various
arrangements.

**Centre 265**
**Linnhe Marine Boating
Centre** est. 1983
Lettershuna
Appin
Argyllshire PA38 4BL
Tel: 0631 73227
Contact: The Manager
Accommodation: for up to 6, in private
house, self-catering or hotel.

**Centre 266**
**Little Benslow Hills** est. 1929
Benslow Music Trust
Ibberson Way
Hitchin
Hertfordhshire SG4 9RB
Tel: 0462 459446
Contact: Course Administrator
Accommodation: for up to 55, full
board residential at Centre.

**Centre 267**
**Living Wood Training** est. 1985
159 Cotswold Road
Windmill Hill
Bristol
Avon BS3 4PH
Tel: 0272 636244
Contact: Mike Abbott
Accommodation: for 8, B&B in guest
house, or self-catering in camping
facilities.

**Centre 268**
**Llangorse Riding Centre** est. 1960
Gilfach Farm - Llangorse
Brecon
Powys LD3 7UH
Tel: 087 484 272
Contact: Irene Thomas
Accommodation: all types in guest
houses/hotels, or camping.

**Centre 269**
**Loch Insh Watersports
& Skiing Centre** est. 1962
Insh Hall
Kincraig
Inverness-shire PH21 1NU
Tel: 0540 651272
Contact: The Secretary
Accommodation: for 60, all types in
residential hall.

**Centre 270**
**Loch Morar Adventure
Centre** est. 1966
Bracora
Mallaig
Inverness-shire
PH40 4PE
Tel: 0687 2164
Contact: H.R. Jenkins

Accommodation: for 10, self-catering on-site, or various off-site arrangements.

'Tuition or hire- sailing, canoeing, fishing,painting, photography, wild-life observation for small family groups. Magnificent scenic area: inland loch and nearby coastal region.'

## Centre 271

**Logie Farm Riding Centre** est. 1965
Glenferness
Nairn
Nairnshire
IV12 5XA
Tel: 0309 651226
Contact: Mrs Hilleary
Accommodation: for 6, full board/B&B in private house, guest house, or self-catering in cottage or caravan.

'One of Scotlands most beautiful riding centres situated in the lovely Findhorn valley. Riding, fishing, painting, bird watching, golf courses, beaches, castles and theatre.'

## Centre 272

**London Gliding Club** est. 1977
Tring Road
Dunstable
Bedfordshire LU6 2JP
Tel: 0582 663419
Contact: Valerie Abercrombie/ Margaret Clark
Accommodation: for 12, full board, dormitory.

'Stunning scenery, flying facility and walking. Bar and restaurant every evening in season.'

## Centre 273

**Lower Aston House Pottery and Painting School** est. 1981
Aston Bank
Knighton-on-Teme
Tenbury Wells
Worcestershire
WR15 8LW
Tel: 0584 79404
Contact: Tina Homer
Accommodation: for 18, full board in private country houses.

## Centre 274

**Lydbury English Centre** est. 1985
The Old Vicarage
Lydbury North
Shropshire
SY7 8AU
Tel: 05888 233
Contact: Duncan Baker
Accommodation: for 10, full board in residential/private or hotel.

## Centre 275

**Lydford House & Riding Stables** est. 1980
Lydford House Hotel
Lydford
Okehampton
Devon
EX20 4AU
Tel: 082 282 347
Contact: R.E. Boulter
Accommodation: for 23, half board/ B&B in country house hotel.

**Centre 276**
**Lyme Regis Painting**
**Workshops**          est. 1985
Long Close
Clappentail Lane
Lyme Regis
Dorset DT7 3LZ
Tel: 0297 442937
Contact: The Administrator
Accommodation: for 6, full board in
private house.

🏃

**Centre 277**
**Lyncombe Lodge**          est. 1976
Avon Ski Centre-Mendip Riding
Centre
Churchill
Bristol
Avon
BS19 5PG
Tel: 0934 852335
Contact: Helen Tripp/Mrs. Lee
Accommodation: for 35, halfboard or
B&B, in farmhouse hotel.

🏃🐕

**Centre 278**
**Malham Tarn Field Centre** est. 1947
(Field Studies Council)
Malham
Settle
Yorkshire BD24 9PU
Tel: 0729 830331
Contact: Mr Iball
Accommodation: for 80, full board, at
Centre.

🏃♿

**Centre 279**
**Manor School of Fine**
**Cuisine (The)**          est. 1988
Old Melton Road
Widmerpool

Nottinghamshire
NG12 5QL
Tel: 0949 81371
Contact: Claire Gentinetta
Accommodation: for 8, full/halfboard
or B&B in georgian manor house.

🏃♿🐕

**Centre 280**
**Marlborough College Summer**
**School**          est. 1975
Marlborough
Wiltshire
SN8 1PA
Tel: 0672 513888
Contact: David Green/Glynis Lewis
Accommodation: for 500, full board, in
school boarding houses.

🏃

**Centre 281**
**Maryland Residential**
**College**          est. 1967
Leighton Street
Woburn
Milton Keynes
Buckinghamshire
MK17 9JD
Tel: 525 290688
Contact: Mary Rolls
Accommodation: for 38, full board,
residential at the college.

♿

*'The food is excellent, the lectures of
the highest standard and make learning
experiences easy. The setting in the
countryside is idyllic. Full brochure
sent free.'*

**Centre 282**
**Medway Sea School**          est. 1987
7 Covered Slip
Historic Dockyard

Chatham
Kent
ME4 4TE
0634 402518
Contact: C. Mason
Accommodation: for 5, full board on
yachts.

**Centre 283**
**Mendip Gliding Club**       est. 1975
Halesland Airfield
New Road
Draycott
Somerset
BS27 3SJ
0934 412728
Contact: Peter Turner
Accommodation: List of recommended
B&Bs, and camping. Ring for details.

*'Mendip Gliding Club is situated on the
top of the Mendip Hills near Cheddar
enjoying stunning views across
Somerset. There are many local tourist
attractions.'*

**Centre 284**
**Mendip Outdoor Pursuits**   est. 1987
Laurel Farmhouse - Summer Lane
Banwell
Weston-super-Mare
Avon
BS24 6LP
0934 820518
Contact: Jim Hayward
Accommodation: for 40, all types,
camping, bunkhouse, YHA or hotel.

**Centre 285**
**Merlin Mountain Activities** est. 1990
PO Box 726

Llanrwst
Gwynedd
LL26 0PZ
0492 641241
Contact: David Taylor
Accommodation: for 50, all types at
guest and bunk houses.

**Centre 286**
**Merlin Parachute Centre**   est. 1982
4 Manfield Terrace
Carlton Miniott
Thirsk
Yorkshire
YO7 4NE
0845 524713
Contact: Janet Rawlinson
Accommodation: for 36, B&B in local
guest houses, or camping.

**Centre 287**
**Metamorphic Association**   est. 1979
67 Ritherdon Road
Tooting
London SW17 8QE
081 672 5951
Contact: G. St-Pierre
Accommodation: for 3, B&B in private
house.

**Centre 289**
**Michael O'Donnell -
Woodturner**                 est. 1984
The Croft
Brough
Thurso
CaithnessKW14 8YE
084 785 605
Contact: Claire Miller
Accommodation: varying in off-site
hotel, guest house, or camping.

## Centre 289

**Middlewich Narrowboats**   est. 1971
66 Canal Terrace
Middlewich
Cheshire
CW10 9BD
Tel: 060 684 2460
Contact: Mr Cliff/Mrs Cormack
Accommodation: for 12, self-catering in canal boat.

*'Relaxing canal holidays on comfortable 4-12 berth traditional narrowboats. Cruise through our beautiful countryside and pretty villages. No experience required. Full tuition given.'*

## Centre 290

**Midland Gliding Club**   est. 1934
Long Mynd
Church Stretton
Shropshire SY6 6TA
Tel: 058861 206
Contact: Janet Stuart
Accommodation: for 20+, full board in on-site bunk houses or private rooms.

## Centre 291

**Mill Farm Riding Centre**   est. 1976
Hughley
Shrewsbury
Shropshire
SY5 6NT
Tel: 074636 645
Contact: Elizabeth Bosworth
Accommodation: for 6, full board/B&B in farmhouse, camping also available for up to 20.

## Centre 292

**Mill on the Brue Activity Centre**   est. 1982
Trendle Farm - Tower Hill
Bruton
Somerset BA10 OBA
Tel: 0749 812307
Contact: T. Rawlinson Plant
Accommodation: for 50, full board at Centre.

*'Based in 20 acres of its own fields, woods and river. There are over 30 activities on-site. Qualified, experienced instructors, comfortable accommodation, excellent food. Winner of National Heartbeat Award.'*

## Centre 293

**Millfield School Village of Education**   est. 1971
Millfield School
Street
Somerset
BA16 0YD
Tel: 0458 45823
Contact: Carolyn Steer
Accommodation: for 900, full board in residential boarding schoolhouses.

## Centre 294

**Millnain**   est. 1990
Blackwater
Tarvie
Strathpeffer
Ross-shire
IV14 9EJ
Tel: 0997 414331
Contact: Martin Sedgley
Accommodation: for 6, full/half board or B&B in guest house.

*View from Millnain guest house.*

## Centre 295
**Minerva Training**          est. 1975
Plas Glansevin
Llangadog
Dyfed
SA19 9HY
Tel: 0550 777121
Contact: Gill Thornton
Accommodation: for 40, full board at
residential centre.

## Centre 296
**Missenden Abbey**          est. 1979
Great Missenden
Buckinghamshire
HP16 0BD
Tel: 02406 6811
Contact: Barbara Cooke
Accommodation: for 63, full board at
abbey or B&B in village.

*'Missenden Abbey for weekend
courses, Easter and Summer Schools.
Arts, crafts, textiles, music, natural
sciences, sport for beginners and more
advanced students.'*

## Centre 297
**Monmouth Canoe Hire &
Activities Centre**          est. 1981
Castle Yard
Old Dixton Road
Monmouth
Gwent
NP5 3DP
Tel: 0600 713461
Contact: Sue or Graham Symonds
Accommodation: youth hostel or B&B.
Ring for details.

## Centre 298
**Moonfleet Manor Hotel &**
**Sports Resort**        est. 1986
Weymouth
Dorset
DT3 4ED
Tel: 0305 786948
Contact: B. Hemingway
Accommodation: for 60, all types in
on-site hotel.

*'Georgian Manor House, 5 acres
countryside alongside the English
Channel. Many sporting facilities,
indoor pool, bowls, squash, tennis,
snooker, automatic skittles.'*

## Centre 299
**Moss Farm Riding**        est. 1986
Bradford
Blisland
Bodmin
Cornwall
PL30 4LF
Tel: 0208 850628
Contact: Mrs Dibbs/Mrs Corney
Accommodation: for 6, half board/
B&B in farmhouse, and self-catering in
various arrangements for an additional 6.

## Centre 300
**Motherby House Activities**   est. 1981
Motherby
Penrith
Cumbria CA11 0RJ
Tel: 07684 83368
Contact: Jacqui Freeborn
Accommodation: for 72, all types at on-
site guest house and nearby youth hostel.

## Centre 301
**Motor Safari**        est. 1983
Pinfold Lane
Buckley
Clwyd CM7 3NW
Tel: 0244 550440
Contact: Stephanie Thomas
Accommodation: variety of local
establishments to choose from.

## Centre 302
**Mountain & Water**        est. 1989
3a Riverside Business Park
New Road
Crickhowell
Powys NP8 1AT
Tel: 0873 811 887
Contact: Pam Bell/Phil Swaine
Accommodation: all types at various
off-site locations.

## Centre 303
**Mountain Adventure Guides**   est. 1985
Eel Crag
Melbecks
Braithwaite
Cumbria CA12 5TL
Tel: 07687 78517
Contact: Stuart Miller
Accommodation: all types available as
required.

## Centre 304
**Mountain Craft**        est. 1986
Glenfinnan
Fort William
Inverness-shire PH37 4LT
Tel: 039783 213
Contact: Simon Powell
Accommodation: various, ring for
details.

## Centre 305

**Mountain Stream Activities** est. 1987
Wydemeet
Hexworthy
Yelverton
Devon
PL20 6SF
Tel: 03643 215
Contact: Kevin Chamberlain
Accommodation: for 34, all types, in
private house and chalet.

## Centre 306

**Mountain Ventures Ltd**    est. 1981
120 Allerton Road
Liverpool
L18 2DG
Tel: 051 734 2477
Contact: The Manager
Accommodation: for 47, full/half board
in hostel/hotel or camping.

## Centre 307

**Mounts Bay Art Centre**    est. 1977
Trevatha
Newlyn
Penzance
Cornwall
TR18 5DJ
Tel: 0736 66284
Contact: Bernard Evans
Accommodation: for 12, full board in
private house or hotel.

*'Landscape painting weeks on the
superb coastline of West Cornwall.
Fishing ports, caves and rugged cliffs.
Individual tuition, illustrated talks and
studio. Beginners welcome.'*

## Centre 308

**Mowbray School of Porcelain
Restoration**    est. 1989
Flint Barn
West End Lane
Essendon
Hertfordshire AL9 5RQ
Tel: 081 367 1786
Contact: Maureen Aldridge
Accommodation: half board/B&B
available in hotels or guest houses.

*'Studio located in tranquil Hertford-
shire countryside offering a relaxed
atmosphere and skilled tuition. A very
spacious and well equipped school.
Central London just 40 minutes by
train from local station.'*

## Centre 309

**Mulberry House Studio**    est. 1987
Mulberry House
The Ridings
Headington
Oxon
OX3 8TB
Tel: 0865 61033
Contact: Joanna Seaward
Accommodation: various local options,
contact organisation for information.

## Centre 310

**Mylor Sailing School**    est. 1970
Mylor Yacht Harbour
Nr. Falmouth
Cornwall
TR11 5UF
Tel: 0326 377633
Contact: Jan Robson
Accommodation: for 20, various
arrangements in hotel, cottages, flats,
guest houses or camping.

## Centre 311

**Nairn Craft Holidays**          est. 1991
The Court House
High Street
Nairn
Inverness-shire IV12 4AU
Tel: 0667 56144
Contact: Hugh Allison
Accommodation: for 80, self-catering or
B&B in hotel, guest house or caravan.
🧍♿🐎

## Centre 312

**National Operatic & Dramatic
Association**          est. 1899
NODA House
1 Crestfield Street
London WC1H 8AU
Tel: 071 837 5655
Contact: The Administrator
Accommodation: for 150, full board at
university halls of residence.

## Centre 313

**National Trust**          est. 1895
PO Box 12
Westbury
Wiltshire BA13 4NA
Tel: 0373 826826
Contact: Beryl Sims
Accommodation: for 20, full board at
base camps and bunk houses.

## Centre 314

**Nettlecombe Court**          est. 1968
The Leonard Wills Field Centre
Field Studies Council
Williton
Taunton
Somerset TA4 4HT
Tel: 0984 40320
Contact: The Warden
Accommodation: for 80, full board at
residential centre.

## Centre 315

**Newlyn Workshops**          est. 1991
Tolcarne Farmhouse
Newlyn
Penzance
Cornwall
TR18 5QH
Tel: 0736 330284
Contact: Mary Oliver/Piers Owen
Accommodation: for 8, full/half board
or B&B in private house.
🧍

## Centre 316

**Newton Ferrers Sailing School** est. 1956
Westerly
Yealm Road
Newton Ferrers
Devon
PL8 1BJ
Tel: 0752 872 375
Contact: A. Thomson
Accommodation: for 12, full board on-
site, or B&B at local guest houses,
hotels or camping.

## Centre 317

**Norfolk Cycling Holidays**          est. 1987
Sandy Way
Ingoldisthorpe
King's Lynn
Norfolk
PE31 6NJ
Tel: 0485 540642
Contact: Ken or Suzanne Gibson
Accommodation: for 16, B&B in guest
house/private house or hotel.
🧍

## Centre 318

**North-West Frontiers**          est. 1985
19 West Terrace
Ullapool
Ross-shire

IV26 2UU
Tel: 0854 612571
Contact: Andrew Bluefield
Accommodation: for 8, half board/
B&B in hotel or guest house.

## Centre 319
**North Wheddon Farm Riding**
**Holidays** est. 1972
Wheddon Cross
Minehead
Somerset
TA24 7EX
Tel: 0643 841224
Contact: Jon Trouton
Accommodation: for 8, half board/
B&B at guest house or hotel.

## Centre 320
**North York Moors Adventure**
**Centre** est. 1978
Ingleby Cross
Northallerton
Yorkshire
DL6 3PE
Tel: 060982 571
Contact: Ewen Bennett
Accommodation: for 24, full board/
B&B at outdoor activity Centre.

## Centre 321
**Northern Microlight School** est. 1982
89a Croston Road
Garstang
Preston
Lancashire
PR3 1HQ
Tel: 0995 604694
Contact: Graham or Claire Hobson
Accommodation: B&B or camping.

## Centre 322
**Northfield Farm Riding**
**Centre** est. 1976
Flash
Nr Buxton
Derbyshire
SK17 0SW
Tel: 0298 22543
Contact: E. Andrews
Accommodation: B&B in guest house
or self-catering.

## Centre 323
**Northumbria Experience**
**(The)** est. 1989
Marketing Office - University of
Durham
Co Durham
DH1 3PH
Tel: 091 374 3454
Contact: Margery Gill
Accommodation: full board at residen-
tial college.

*'The Northumbria Experience holidays*
*include full board, tours led by*
*university accredited guides, evening*
*talks and entertainment, centred in*
*modern university accommodation in*
*historic Durham.'*

## Centre 324
**Northumbria Horse Holidays** est. 1975
East Castle
Annfield Plain
Stanley
Co Durham
DH9 8PH
Tel: 0207 235354/230555
Contact: The Booking Department
Accommodation: for 80, full board in
hotel.

**Centre 325**
**Northumbrian Recorder & Violin School** est. 1971
College of St Hild & St Bede
5 Birchgrove Avenue
Durham
Co Durham
DH1 1DE
Tel: 091 374 3000
Contact: Marlene Austin
Accommodation: for 100+, full/half board in university hall of residence.

**Centre 326**
**Oathill Farm Riding Centre** est. 1982
Pound Lane
Molash
Canterbury
Kent
CT4 8HQ
Tel: 0233 740573
Contact: A.J. Doree
Accommodation: for 18 up to, full board in farmhouse.

**Centre 327**
**Ocean Youth Club** est. 1960
The Bus Station
South Street
Gosport
Hampshire
PO12 1EP
Tel: 0705 528421
Contact: The Manager
Accommodation: for 12, full board on board a range of vessels.

'Ocean Youth Club exists to help all young people, especially those disadvantaged by discrimination or social or financial circumstances to develop *responsibility about themselves and others.'*

**Centre 328**
**Old Vicarage (The)** est. 1985
Kirkwhelpington
Northumberland
NE19 2RT
Tel: 0830 40319
Contact: Hilary Wells
Accommodation: for 10, full board in a private house.

**Centre 329**
**Orielton Field Centre** est. 1958
(Field Studies Council)
Pembroke
Dyfed
SA71 5EZ
Tel: 0646 661225
Contact: The Warden
Accommodation: for 40, full board at Centre.

**Centre 330**
**Ossian Guides** est. 1988
Sanna
Newtonmore
Inverness-shire
PH20 1DT
Tel: 0540 673402
Contact: Dig Bulmer/Jim Neill
Accommodation: for 24, full board in hotels/guest houses, camping on trek.

**Centre 331**
**Outdoor Adventure** est. 1981
Atlantic Court
Widemouth Bay
Bude
Cornwall
EX23 0DF
Tel: 0288 361312

Contact: R.H. Gill
Accommodation: for 26, full board at residential activities centre.

*'Adventure Sports Holidays and Windsurfing courses. Weeks and weekends. 16+ individual groups. Windsurfing canoeing surfing ski-surfing climbing mountain biking. Seafront centre. Lively evenings and bar.'*

### Centre 332
**Outward Bound Trust**    est. 1941
Chestnut Field
Regent Place
Rugby
Warwickshire
CV21 2PJ
Tel: 0788 560423
Contact: Niki Brisby
Accommodation: full board at residential centre.

&

### Centre 333
**Oystercat Cruises**    est. 1984
5 Poundfield Gardens
Woking
Surrey
GU22 8JP
Tel: 0483 772442
Contact: Brian Huntley
Accommodation: for 4, full board on board catamaran.

### Centre 334
**P&Q Sailing Centre**    est. 1974
Deer Park Lodge
Mannings Lane
Woolverstone
Suffolk
IP9 1AP
Tel: 0473 780293

Contact: Cy Blackwell
Accommodation: for 5, full board on yacht or self-catering in caravan.

*'Delightful river-side base. Cruising in sheltered inland rivers and estuary with fully qualified RYA Doft Skipper. Tuition to Royal Yachting Association Certificate Standard if required.'*

### Centre 335
**Parc-le-Breos Riding & Holiday Centre**    est. 1963
Parc-le-Breos House
Parkmill
Gower
West Glamorgan
SA3 2HA
Tel: 0792 371636
Contact: O. Edwards
Accommodation: for 30-40, full/half board/B&B in farmhouse.

*'18th century farmhouse on beautiful Gower Peninsula 10 miles from Swansea. Riding holidays our speciality other activities by arrangement.'*

### Centre 336
**Park Farm Studios Ltd**    est. 1985
Riseley Road
Bletsoe
Bedford
Bedfordshire
MK44 1QU
Tel: 0234 708132
Contact: Ian & Elisabeth Davies
Accommodation: for 12, varies, off-site private house/hotel.

**Centre 337**
**Park Grove Hotel (The)**    est. 1987
Kimberley Park Road
Falmouth
Cornwall
TR11 2DD
Tel: 0326 313276
Contact: Ian Dempsey
Accommodation: for 32, half board/ .
self-catering at hotel.
斺 ♞

**Centre 338**
**Paul San Casciani Stained Glass**
**Activities**    est. 1982
11 Dale Close
Thames Street
Oxford
Oxon
OX1 1TU
Tel: 0865 727529
Contact: Paul San Casciani
Accommodation: for 6, B&B at
college.

**Centre 339**
**Peak Hang Gliding Ltd**    est. 1977
4B Abbey Units
Macclesfield Road
Leek
Staffordshire
ST13 8LD
Tel: 0538 383659
Contact: Mike Orr
Accommodation: various, contact
organisation for details.

**Centre 340**
**Peak National Park Study**
**Centre**    est. 1972
Losehill Hall
Castleton
Derbyshire
S30 2WB

Tel: 0433 620373
Contact: Patsy Smith
Accommodation: for 60, full board in
country house hotel.
斺

**Centre 341**
**Peak School of Hang Gliding** est. 1978
The Elms
Wetton
Nr. Ashbourne
Derbyshire
DE6 2AF
Tel: 033 527 257
Contact: John Clarke
Accommodation: for 30, various types
including youth hostels.

*'2,5 day courses to BHGA certificate
levels in the Peak National Park. Open
all year. Featured on BBC2 Alternative
Holiday Show. Contact the friendly
professionals.'*

**Centre 342**
**Pedalaway**    est. 1987
Trereece Barn
Llangarron
Ross-on-Wye
Herefordshire HR9 6NH
Tel: 0989 770 357
Contact: Hilary Carpenter
Accommodation: various, arranged by
request.
斺 ♿

**Centre 343**
**Pencerrig Walking Holidays** est. 1991
Pencerrig Country House Hotel
Pencerrig
Bulith Wells
Powys LD2 3TF
Tel: 0982 553226
Contact: Peter Bennett

Accommodation: for 20, full board at Hotel.

人 占 🐎

*'Luxury accommodation amid the rolling hills of mid Wales. An ideal setting and location for the Brecon Beacons, Elan Valley and the Black Mountains.'*

### Centre 344
**Pennine Hang Gliding Centre** est. 1983
18 Scape View
Golcar
Huddersfield
Yorkshire
HD7 4DH
Tel: 0484 641306
Contact: Keith Cockroft
Accommodation: for 24, all types, in guest house or camping.

### Centre 345
**PGL Adventure Holidays** est. 1957
Alton Court
990 Penyard Lane
Ross-on-Wye
Herefordshire HR9 5NR
Tel: 0989 768768
Contact: The Reservations Department
Accommodation: full board at activity centres and summer schools for 6 - 18 year olds.

### Centre 346
**PGL Family Adventure** est. 1957
Alton Court
990 Penyard Lane
Ross-on-Wye
Herefordshire HR9 5NR
Tel: 0989 768768
Contact: The Reservations Department
Accommodation: full board or self-

catering at family centres, colleges and summer schools.

人

### Centre 347
**Philharmonic Study Tour Club** est. 1992
47 King Edward's Gardens
London W3 9RF
Tel: 081 993 2196
Contact: Alastair Mitchell
Accommodation: for 15, full/half board at hotel.

占

### Centre 348
**Photographer's Place (The)** est. 1976
Bradbourne
Ashbourne
Derbyshire DE6 1PB
Tel: 033525 392
Contact Paul or Angela Hill
Accommodation: for 12, full board, shared residential area at Place, or camping.

### Centre 349
**Pitlochry Angling** est. 1989
Pluscarden Cuilc Brae
Pitlochry
Perthshire PH16 5QS
Tel: 0796 472567
Contact: Ian Jeffrey
Accommodation: Ring organisation for recommendations.

### Centre 350
**Plant Papers** est. 1983
Romilly
Brilley
Hereford
Herefordshire HR3 6HE
Tel: 0497 831546
Contact: Maureen Richardson

# Centres Index

## Centre 351
**Plas Menai National Watersports Centre** est. 1982
Caernarfon
Gwynedd
LL55 1UE
Tel: 0248 670964
Contact: Bob Bond
Accommodation: for 115, full/half board or B&B at hotel in on-site houses.

*'The UK's leading watersports centre, ideally located on the scenic Menai Strait. Award-winning residential complex includes heated indoor pool, residents' lounge and bar.'*

## Centre 352
**Pointdrake Ltd** est. 1988
Manor Farm
Chaigley
Clitheroe
Lancashire
BB7 3LS
Tel: 0254 826591
Contact: Amelia Dalton
Accommodation: for 12, full board on board cruise boat.

*'We offer activity holidays from a comfortable boat on the West coast of Scotland visiting remote islands and lochs including St Kilda and the Outer Hebrides.'*

## Centre 353
**Port Edgar Sailing School** est. 1979
Shore Road
South Queensferry
West Lothian EH30 9SQ
Tel: 031 331 3330

Contact: Oliver Ludlow
Accommodation: varies, contact organisation for list of local guest houses, hotels and camping sites.

*'Scotland's largest sailing school offering a wide range of courses at all levels. An excellent area for family holidays or combining sailing with the Edinburgh Festival.'*

## Centre 354
**Pound Cottage Riding Centre** est. 1985
Luccombe Farm
Milton Abbas
Dorset
DT11 0QB
Tel: 0258 880057/451240
Contact: Jacky Hardy
Accommodation: for 4 children, full board, with family; there are local guest houses for adults.

## Centre 355
**Premier** est. 1988
138 Lynn Road
Wisbech
Cambridgeshire
PE13 3DP
Tel: 0945 585052
Contact: P.J. Parish
Accommodation: for 12, B&B in guest house, or self-catering.

## Centre 356
**Preseli Mountain Bikes & Sea Kayaking** est. 1988
Parcynole Fach
Mathry
Haverfordwest
Pembrokeshire
SA62 5HN

Tel: 0348 837709
Contact: Sophie Parker
Accommodation: for 10, half board/
self-catering at centre.

## Centre 357
**Preston Montford Field
Centre** est. 1943
(Field Studies Council)
Montford Bridge
Nr. Shrewbury
Shropshire
SY4 1DX
Tel: 0743 850380
Contact: J.A. Bayley
Accommodation: for 100+, full board,
at Centre.

## Centre 358
**Prime Leisure Activity
Holidays Ltd** est. 1986
7 Streatfield House
Alvescot Road
Carterton
Oxon
OX18 3X2
Tel: 0993 840192
Contact: Caroline or Ben
Accommodation: for 100, full board,
residential at school.

## Centre 359
**Professional Mountaineering
Services** est. 1988
Calluna
Heathercroft
Fort William
Inverness-shire
PH33 6RE
Tel: 0397 700451
Contact: Alan Kimber

Accommodation: for 8, self-catering
flat or B&B, guest houses also
available in area.

## Centre 360
**Purple Flame School of
Aromatherapy** est. 1980
61 Clinton Lane
Kenilworth
Warwickshire
CV8 2 BY
Tel: 0926 55980
Contact: Christine Sapsford
Accommodation: for 20, full/half board
at hotel.

## Centre 361
**Queen Mary Sailsports** est. 1982
Queen Mary Sailing Club
Ashford Road
Ashford
Middlesex
TW15 1UA
Tel: 0784 248881
Contact: C. Wand-Tetley
Accommodation: half board/B&B at
hotel or guest house.

## Centre 362
**R & L Adventures** est. 1979
Knotts Farm
Patterdale Road
Windermere
Cumbria LA23 1NL
Tel: 053 94 45104
Contact: Linda Rutland

## Centre 363
**Raasay Outdoor Centre** est. 1984
Raasay House
Isle of Raasay
Ross-shire
IV40 8PB

Tel: 047 862 266
Contact: Kathryn MacNeil
Accommodation: for 60, all types in
bunk house, or camping.

🚶🐕

*'The centre is based in a georgian
mansion on Raasay (off Skye). Spec-'
tacular views, wide and varied wildlife.
Accommodation is bunkroom style with
excellent food.'*

## Centre 364
**Ramblers Holidays Ltd**       est. 1946
PO Box 43
Welwyn Garden City
Hertfordshire AL8 6PQ
Tel: 0707 331133
Contact: E.A. Chamberlain
Accommodation: for 20, full board in
guest house.

## Centre 365
**Ranch Adventure**       est. 1973
The Wharf
Pensarn Harbour
Llanbedr
Gwynedd LL45 2HS
Tel: 034 123 358
Contact: Dave Newbould
Accommodation: for 92, full board at
residential centre.

🚶♿

## Centre 366
**Recollect Doll Studios**       est. 1968
The Old School
London Road
Sayers Common
Sussex BN6 9HX
Tel: 0273 833314
Contact: Carol Jackman
Accommodation: suggestions are
included in application form.

## Centre 367
**Redfern Hotel (The)**       est. 1974
Cleobury Mortimer
Shropshire
DY14 8AA
Tel: 0299 270395
Contact: Jon Redfern
Accommodation: for 22, full/half board
or B&B at Hotel.

🚶🐕

## Centre 368
**Rhiwiau Riding Centre**       est. 1972
Llanfairechan
Gwynedd
LL33 0EH
Tel: 0248 680094
Contact: Ruth Hill
Accommodation: for 25, full board in
on-site farm guest house.

🚶

## Centre 369
**Roaches Leisure**       est. 1988
Roaches House
Upper Hulme
Leek
Staffordshire ST13 8TZ
Tel: 0538 300232
Contact: Jacqueline Wildman
Accommodation: for 12-15, 3 self-
catering units on-site.

## Centre 370
**Rob Hastings Adventure**       est. 1986
25 Southcourt Avenue
Leighton Buzzard
Bedfordshire
LU7 7QD
Tel: 0525 379881
Contact: The Manager
Accommodation: full board at guest
house or dormitory.

🚶♿

## Centre 371

**Robingarth Lace**       est. 1988
46 Edinburgh Road
Peebles
Tweeddale EH45 8EB
Tel: 0721 720226
Contact: Evelyn Inglis
Accommodation: for 5, B&B in private
house.

## Centre 372

**Rock Lea Activity Centre**   est. 1978
Station Road
Hathersage
Sheffield
Yorkshire S30 1DD
Tel: 0433 650345
Contact: Iain Jennings
Accommodation: for up to 90, all types
at outdoor Centre.

## Centre 373

**Rockley Point Sailing
School**       est. 1976
Rockley Sands
Poole
Dorset BH15 4LZ
Tel: 0202 677272
Contact: Barbara Gordon
Accommodation: for 80, all types
available.

*'Sailing holidays courses for all ages
and abilities. Accommodation can be
provided. Residential children welcome. RYA recognised.'*

## Centre 374

**Rose Narrowboats Ltd**    est. 1974
Fosse Way
Stretton-under-Fosse

Nr. Rugby
Warwickshire CV23 0PU
Tel: 0788 832449
Contact: Bryan Ambrose
Accommodation: for 12, self-catering
on board a boat.

## Centre 375

**Rosebrook Equestrian Centre** est. 1979
South Lopham
Nr. Diss
Norfolk IP22 2JP
Tel: 0379 88 592
Contact: Diane Elliott
Accommodation: local B&B.

## Centre 376

**Rua Fiola Island Exploration
Centre**       est. 1975
Cullipool
Oban
Argyllshire PA34 4TZ
Tel: 03873 72240
Contact: Margaret or Torquil Johnson-
Ferguson
Accommodation: for 40, full board in
private hostel.

## Centre 377

**Sail Training Association**   est. 1956
2a The Hard
Portsmouth
Hampshire PO1 3PT
Tel: 0705 832055/6
Contact: Esther Tibbs
Accommodation: for 39, full board on
board 3-masted 150 ft topsail schooner.

*'Become the crew of Britain's largest
schooners 'Sir Winston Churchill' and
'Malcolm Miller'. Adventure voyages
for those aged 16-24 and 21-69.'*

## Centre 368

**Saltglaze Workshops**       est 1991
Bo-Peep Lane
Selmeston
Nr. Polegate
Sussex BN26 6UH
Tel: 0323 811517
Contact: Sarah Walton
Accommodation: for 6, B&B in local
guest houses, or camping.

*'The workshop is sited 3/4 mile from the
South Downs amongst beautiful farmland. Places of local interest include
Saxon churches, country houses,
including Charleston Farmhouse, and the
towns of Eastbourne, Lewes and Brighton.'*

## Centre 379

**Sancreed School of Painting** est. 1991
The High Barn
Sancreed
Penzance
Cornwall
TR20 8QY
Tel: 0736 788 705
Contact: Dee or Robin Hirtenstein
Accommodation: for 8, B&B in private
house.

## Centre 380

**Sceptre Promotions**       est. 1985
97 Elton Road
Stibbington
Peterborough
Cambridgeshire PE8 6JX
Tel: 0780 782093
Contact: B. or G. Neal
Accommodation: for 1000, full/half
board or self-catering in holiday camps.

## Centre 381

**School of Casting, Salmon & Trout
Fishing**                    est. 1962
Station House
Clovenfords
Galashiels
Selkirkshire TD1 3LU
Tel: 089685 293
Contact: Michael Waller/Margaret
Cockburn
Accommodation: for 8, full board in
off-site hotel.

## Centre 382

**Scope Sport - Redesdale Riding
Centre**                     est. 1987
Soppitt Farm
Otterburn
Northumberland NE19 1AF
Tel: 0830 20276 before May 1993
Tel: 0830 520276 after May 1993
Contact: Jo Deniel-Rowe
Accommodation: all types, and on-site
dormitory for unaccompanied children.

*'Situated in beautiful North Northum-
berland, surrounded by farmland,
forestry, moorland, the peace and
tranquility suits all. All staff are
suitably qualified.'*

## Centre 383

**Scot-Ed Courses**          est. 1985
7 Kew Terrace
Edinburgh
EH12 5JE
Tel: 031 346 0150
Contact: John or Christine Young
Accommodation: all types, hotel, guest
house, college residential or host
family.

## Centre 384
**Scotsell Ltd**                  est. 1980
2D Churchill Way
Bishopbriggs
Glasgow
G64 2RH
Tel: 041 772 5928
Contact: T. Hart
Accommodation: for 10/20, full board
at hotel.

🏃

## Centre 385
**Scottish Centres**              est. 1947
Loaningdale House
Carwood Road
Biggar
Lanarkshire
ML12 6LX
Tel: 0899 21115
Contact: Karen Lamb
Accommodation: for 250, all types in
cedar wood chalets at Centre.

🏃 ♿

## Centre 386
**Scottish Cycling Holidays**   est. 1979
Ballintuim
Nr. Blairgowrie
Perthshire
PH10 7NJ
Tel: 0250886 201
Contact: Kenneth Todd
Accommodation:  youth hostels, guest
houses or hotels.

## Centre 387
**Scottish Parachute Club**      est. 1962
Strathallan Airfield
Auchterarder
Perthshire
PH3 1LA
Tel: 0764 62572/63430
Contact: Fiona Davidson

Accommodation: all types at local
guest houses.

## Centre 388
**Scottish Youth Hostels**       est. 1931
7 Glebe Crescent
Stirling
Stirlingshire
FK8 2JA
Tel: 0786 51181
Contact: Alan Mitchell
Accommodation: full board or self-
catering at youth hostel.
♿ (at certain locations)

## Centre 389
**Scottish-Norwegian Ski
School**                         est. 1957
Speyside Sports
Main Road
Aviemore
Inverness-shire
PH22 1PD
Tel: 0479 810656
Contact: C. Sutton
Accommodation: Ring Scottish tourist
office for information on 0479 810363.

## Centre 390
**Sealyham Activity Centre**     est. 1986
Wolfscastle
Haverfordwest
Pembrokeshire
SA62 5NF
Tel: 0348 840763
Contact: Mrs Richards
Accommodation: for 100, all types, in
mansion house dormitory at Centre.

🏃

*'Multi-activity holidays for all ages.
Groups and individuals catered for.
Activites include canoeing, sailing,
rock climbing and pony trekking.'*

## Centre 391
**Seaways - Truro Diving**
**Services** est. 1980
38 Lemon Street
Truro
Cornwall
TR1 2NS
Tel: 0872 77652
Contact: J.R. or S.J. Ellis
Accommodation: all types available,
contact organisation for recommenda-
tions.

## Centre 392
**Severn Valley Sports** est. 1983
9 Orchard Street
Wotton-under-Edge
Gloucestershire
GL12 7EZ
Tel: 0453 842892
Contact: Stephen Carter
Accommodation: for 65 aged 6-17, full
board in private school dormitory.
🏃

## Centre 393
**Shaftesbury Homes Venture**
**Centre** est. 1975
Lower Upnor
Rochester
Kent
ME2 4XB
Tel: 0634 719933
Contact: David Hudson/Martin Smith
Accommodation: for 80, full board or
self-catering in on-site dormitory and
small bunk rooms.
🏃

*'Courses are mainly for schools and
youth organisations from disadvantaged city areas. Situated in a rural
environment beside River Medway
close to historic Rochester.'*

## Centre 394
**Shinafoot Fine Art Studios** est. 1988
Shinafoot
Auchterarder
Perthshire PH3 1DU
Tel: 0764 63639
Contact: Margaret Evans
Accommodation: for 12, any type,
arrange to suit all price brackets.
♿

## Centre 395
**Shorelands** est. 1988
Malltraeth
Anglesey
Gwynedd LL62 5AT
Tel: 0407 840396
Contact: Paul Rogers
Accommodation: for 6, full board or
B&B in guest house.
🏃

## Centre 396
**Shoreline Leisure** est. 1979
15 Crooklets
Bude
Cornwall EX23 8NE
Tel: 0288 354039/352452
Contact: Simon Hammond
Accommodation: for 45, half board in
hotel.
🏃

*'Hotel situated in superb beach/town
location. Magnificent unspoilt countryside. 5 choice menu daily, colour T.V.,
tea/coffee in all rooms.'*

## Centre 397
**Silverweed** est. 1987
Post Office House
Parc-y-Rhos
Cwmann
Lampeter

Dyfed
SA48 8DZ
Tel: 0570 423 254
Contact: Hanna Lindenberg
Accommodation: for 2, B&B for
females only in private house.

## Centre 398

**Sinbad Charters**　　　　est. 1983
Aidenkyle House
Aidenkyle Road
Kilcreggan
Nr. Helensburgh
Dunbartonshire
G84 0HP
Tel: 0436 84 2247
Contact: Peter Waddington
Accommodation: for 5, self-catering on
board 36' yacht.
人 と (limited) 🐑

## Centre 399

**SKADI - Women's Walking
Holidays**　　　　est. 1985
High Grassrigg Barn
Killington
Sedbergh
Cumbria LA10 5EN
Tel: 05396 21188
Contact: Paula Day
Accommodation: for 6, full board in
private house.
人

## Centre 400

**Skaigh Stables Farm**　　est. 1964
Belstone
Okehampton
Devon EX20 1RD
Tel: 0837 840429
Contact: Rosemary Hooley
Accommodation: for 10, full board or
B&B, chalet at Farm.

*'Residential riding holidays on a
Dartmoor farm. Also riding for non-
residents. Good fit horses. Unrivalled
natural riding country.'*

## Centre 401

**Skern Lodge**　　　　est. 1976
Appledore
Bideford
Devon EX39 1NG
Tel: 0237 475992
Contact: Jenny Prince
Accommodation: for 140, full board at
outdoor activity and training centre.
人 と

*'Over twenty exciting activities including
canoeing, surfing, sailing, and climbing.
Qualified staff, all equipment provided,
excellent staff ratios. The professional
outdoor centre.'*

## Centre 402

**Ski Wildcountry**　　　　est. 1987
Alvey House Hotel
Golf Course Road
Newtonmore
Inverness-shire PH20 1AT
Tel: 0540673 260
Contact: Andy McLay
Accommodation: for 14, full board, in
family run small hotel.

## Centre 403

**Skydragons Paragliding**　est. 1989
43 Tan Y Bryn
Pwllglas
Ruthin
Clwyd LL15 2PJ
Tel: 082 42 7171
Contact: Audrey or Noel Humphreys
Accommodation: various off-site
arrangements can be arranged to suit
needs.

# Centres Index

## Centre 404
**Skyes'l Charters**   est. 1987
36 Bernisdale
Nr. Portree
Isle of Skye IV51 9NS
Tel: 047 032 413
Contact: Vicki Samuels
Accommodation: for 6, full board on board sailing boat.

🚶🏻

*'Help us to sail a 1915 traditional 60' Gaff Cutter amongst the most magnificent scenery in Britain! Warm companionship, wholesome food and exciting sailing.'*

## Centre 405
**Skysports**   est. 1978
36 Hatherleigh Road
Abergavenny
Gwent NP7 7RG
Tel: 0873 856112
Contact: Ian Phillips
Accommodation: for 12, all types available.

## Centre 406
**Slapton Ley Field Centre**   est. 1959
(Field Studies Council)
Kingsbridge
Devon TQ7 1QP
Tel: 0548 580466
Contact: The Warden
Accommodation: for 87, full board, residential in centre.

## Centre 407
**Slate Hall Riding Centre**   est. 1973
Main Street
Nr. Seahouses
Northumberland
NE68 7UA
Tel: 0665 720320

Contact: M. Nicol
Accommodation: for 6, B&B at farmhouse, or self-catering.

## Centre 408
**Sleat Marine Services**   est. 1983
Ardvasar
Isle of Skye
IV45 8RU
Tel: 047 14 216/387
Contact: John Mannall
Accommodation: for 6-8, self-catering on board cruising yachts.

*'Yachts bare boat or skippered off West Coast of Scotland including Saint Kilda. Charts also available for very experienced crews to Orkney, Shetland, Faeroes and Iceland.'*

## Centre 409
**Smithy Art Studio (The)**   est. 1991
Stowford Moor Cottage
Collingsdown Cross
Buckland Brewer
Bideford
Devon
EX39 5NN
Tel: 0409 261325
Contact: Trudy Friend
Accommodation: for 5, full/half board or B&B in guest house.

## Centre 410
**Snail Trail Handweavers**   est. 1976
Penwenallt Farm
Cilgerran
Cardigan
Dyfed
SA43 2TP
Tel: 0239 841228
Contact: Martin or Nina Weatherhead

Accommodation: for 12, (6) full board at guest house and (6) self-catering in 5 berth caravan or camping.

🚶‍♂️ ♿ 🐕

## Centre 411
**Snape Maltings**
Riverside Centre      est. 1981
Snape Maltings
Nr. Saxmundham
Suffolk
IP17 1SR
Tel: 0728 688305
Contact: Julia Pipe
Accommodation: off-site locations can be recommended by organisation.

## Centre 412
**Solent Coastal & Offshore Sailing School**      est. 1975
48 Cranford Road
Petersfield
Hampshire GU32 3NA
Tel: 0730 262531
Contact: Mike or Mo Burt
Accommodation: for 5, full board on board training yacht.

🚶‍♂️

## Centre 413
**SPICE**      est. 1982
26 Mount Road
Dagenham
Essex
RM8 1NA
Tel: 081 595 4403
Contact: June Tuck
Accommodations: varies with each activity.

*'SPICE - the multi adventure club for those would like to eat fire, balloon, wet bike, bungee, rally and so much more.' Phone 081 595 4403.*

## Centre 414
**St. George's Island Craft Centre**      est. 1965
St. George's Island
The Craft Centre
Looe
Cornwall
PL13 2AB
Tel: 0836 522919
Contact: R.A. or E.E. Atkins
Accommodation: for 8, self-catering in cottage or chalet.

🚶‍♂️

## Centre 415
**St. Michaels of Falmouth**      est. 1982
Gyllyngvase Beach
Seafront
Falmouth
Cornwall TR11 4NB
Tel: 0326 312707
Contact: David Glover/Eleanor Hodges
Accommodation: various options at Hotel. Ring for details.

🚶‍♂️ ♿ 🐕

## Centre 416
**Starlight Studio**      est. 1989
Hilles Cottage
Edge
Gloucestershire
GL6 6NU
Tel: 0453 750919
Contact: Rod Friend
Accommodation: local B&Bs.

## Centre 417
**Step by Step Walking**      est. 1986
Hambledon Hotel
11 Queens Road
Shanklin
Isle of Wight
PO37 6AW
Tel: 0983 862403

Contact: Norman Birch
Accommodation: for 22, full/half board
or B&B in hotel.

ᛘᛘ

*'Discover unspoilt beauty on the Isle of
Wight - superb views and scenery. Stay
in quality en-suite accommodation.
Walkers welcomed at all times. Open
all year. We understand your needs.'*

## Centre 418
**Stonelands Activity Holidays**  est. 1986
Stonelands School of Dance & Drama
Ashcombe Road
Dawlish
Devon
EX7 9BL
Tel: 0626 866708
Contact: Liz Filpi
Accommodation: for 50, full board,
residential vocational school.

ᛘᛘ

## Centre 419
**Straw Craft Studios**        est. 1978
Cowarne Hall Cottages
Much Cowarne
Herefordshire HR7 4JQ
Tel: 0432 820317
Contact: Mrs Bradbury
Accommodation: for 8, all types in
school house and cottages.

ᛘᛘ

## Centre 420
**Stubbers Outdoor Centre**    est. 1973
Ockendon Road
Upminister
Essex RM14 2TY
Tel: 04022 24753
Contact: The Secretary
Accommodation: for 200, all types in
residential hostel, self-contained

cottage, or camping.

ᛘᛘ

*'Full range of outdoor and adventure
activities organised by highly qualified
staff: abseiling, climbing, canoeing,
windsurfing, archery and campcraft.
Environmental base and cultural visits
to London.'*

## Centre 421
**Styal Workshop**             est. 1977
Quarry Bank Mill
Styal
Cheshire SK9 4LA
Tel: 0625 527468
Contact: Alice Uren
Accommodation: a list of local lodgings
is available from the organisation.

&

## Centre 422
**Suffolk College Summer
School**                       est. 1986
Argyle Street
Ipswich
Suffolk
IP4 2NA
Tel: 0473 255885 x 203/434
Contact: Audrey Semple/Lindsey Webb
Accommodation: all off campus.

*'Two weeks of leisure learning in July
with over 100 courses based in
Ipswich, Norwich (in conjunction with
the University of East Anglia) and
abroad'*

## Centre 423
**Summer Academy**             est. 1986
School of Continuing Education
The University of Canterbury
Kent
CT2 7PD

Tel: 0227 470402
Contact: Andrea Nicholaides
Accommodation: full board at university halls of residence.
&(at Sheffield & Stirling only) 🐏

## Centre 424
**Summer Isles Marine**          est. 1974
119 Polglass
Achiltibuie
Ross-shire IV26 2YG
Tel: 085 482 366
Contact: Neil Murray
Accommodation: for 6, B&B, in guest house or hotel, or camping.

## Centre 425
**Summer University**          est. 1968
University of Loughborough
Leicstershire LE11 3TU
Tel: 0509 222189
Contact: Colin Groves
Accommodation: for 2000, full board in residential student blocks or at a 5-star short course centre.

## Centre 426
**Sunnybanks Tennis Farm**     est. 1975
Fletchers Bridge
Bodmin
Cornwall PL30 4AN
Tel: 0208 75048
Contact: James Webster
Accommodation: for 20, full board at Tennis Farm.

## Centre 427
**Surface Watersports**        est. 1981
Whitwell Sailing Centre
Rutland Water
Empingham

Leicestershire
LE15 8QS
Tel: 078 086 464
Contact: David Hales

## Centre 428
**Surfrider Activity Holidays** est. 1990
Montague Farm
6 Watery Lane
Croyde
Devon
EX33 1NQ
Tel: 0271 890083
Contact: Steve Rosenbaum
Accommodation: for 30, all types, guest houses and camping.

## Centre 429
**Sussex College of Hang Gliding & Paragliding**          est. 1980
10 Crescent Road
Brighton
Sussex BN2 3RP
Tel: 0273 609925
Contact: Tim Cox
Accommodation: for 12, all types, organisation will help in placement.

## Centre 430
**Sussex Seen**                est. 1981
14 Maltravers Street
Arundel
Sussex BN18 9BU
Tel: 0903 882474
Contact: Sally Godfrey
Accommodation: for 15, full board in private, mainly period, houses.

## Centre 431
**Swansea Parachute Club**     est. 1983
Swansea Airport
Fairwood Common
Swansea

West Glamorgan
SA2 7JU
Tel: 0792 296464
Contact: David Howerski
Accommodation: various types
available locally.

## Centre 432
**Taliesin Trust**          est. 1990
Ty Newydd
Llanystumdwy
Cricieth
Gwynedd LL52 0LW
Tel: 0766 522811
Contact: Sally Baker
Accommodation: for 16, full board at
the centre.

## Centre 433
**Talland Bay Hotel**        est. 1972
Talland Bay
Nr Looe
Cornwall
PL13 2JB
Tel: 0503 72667
Contact: The Manager
Accommodation: for 50, half board or
B&B at hotel.

## Centre 434
**Tama Sailing**           est. 1970
55 Eastern Road
Thorpe St Andrew
Norwich
Norfolk
NR7 0UJ
Tel: 0603 35431
Contact: Tony Cannell
Accommodation: full/half board or
self-catering on board yacht.

*'Sail the beautiful East Coast. Full
range of RYA cruising courses, novice
to yachtmaster. Also holiday cruises.
For friendly expert tuition by professional instructors.'*

## Centre 435
**Taunton Summer School**      est. 1980
Room 11
Taunton School
Staplegrove Road
Taunton
Somerset
TA2 6AD
Tel: 0823 276543
Contact: Diana Atkinson
Accommodation: for 250, full board in
independent boarding school.

*'Over 60 courses to suit 7-70+.
Situated on the outskirts of Taunton, it
is ideal for excursions into the surrounding countryside. All inclusive
prices: food, accommodation, course
tuition, evening entertainments, use of
sports facilities.'*

## Centre 436
**Temewalk**             est. 1987
Sunny Side
Knucklas
Knighton
Powys LD7 1PR
Tel: 0547 520363
Contact: Angie Davies
Accommodation: 8 full board or B&B
in guest house.

## Centre 437
**Tennis Coaching
International**           est. 1965
Woodlands Tennis Centre

15 Thurleigh Road
Milton Ernest
Bedfordshire
MK44 1RF
Tel: 02302 2914
Contact: Peter G. Smith
Accommodation: for 43, all types,
residential at centre or in guest house,
hotel or private houses.

## Centre 438
**Terrick Hall Country
Hotel (The)**          est. 1987
Hill Valley
Whitchurch
Shropshire
SY13 4JZ
Tel: 0948 3031
Contact: A. or H.C. Hotham
Accommodation: for 48, full/half board
or B&B in hotel.

## Centre 439
**Tighnabruaich Sailing
School**          est. 1965
Tighnabruaich
Argyll
PA21 2BD
Tel: 0700 811396
Contact: D R Stephens
Accommodation: all types in hotel,
guest house, camping, hostel or private
house.

*'Tighnabruaich Sailing School is well
known for high quality instruction in a
holiday setting amidst the beautiful
Kyles of Bute. Based in quiet Scottish
village.'*

## Centre 440
**TM International School of
Horsemanship**          est. 1983
Sunrising Riding Centre
Henwood
Nr. Liskeard
Cornwall
PL14 5BP
Tel: 0579 62895
Contact: Captain E.W.R. Moore
Accommodation: for 20, full board, in
private house.

*'Instruction in riding and jumping to
all levels, novices and unaccompanied
youngsters welcome. Wonderful
hacking on Bodmin Moor. Approved by
the British Horse Society, A.B.R.S., and
Ponies Ass. (U.K.).'*

## Centre 441
**Torquay Boardsailing Centre &
School**          est. 1978
55 Victoria Road
Ellacombe
Torquay
Devon TQ1 1HX
Tel: 0803 212411
Contact: A.R. or M.D. Shorland
Accommodation: ring for details.

## Centre 442
**Towers Adventure Centre** est. 1978
Promenade
Llanfairfechen
Gwynedd
LL33 0DA
Tel: 0248 680012
Contact: L.C. Goodey
Accommodation: for 20, all types in
guest house or self-catering in apart-
ments.

## Centre 443
**Traditional School of Falconry**
6 Wilson Road
Coseley
Bilston
West Midlands
WV14 9NE
Write for details.
Contact: Mr W. Hawkins-Pinchers
Accommodation: for 4, half board or
B&B in guest house.

*'W. Hawkins-Pinchers teach's falconry at a professional level, incorporating North American, European and Middle East traditions. Enjoy these activities in wonderful English countryside and the spectacular sights of the Middle East.'*

## Centre 444
**Trans-Wales Trails**          est. 1972
Cwmfforest Riding Centre
Nr. Talgarth
Brecon
Powys LD3 0EU
Tel: 0874 711398
Contact: Michael or Maria Turner
Accommodation: for 10, full board or
B&B in guest house.

## Centre 445
**Transcotland Holiday
Expeditions**          est. 1985
216 Newhaven Road
Edinburgh
EH6 4QE
Tel: 031 552 8360
Contact: Chris Gurner
Accommodation: for 12, full board in
hotel or guest house.

## Centre 446
**Trevone Hotel**          est. 1924
Mount Wise
Newquay
Cornwall
TR7 2BP
Tel: 0637 873039
Contact: Pam Chegwin
Accommodation: for 50+, half board in
hotel.

*'Guests are given a weekly programme for each holiday with expert local leaders for each subject. It is accepted that they may opt out at any time if they wish to do so. Friendly house party atmosphere with many returning guests.'*

## Centre 447
**Trewysgoed Riding Centre**   est. 1976
Fforest
Nr. Abergavenny
Gwent
NP7 7LW
Tel: 0873 890296
Contact: Sarah Fetherstonhaugh
Accommodation: for 15, full/half board
or B&B in private house.

*'Trewysgoed offers B.H.S. qualified instruction and mountain hacks in the heart of the unspoilt Black Mountains. Comfortable farmhouse accommodation with swimming pool. Trout fishing.'*

## Centre 448
**Tufton Arm Hotel (The)**     est. 1989
Market Square
Appleby-in-Westmorland
Cumbria
CA16 6XA

Tel: 07683 51593
Contact: Nigel or Bill Milsom
Accommodation: for 33 full/half board
or B&B in hotel.

**Centre 449**
**Turret Art Holidays**    est. 1989
The Heugh
Gwydyr Road
Crieff
Perthshire
PH7 4EX
Tel: 0764 2523
Contact: Alison Shand
Accommodation: for 12, full board in
private house or guest house.

**Centre 450**
**Tweed Valley Hotel**    est. 1973
Tweed Valley Hotel
Galashiels Road
Walkerburn
Peebles-shire
EH43 6AA
Tel: 089 687 636
Contact: Charles or Keith Miller
Accommodation: for 32, half board in
hotel.

**Centre 451**
**Twr-y-Felin Outdoor**
**Centre**    est. 1986
St Davids
Pembrokeshire
Dyfed
SA62 6QS
Tel: 0437 720391
Contact: Marion Coombes
Accommodation: for 32 full/half board
or B&B in hotel, or camping.

*'Range of activities including canoe-
ing, climbing, surfing, windsurfing and
orienteering, within a few minutes
drive. Courses tailored to your
requirements in the Pembrokeshire
Coast National Park.'*

**Centre 452**
**Tymawr Farm**    est. 1990
Glascoed
Pontypool
Gwent
NP4 0TF
Tel: 049528 243
Contact: C. Sainsbury
Accommodation: for 3, self-catering in
converted byre.

**Centre 453**
**U.K. Sailing Centre**    est. 1988
West Cowes
Isle of Wight
PO31 7PQ
Tel: 0983 294 941
Contact: Linda Dixons
Accommodation: for 134, full board,
residential at Centre.

**Centre 454**
**Uist Outdoor Centre**    est. 1992
Oern Dusgaidh
Lochmaddy
Isle of North Uist
Outer Hebrides
PA82 5AE
Tel: 08763 480
Contact: Niall Johnson
Accommodation: for 20, full board or
self-catering at residential centre.

## Centre 455
**University of Birmingham**
School of Continuing Studies
Edgbaston
Birmingham
West Midlands
B15 2TT
Tel: 021 414 5615
Contact: Judith Burl
Accommodation: for 30, full/half board
in university halls of residence.

## Centre 456
**University of Cambridge**
Board of Extra Mural Studies
Madingley Hall
Cambridge
Cambridgeshire
CB3 8AQ
Tel: 0954 210636
Contact: The Courses Registrar
Accommodation: for 53, full board in
residential Centre.
♿

## Centre 457
**University of Manchester**
Department of Extra Mural Studies
Manchester
M13 9PL
Tel: 061 275 3273
Contact: Jackie Boyd
Accommodation: self-catering in
university halls of residence.

## Centre 458
**University of Oxford**
**Summer School**
Department for Continuing Education
1 Wellington Square
Oxford
Oxon
OX1 2JA
Tel: 0865 270396

Contact: Anna Sandham
Accommodation: for 48, full board in
residential cente.
♿

*'Oxford University welcomes anyone
who enjoys serious study to join a wide
range of seminars conducted by some
of the finest tutors in the country.'*

## Centre 459
**University of Stirling**
Department of Continuing Education
Stirling
Stirlingshire
FK9 4LA
Tel: 0786 67940
Contact: The Administrator
Accommodation: full board in univer-
sity halls of residence.

## Centre 460
**Upper House Farm**     est. 1988
Dilwyn
Hereford
Herefordshire HR4 8JJ
Tel: 05447 245
Contact: Diana Hoare
Accommodation: for 6, full/half board,
B&B in farmhouse.
🧍🐕

## Centre 461
**Urchfont Manor College**     est. 1950
Urchfont
Nr. Devizes
Wiltshire
SN10 4RG
Tel: 0380 840495
Contact: Gill Reed
Accommodation: for 55, full board in
residential college.

## Centre 462
**Urchinwood Manor Equitation**
**Centre**                    est. 1979
Congresbury
Bristol
Avon BS19 5AP
Tel: 0934 833248
Contact: H.C. Watts
Accommodation: for 10, full board or
B&B in private house.

## Centre 463
**Valley School of Floristry**   est. 1985
12 Cann Hall Drive
Bridgnorth
Shropshire WV15 5BG
Tel: 0746 761302
Contact: D.R. Cardwell
Accommodation: half board in small
family hotel.

*'Bridgnorth neighbours areas of
outstanding natural beauty and great
historic interest (e.g. Ironbridge). Itself
boasting a steam railway, river, cliff
railway, leisure centre, cinema,
theatre.'*

## Centre 464
**Wales Wildlife Holidays**     est. 1987
Tainewyddion-Uchaf
Cwymstwyth
Dyfed
SY23 4AF
Tel: 097422 672
Contact: Mr or Mrs Liford
Accommodation: for 6, full board in
guest house.

## Centre 465
**Walkers' Britain**            est. 1990
131a Heston Road
Hounslow
Middlesex
TW5 0RD
Tel: 081 569 6627
Contact: Trina Willis
Accommodation: for escorted groups
of up to 15, B&B in hotel.

*'Walk along ancient trails and discover
Britain's history the real way. Dramatic scenery, age-old castles and
churches and much, much more! All
luggage is transported for you.
Escorted and unescorted walks
available.'*

## Centre 466
**Wansfell College**            est. 1949
30 Piercing Hill
Theydon Bois
Epping
Essex CM16 7LF
Tel: 0992 813027
Contact: The Principal
Accommodation: for 50+, full board,
residential at College.

## Centre 467
**Wasdale Mountain Walking**
**Holidays**                    est. 1980
Old Strands Cottage
Wasdale
Cumbria
CA20 1ET
Tel: 09467 26258
Contact: David Killick
Accommodation: for 4, full board in
private cottage.

**Centre 468**

**Water Lily Weavers**          est. 1987
Homestead Craft Centre
The Hirsel
Coldstream
Berwickshire
TD12 4LR
Tel: 0890 2977
Contact: Val or Theo Dykman
Accommodation: all types in hotel,
guest house or camping.
🚶🏍 ♿

**Centre 469**

**Watercolour Weeks at
Weobley**          est. 1982
The Old Corner House
Broad Street
Weobley
Herefordshire
HR4 8SA
Tel: 0544 318
Contact: R. Kilvert/C. Wylie
Accommodation: for 18, half board in
private house or guest house.

**Centre 470**

**Waternish Workshop**          est. 1991
Old Church
Hallin
Waternish
Isle of Skye IV55 8GH
Tel: 047 083 307
Contact: Marie Ashwood
Accommodation: for 8, full board or
B&B in private house, or camping.
🚶🏍

**Centre 471**

**Wave Yacht Charters**          est. 1990
1 Hazel Drive
Dundee
Perthshire DD2 1QQ

Tel: 0382 68501
Contact: Joan Bruce
Accommodation: for 7 full/half board
or self-catering on board yacht.

**Centre 472**

**Wayford Watersports**          est. 1988
Wayford Bridge
Stalham
Norfolk NR12 9LL
Tel: 0692 582741
Contact: Les Cole
Accommodation: for 30, full board or
self-catering in 6 bed tents.
🚶🏍

**Centre 473**

**Wellington Riding**          est. 1972
Basingstoke Road
Heckfield
Hampshire
RG27 0LJ
Tel: 0734 326308
Contact: Suzanne Green
Accommodation: for 40, full board,
residential for children, or hotel for
adults.
🚶🏍

**Centre 474**

**Welsh Hang Gliding Centre** est. 1975
Bryn Bach Park
Tredegar
Gwent
NP2 3AY
Tel: 0873 832100
Contact: Paul Farley
Accommodation: ring for details.

**Centre 475**

**Welsh Horse Drawn
Holidays**          est. 1968
Greystones
Talgarth

LD3 0BP
Tel: 0874 711346
Contact: Austin Gwillim
Accommodation: self-catering in 4-berth horse-drawn caravan (1 person must be over 18).

## Centre 476
**The Welsh Woodland Skills Centre**                est. 1989
Ty-Gwillum
Llanfihangel-Bryn-Pabvan
Builth Wells
Powys
LD2 3SH
Tel: 059 789 469
Contact: Tim Wade
Accommodation: all types in local B&B's, pubs or camping.

*'A holiday with a difference where you can learn new skills and produce something unique for your home. Meet new friends. Set in a quiet wood in mid-Wales.'*

## Centre 477
**Wenford Bridge Pottery**        est. 1939
Wenford Bridge
St Breward
Nr. Bodmin
Cornwall
PL30 3PN
Tel: 0208 851 038
Contact: Ara Cardew
Accommodation: for 6, half board in private 18th century cottage.

*'Pottery holiday courses. In Cornish wooded valley. Tuition for all levels. Partners welcome. Enjoy good food*

*wine and relax in tranquil riverside garden.' Tel. 028 851 038.*

## Centre 478
**Wessex Fine Arts Summer Study Courses**        est. 1982
c/o Dr. Sweetman, Dept of History
The University
Southampton
Hampshire
SO9 5NH
Tel: 0703 769493
Contact: Barbara Hutton
Accommodation: for 42, full board in hotel or university halls of residence.

## Centre 479
**West Cornwall Learning Holidays**        est. 1988
Tregeraint House
Zennor
St Ives
Cornwall
TR26 3DB
Tel: 0736 797061
Contact: John or Sue Wilson
Accommodation: for 10, full board in private house or guest houses.

## Centre 480
**West Country Wildlife**        est. 1984
Courtlans
Old Tiverton Road
Crediton
Devon EX17 1EE
Tel: 0363 775459
Contact: Janet Lawrence
Accommodation: for 4, half board in farmhouse.

*Badger watching with West Cornwall Leaning Holidays*

## Centre 481
**West Dean College**
of Crafts Arts & Music          est. 1964
West Dean
Chichester
Sussex PO18 0QZ
Tel: 0243 63 301
Contact: The Administrator
Accommodation: for 60-120, full
board, residential at college.

## Centre 482
**Wetherby**          est. 1988
35 The Avenue
Mortimer
Reading
Berkshire RG7 3QU
Tel: 0734 333166
Contact: Valerie Keast
Accommodation: for 6 full/half board
in guest house.

## Centre 483
**Wethersfield Arts Centre**    est. 1987
Upperbarns
Hedingham Road
Wethersfield
Braintree
Essex CM7 4EQ
Tel: 0371 851054
Contact: Diana Bryant
Accommodation: for 12, full/half board
or B&B in residential guest house.

*'Lovely rural location. Stimulating,
excellent and understanding tuition.
Superb food. Friendly atmosphere.
Based in converted tudor barns of
great character and comfort. Brochure
on request.'*

## Centre 484
**Wharton Lodge**  est. 1989
Weston-under-Penyard
Ross-on-Wye
Herefordshire HR9 7JX
Tel: 0989 81795
Contact: Tracie Oldfield
Accommodation: for 16, full/half board
or B&B in country house hotel.

## Centre 485
**Wheal Buller Riding School** est. 1984
Buller Hill
Redruth
Cornwall TR16 6ST
Tel: 0209 211852
Contact: Janet Vernon
Accommodation: for 24, full board in
private house.

## Centre 486
**White Hall Centre**  est. 1951
Long Hill
Buxton
Derbyshire SK17 6SX
Tel: 0298 23260
Contact: Doug Jones
Accommodation: full board or self-catering
at residential outdoor centre or camping.

## Centre 487
**White Horse Riding Centre**  est. 1985
White Horse Stables
Goosey Glebe Small Holding
Nr. Faringdon
Oxon SN7 8PA
Tel: 0367 718806
Contact: The Manager
Accommodation: for 8, half board in
off-site guest house, or camping.

## Centre 488
**White Horse Trail Rides**  est. 1987
The Stables
Sherborne Cottage
Uffington
Oxon
SN7 7RA
Tel: 0367 820 783
Contact: David Morfee
Accommodation: for 12, B&B in
private house.

## Centre 489
**White Roding Pottery**  est. 1971
Brett's Farm
White Roding
Gt Dunmow
Essex
CM6 1RF
Tel: 0279 876326
Contact: Deborah Baynes
Accommodation: for 9, half board in
private house.

*'Creative fun in the Essex countryside.
Ideal for beginners and more experienced potters. Friendly tuition hot-tips
and cheating! Throwing, handbuilding,
decorating and firing every week.'*

## Centre 490
**Whizz-Kid Sailing**  est. 1988
Badgers - Trewint Lane
Rock
Wadebridge
Cornwall PL27 6LT
Tel: 0208 862854
Contact: Ted Finch
Accommodation: for 4-6, half board on
board yacht or B&B can be arranged.

*'Cornwall offers an infinite variety of scenery. The home port, Padstow, a fishing village, has good sailing, sandy beaches, water sports etc, in a wide estuary.'*

## Centre 491
**Wight Water Adventure Sports** est. 1984
19 Orchardleigh Road
Shanklin
Isle of Wight PO37 7NP
Tel: 0983 866269
Contact: I. D. Williams
Accommodation: ring for details.

## Centre 492
**Wild Explorer Holidays** est. 1984
Skye Environment Centre Ltd
Broadford
Isle of Skye IV49 9AQ
Tel: 0471 822 487
Contact: Grace Yoxon
Accommodation: for 11, full board in hotel or guest house.

*'Holidays are designed particularly for those who take pleasure in the country-side and its wildlife. All profits go towards the charities work in wildlife conservation.'*

## Centre 493
**Wildquest** est. 1986
31 Laneside Road
New Mills
Via Stockport
Derbyshire SK12 4LT
Tel: 0663 741578
Contact: Barry Marshall
Accommodation: for 16, full board in country inn.

## Centre 494
**Wiltshire Hang Gliding, Paragliding & Microlight Centre** est. 1980
The Old Barn - Rhyls Lane
Lockeridge
Nr. Marlborough
Wiltshire
SN8 4EE
Tel: 0672 86 555/4
Contact: Tony Hughes
Accommodation: for 7, self-catering residential at centre or B&B in guest house.

## Centre 495
**Wiltshire Painting Holidays** est. 1985
18 Broadacres
Broadtown
Swindon
Wiltshire
SN4 7RP
Tel: 0793 731519
Contact: Cameron Street
Accommodation: ring for details.

## Centre 496
**Windermere Lake Holidays Afloat** est. 1957
Glebe Road
Bowness Bay
Windermere
Cumbria LA23 3HE
Tel: 05394 43415
Contact: Michelle Dixon
Accommodation: self-catering on board motor or sailing cruiser.

## Centre 497
**Windmill Ways** est. 1992
50 Bircham Road
Reepham
Norfolk NR10 4NQ
Tel: 00603 871111

Contact: Veronica Booth
Accommodation: B&B in small guest houses or country hotels.

🚶 🐑

## Centre 498
**Windsports Centre**   est. 1982
The Control Tower
Wombleton Aerodrome
Kirkbymoorside
Yorkshire
YO6 5RY
Tel: 0751 33358/32356
Contact: John Teesdale/Eden Bly
Accommodation: half board or B&B in local guest house or camping.

🚶

## Centre 499
**Windsurfing Worcester**   est. 1984
Worcester Road
Holt
Worcester
Worcestershire
WR6 6NH
Tel: 0905 620044
Contact: The Administrator
Accommodation: ring for details.

## Centre 500
**Wine Weekends**   est. 1973
Upper Orchard
Hoarwithy
Herefordshire
HR2 6QR
Tel: 0432 840649
Contact: Jon or Heather Hurley
Accommodation: for 12, half board or B&B in guest house.

🚶 🐑

## Centre 501
**Wolds Silver**   est. 1986
Rothay Cottage

Leppington
Malton
Yorkshire YO17 9RL
Tel: 065 385 485
Contact: V. or M. Ashworth
Accommodation: for 5, full board or B&B.

🚶

## Centre 502
**Wolfscastle Pottery**   est. 1977
The Pottery
Wolfscastle
Pembrokeshire SA62 5LZ
Tel: 0437 87609
Contact: Philip Cunningham
Accommodation: for 7, full board in cottage.

## Centre 503
**Woodcarving**   est. 1982
Sycamore Cottage
Traboe
St Martin
Helston
Cornwall TR12 6EA
Tel: 0326 23 609
Contact: Jeremy Williams
Accommodation: half board off-site in hotel or guest house.

## Centre 504
**Working Weekends on Organic Farms (WWOOF)**   est. 1971
19 Bradford Road
Lewes
Sussex BN7 1RB
Tel: 0273 476286
Contact: Don or Maureen Pynches
Accommodation: for 2-4, full board in private house. Long stays arranged.

🚶

---

## WYCOMBE MUSIC SUMMER SCHOOL

7 - 14 August 1993
Wycombe Abbey, Buckinghamshire

SYMPHONY ORCHESTRA ❏     ❏ CHORAL COURSE
YOUNG MUSIC MAKERS (8 to 14) ❏     ❏ CONDUCTING COURSE
LATE LEARNER STRING ENSEMBLE ❏     ❏ LATE LEARNER WIND ENSEMBLE

*To enjoy a stimulating week of music making, get your brochure now from:*
***Wycombe Music Summer School,***
*3 Lynwood Road, Thames Ditton, Surrey, KT7 0DN. Tel: 081 398 3227*

---

### Centre 505
**Worlds End Lodge**
Staunton-on-Wye
Hereford
HR4 7NF
Tel: 09817 308
Contact: Course Organiser
Accommodation: for 70, in outdoor
centre or camping.

### Centre 506
**Wycombe Music Summer
School**                          est. 1982
New London Music Society
3 Lynwood Road
Thames Ditton
Surrey
KT7 0DN
Tel: 081 398 3227
Contact: Cynthia Gomme
Accommodation: for 150, full board or
self-catering in school.

### Centre 507
**Wyedean Canoe & Adventure
Centre**                          est. 1987
Holly Barn
Symonds Yat
Coleford
Gloucestershire
GL16 7NZ
Tel: 0594 833238

Contact: Paul or Jane Howells
Accommodation: for 50, self-catering
in converted barn or camping.

*'Holly Barn situated on top of Symonds
Yat rock and in the Forest of Dean.
Adventure activities provided, canoe-
ing, climbing etc. Simply the best.'*

### Centre 508
**Wynn Bishop**                   est. 1982
Bishop's Wynd
Market Place
Middleham
Yorkshire DL8 4RD
Tel: 0969 22418
Contact: Wynn Bishop
Accommodation: for 2, self-catering.

### Centre 509
**Y Neuadd Guest House &
Photography Holidays**            est. 1987
Pentre Ty Gwyn
Llandovery
Dyfed SA20 0RN
Tel: 0550 20603
Contact: Sue or Dave Farrants
Accommodation: for 6, half board or
B&B in guest house.

## Centre 510
**Yacht Corryvreckan**    est. 1980
Isle of Kerrera
Oban
Argyll PA34 4SX
Tel: 0631 64371
Contact: D. Lindsay
Accommodation: for 10, full board on
board 60ft sailing yacht.

## Centre 511
**Yeolden Country House**
**Hotel**    est. 1985
Durrant Lane
Northam
Bideford
Devon EX39 2RL
Tel: 0237 474400
Contact: N. M. Turner
Accommodation: for 20, half board in
hotel.

## Centre 512
**YMCA National Centre**    est. 1962
Lakeside
Ulverston
Cumbria LA12 8BD
Tel: 05395 31758
Contact: Bob Pilbeam
Accommodation: for 300 full board in
chalets, or camping in summer.

## Centre 513
**Ynys Hywel Countryside**
**Centre**    est. 1988
Cwmfelinfach
Crosskeys
Gwent NP1 7JX
Tel: 0495 200113
Contact: Nina Finnigan
Accommodation: full/half board in
hotel, or camping.

*'Winner of WTB 'Green' award, highly
commended three crown. 'Tourism for
tomorrow' awards. Set in beautiful
surroundings. Licensed restaurant
serves Welsh food. Vegetarian Menu.
Landrover rides.'*

## Centre 514
**Yoga for Health Foundation** est. 1978
Ickwell Bury
Biggleswade
Bedfordshire
SE18 9EF
Tel: 0767 627271
Contact: The Booking Office
Accommodation: for 40, full board in
residential centre.

## Centre 515
**Yorkshire Riding Centre** est. 1963
Markington
Harrogate
Yorkshire
H63 3PE
Tel: 0765 677207
Contact: Belinda Wilson
Accommodation: for 32, full board or
B&B, in guest house or hostel.

## Centre 516
**Young Cooks of Britain** est. 1983
2 Terminus Road
Chichester
Sussex
PO19 2DR
Tel: 0243 779239
Contact: Anna Best/Peta Brown
Accommodation: for 20, full board, at
country school dormitory.

## Centre 517
**Youth Hostels Association**   est. 1930
Trevelyan House
8 St Stephen's Hill
St Albans
Hertfordshire
AL1 2DY
Tel: 0727 55215
Contact: Reservations Department
Accommodation: for 18-120, all types,
in youth hostel.

## Centre 518
**Zara Training Centre**   est. 1980
Highleigh Road
Sidleham
Chichester
Sussex
PO20 7NR
Tel: 0243 641662
Contact: P. Brown
Accommodation: for 5, half board or
B&B in private house.
kids

## Centre 519
**Zoë Gertner - Woodcarving** est. 1980
Deans Cottage
Bagley
Wedmore
Somerset
BS28 4TD
Tel: 0934 712679
Contact: Zoë Gertner
Accommodation: various off-site
options. Ring for details.

# Index

# Index

*The Lutterworth Guide to* Activity and Study Holidays

# Index